Gerald Hartung and Valentin Pluder
From Hegel to Windelband

New Studies in the History and Historiography of Philosophy

Edited by
Gerald Hartung and Sebastian Luft

Volume 1

From Hegel to Windelband

Historiography of Philosophy in the 19th Century

Edited by
Gerald Hartung and Valentin Pluder

DE GRUYTER

ISBN 978-3-11-055454-0
e-ISBN (PDF) 978-3-11-032482-2
e-ISBN (EPUB) 978-3-11-038986-9
ISSN 0340-6059

Library of Congress Cataloging-in-Publication Data
A CIP catalog record for this book has been applied for at the Library of Congress.

Bibliographic information published by the Deutsche Nationalbibliothek
The Deutsche Nationalbibliothek lists this publication in the Deutsche Nationalbibliografie; detailed bibliographic data are available on the internet at http://dnb.dnb.de.

© 2017 Walter de Gruyter GmbH, Berlin/Boston
This volume is text- and page-identical with the hardback published in 2015.
Printing and binding: CPI books GmbH, Leck
♾ Printed on acid-free paper
Printed in Germany

www.degruyter.com

Contents

Gerald Hartung, Valentin Pluder
From Hegel to Windelband: The Classical Epoch of Philosophical Historiography —— 1

Gerald Hartung
Philosophical Historiography in the 19th century: A Provisional Typology —— 9

Gunter Scholtz
From Philosophical Historiography to Historical Philosophy —— 25

Emil Angehrn
On the Meaning of the History of Philosophy —— 45

Martin Bondeli
The History of Philosophy as Progress towards a System of Reason —— 63

Frederick Beiser
Two Traditions of Idealism —— 81

Valentin Pluder
The End of the Story, the End of History —— 99

Helmut Heit
Hegel, Zeller and Nietzsche: Alternative Approaches to Philosophical Historiography —— 117

Michael Forster
Does Western Philosophy Have Non-Western Roots? —— 141

Andreas Urs Sommer
The History of Philosophy as Counter- History: Strategies of Philosophico-Historiographical Dissidence —— 159

Sebastian Luft
Philosophical Historiography in Marburg Neo-Kantianism: The Example of Cassirer's *Erkenntnisproblem* —— 181

Paul Ziche
Indecisionism and Anti-Relativism: Wilhelm Windelband as a Philosophical Historiographer of Philosophy —— 207

Tim-Florian Goslar
On the Culturalization of Philosophical Historiography: Hermeneutics and Philosophical Historiography in Feuerbach, Dilthey and Blumenberg —— 227

Index —— 245

Gerald Hartung, Valentin Pluder
From Hegel to Windelband: The Classical Epoch of Philosophical Historiography

The question "what is history and how should it be written?" was posed anew in the middle of the 18th century and its answers contrasted with preceding notions of history which had ranged from chronicle to narrative. What is characteristic of this new form of historiography, as Enlightenment historiography, is an understanding of history as linear and causally linked or through its showing the grounds for history's course and development in time. This latter is itself understood as universal-historical progress towards a secular end of history. This historiography grasps the past because its practical effects on the present and the present becomes an expedient transitional stage on the way to the expected future.

This concept of history changes in the 19th century. It is true the developing historicism retains the idea of a completion of history that moves ever forward. However the activity-oriented and didactic impetus of historiography retreats in favour of a striving towards objectivity and impartiality founded on the sources. The general-universal aspect loses its leading significance in this conception of history. The pre-eminent object of such historiography is particular and, in the best case, empirically proven historical data, a focus that leads to almost positivist practices in the middle of the 19th century. Thus freed from the universal-historical claim of the Enlightenment, this tendency to prefer the particular over the general leads to a gradual—and of course persistently Euro-centric—pluralisation of historiography. A consciousness of its own historicity can be seen within historiography itself and hence an awareness of the relativity of its own statements which up to this point were explicated with objectivity and universality as the goal. At the end of the 19th century this development moves into the centre of reflective discourses not only in philosophy but also within the framework of historiography itself, which adds a further meta-discourse to the already multi-faceted historiography of the 19th century.

The philosophical historiography of the 19th century is embedded within this general development of the conception of history from the Enlightenment to historicism and beyond. However, the investigation of the philosophical-historical texts of the 19th century is not only a concretion of a general conception of history but it is also based on the historical understanding of philosophy as such and to making the understanding of philosophy as historical fruitful. For these texts not only need to exhibit a concept of the temporal succession and development of events, that is, in this case, of intellectual work manifested as transmitted texts. The philosophical-historical texts must also define what exactly qualifies these events and texts to appear in a history of philosophy. Accordingly every history of philosophy not only implies a specific philosophy of history—even a philosophy of the history of philosophy—but it must also include a philosophy of philosophy, at least insofar as it wants to be able to justify its approach.[1]

When looking at the texts of the 19th century in particular it is certainly an advantage that it is not necessary to subsequently extract its conceptual meta-level from its philosophical historiography. Rather, in these texts this subject-matter is explicitly self-reflective.[2] This is certainly not to say that its statements on the history of philosophy and the conception of history of philosophy that was actually published are in tandem. On the one hand this relation needs to be subjected to a critical analysis and the respective method of the history of philosophy need to be extrapolated. On the other hand it should be noted that the question of the sources of the history of philosophy in the 19th century, a question which includes the analysis of what is accepted as a source in philosophical history, is of equal importance to methodological considerations.

Accordingly when examining the philosophical historiography of the 19th century three interrelated and interlocking approaches or directions of investigation suggest themselves for closer analysis: (1) for one, concrete works and their immanent underlying concepts including their historical location not only in relation to the overall trends of historiography but also with a view to the individual formation of schools and the constellations of protagonists; (2) for another, the explicit reflection of historiography in a genuine philosophical consideration of history, philosophy and the philosophy of history, which does not have to mean that there is a congruence between the proposed conceptual basis of historiography and the way in which it is actually explicated[3] and (3) last but not least the issue of sources of philosophical historiography in the 19th century.

---

[1] This thesis can be found in Goldsetzer (1968), a work that is still indispensible for understanding philosophical historiography in the 19th century. It is taken up again in the studies by Kang (1998) and Beelmann (2011).

[2] On the theory of philosophical historiography in the long 19th century see, in addition to Goldsetzer (1968), Schröpfer (1987); Catana (2008) und Michalski (2010). There are of course studies of the historiography of philosophy in other eras. On antiquity, see Mansfeld (1990); on the philosophy of the Middle Ages see Inglis (1998) and as regards philosophical historiography in the Soviet regime, see Zweerde (1997).

[3] A number of texts have been published on this subject over the years of selection of which are Laerke, Smith and Schliesser (2013); Flasch (2005); Angehrn, Baertschi (2002); Rorty, Schneewind a. Skinner (1984); Gracia (1992); Sandkühler (1991); Holland (1985); Braun (1985); Rée, Ayers a. Westoby (1978); Braun (1973); Passmore (1965).

An assessment of the sources of 19th century philosophical historiography obviously rest on the state of current research. Only through this are we able to understand and if necessary to correct historical interpretations in their possible distortedness due to insufficient sources. In the same manner it is equally impossible to consider the questioning of concepts immanent to 19th century philosophical historiography without explicit reference to the diversity that is the basis of today's interpretations of philosophical historiography. That is why the view of the 19th century must be complemented by reflection on the point of view and the position from which it is viewed, from which the past is judged.

These considerations lead once again to the question concerning historiography in general. However historiography is to be questioned not only with regard to its expression in the 19th century but rather in the face of the obvious fact that the investigation of historiography in history too is a form of historiography and thus itself, because of its own historicity, is carried out within the framework of conceptual parameters of the historicity which is to be questioned. The contributions in the present volume elaborate the questions of what philosophical historiography in its classical epoch between Hegel and Windelband, was and what it could be today, through the critical examination of the 19th century authors. Here, then, the question of the appropriate sensitivity to contexts joins the question of historicity. The analysis of the conditions of the production of philosophical-historical texts (1–3) needs to be complimented by the consideration of appropriate conditions for their reception. With the essays in the present book we also want to face the question of how the history of philosophy should be written to find readers today. Certainly it makes little sense to represent the history of philosophy as a conflict between contradictory theories and systems which has winners and losers. A history of concepts, categories, metaphors, arguments and styles of thinking will be, likewise, of little interest. Rather it is far more likely that a history that enables an "insight into the changes in variables of human life-experience and its fundamental assumptions" will arouse our interest even today because it shows how philosophical thoughts are anchored in the life-world.[4] The philosophical historians of the 19th and early 20th century determined what was to be considered an episode and fragment, what a genuine problem of life or a basic philosophical problem which expresses a determinate historical situation, and what, transcending this latter, expresses a seemingly timeless claim to validity. While we, writing for our time, will most likely emphasize things differently, it is apparent that the problems that we

---

4 Regarding this see Hampe (2014), 437.

encounter on this path are not entirely new. Wilhelm Windelband has circumscribed the scope of our volume by having rightly expressed the following thoughts: "It is Hegel's merit to have consciously understood what philosophy has always been doing. Since then every history of philosophy that does not know how to uncover the intimate vital relation between systems and the cultural interests of their time would seem to us inadequate.[5]

The essays of the present volume cover the path from Hegel to Windelband in a non-linear fashion, threading the side paths of the episodic and the dissident and throwing a critical look at the classical period of philosophical historiography. Gerald Hartung, in *Philosophical Historiography in the 19*th *Century: A Provisional Typology*, brings out how philosophical historiography gradually emancipates itself from the shadow of Hegel and enters the horizon of scientific and cultural history. He illustrates, using the examples of Rudolf Eucken and Wilhelm Windelband, the different approaches taken by a representation of the history of philosophy oriented towards "problems of life and culture".

In *From Philosophical Historiography to Historical Philosophy* Gunter Scholtz describes the turn to a philosophical understanding of the history of philosophy that took place around 1800. This implies the need for a new understanding of philosophy that is to be worked out only through productive philosophizing and through the history of philosophy. In a tour through the 19th century Scoltz shows how precarious the relation between systematicity and history has remained, in spite of all the systematic endeavours between Schleiermacher, Schlegel and Hegel right up to Nietzsche. In spite of all their differences the above named authors' histories of philosophy remain—as was already demanded by Schlegel—a critique as a living examination of the past in the face of the present.

In *On the Meaning of the History of Philosophy*, Emil Angehrn approaches, with systematic and historical intent, the question of the meaning of philosophy being history [*Geschichte*] and its having a history. The entanglement that Hegel had considered between the history of spirit and its reflection is historiography remains a guiding thought for Angehrn. For, according to Hegel it is itself a fact of history [*Geschichte*] that the historiography of philosophy has become possible and necessary in the present. In the *historiography* of philosophy, the progressive condition of the *history* of philosophy, the historical self-explication of spirit is depicted.

In *The History of Philosophy as Progress towards a System of Reason* Martin Bondeli provides a precise representation of Kant, Reinhold and Hegel's philosophical-historical remarks so as to bring out the genesis of a concept of a ration-

---

5 Windelband (1916), 186.

al history of philosophy. Although the overall concept of a linear conception of history must be viewed as a failure, Bondeli notices however that on the one hand that Hegel's perspective already opens up a perspective on other histories of philosophy as equally valuable and not as trivial and that on the other hand the list of demands that a rational history of philosophy makes can even be relevant for the history of philosophy today.

In *Two Traditions of Idealism* Frederick Beiser depicts, in addition to the Hegelian line as regards representing the history of philosophy a second and hitherto insufficiently appreciated line taken in the history of philosophy which is associated with the names Fries, Herbart and Beneke. Using various problems such as the discussion of empirical methods, the critique of the dualist position in epistemology he shows that the victory of the first course was only superficial and that Fries, Herbart and Beneke's lines of argument greatly influenced the 19th century. With regard to this issue another historiography of philosophy is needed for the 19th century.

In *The End of the Story, the End of History* Valentin Pluder responds to the different emphases of the discourse on the end of the history of philosophy as found in Fries, Grohmann, Hegel, Engels and Dilthey. Here, Dilthey appears as the figure who establishes a summation of the previous concepts by detailing a typology of history and who, by recourse to Hegel, seeks to defend himself against the spectre of relativism. The final considerations on this question are left, not without a certain irony, to Frege who does not even declare the end of the history of philosophy but who by disregarding this very question constitutes an endpoint—and enables a new beginning.

Helmut Heit, in *Hegel, Zeller and Nietzsche: Alternative Approaches to Philosophical Historiography*, leaves the monographic concept of philosophical historiography behind and throws light on Hegel's long shadow. For him these three historians of philosophy are paradigms for different perspectives and attitudes. Next to Hegel, the speculative historian, stands Zeller, the scientific historian and Nietzsche, the artistic historian. The independence of these individual ways of thinking leads Heit to sketch a polyphonic philosophical historiography in which, in a last will to representational unity, the historian of philosophy is committed to a tolerant pluralism.

In *Does Western Philosophy Have Non-Western Roots* Michael Forster asks whether Western philosophy has several origins and whether this insight can influence philosophical historiography. With reference to the question concerning the origin of Greek philosophy he shows, through a precise analysis of the philosophical-historical writings of Gladisch, Röth, Zeller and Nietzsche, how opportunities for contextualizing can become opened and adjusted anew. This 19th century debate is paradigmatic for the striving of philosophical historiography towards for linearity and its avoidance of the consideration of contexts (such as religion, architecture and so on).

In *The History of Philosophy as Counter-History: Strategies of Philosophical-Historiography Dissidence* Andreas Urs Sommer lays out the contrast between the monumental philosophico-historical works that were canonical in universities in the time between Hegel and Windelband and the approaches and possibilities of philosophico-historiographical dissidence, the traces of which he uncovers in the writings of the theologian Overbeck. For Overbeck history proves itself to be a discontinuous process in which there is much that simply cannot be sublated even though many moments recur. In Sainte-Beuve and in his reader Nietzsche a philosophical virtuosity as regards media is revealed which, when applied to the history of philosophy, calls for another form of philosophical historiography: the aphorism, the biographical sketch, the portrait—a form that is polyglot and polemical.

In his essay *Indecisionism and Anti-Relativism: Wilhelm Windelband as a Philosophical Historiographer of Philosophy* Paul Ziche introduces Windelband's philosophizing historiography of philosophy. It is often overlooked that Windelband's historiographical and systematic works on philosophy are to be understood as complementary. Ziche works out the main lines of Windelband's empirical philosophy in the light of the idiosyncratic combination of indecisionism and anti-relativism in Windelband's writings. Finally he shows that Windelband, with his concept of philosophical problems, integrates systematic and historical questions and attempts to establish indecisionism as a philosophical virtue.

In his *Philosophical Historiography in Marburg Neo-Kantianism: The Example of Cassirer's Erkenntnisproblem* Sebastian Luft clarifies the autonomous character of Cassirer's studies of the problem of knowledge against the background of the Marburg School of neo-Kantianism. Starting with Windelband's works on a problem oriented philosophical historiography and taking into account Gadamer's critique of this, namely that problem-history is a "bastard of historicism", for Luft what is at stake is representing the systematic and intrinsic value of problem history and building a bridge from this to the development of the history of science.

In *On the Culturalization of Philosophical Historiography: Hermeneutics and Philosophical Historiography in Feuerbach, Dilthey and Blumenberg* Tim-Florian Goslar traces a long arc from the middle of the 19th century up the second half of the 20th century with reference to the fundamental question concerning the relation between philosophical historiography and hermeneutics. Goslar shows, based on three self-contained analyses of Feuerbach, Dilthey and Blumenberg, that the gradual "hermeneuticization of philosophy" provoked an expansion in perspective beyond the limits of the history of philosophy such that the historiography of philosophy becomes cultural historiography.

The editors thank the *Schweizerischen Akademie der Geistes- und Sozialwissenschaften* (SAGW) and especially the president of the *Kuratorium Grundriss der Geschichte der Philosophie*, Herrn Professor Dr. Dr. h.c. Helmuth Holzhey and the Bergische Universität Wuppertal for the financial support for an international conference which was held under the title *Die Facetten der Philosophiegeschichtsschreibung im 19. Jahrhundert* at the Bergische Universität Wuppertal from the 11th to the 13th of September 2013. We are grateful to the team of the Professor for Cultural philosophy and Aesthetics, especially to Ines Bräuniger, Heike Koenig and Daniel Rompf for a wide range of organizational support. Heike Koenig is also responsible for the revision of the manuscript and Dr. Aengus Daly for the translation of the texts. We thank them for their excellent work. Many thanks are also due to the publisher *Verlag De Gruyter* (Boston/ Berlin) and above all to Frau Gertrud Grünkorn for the inclusion of this volume in their publishing programme and for the launch of a new series on the History and Historiography of Philosophy.

Wuppertal/Bochum, December 2014

Bibliography

Angehrn, Baertschi (2002): Emil Angehrn and Bernard Baertschi, *Philosophie und Philosophiegeschichte = La Philosophie et son histoire*, Bern: Verlag P. Haupt.
Beelmann (2001): Axel Beelmann, *Theoretische Philosophiegeschichte: grundsätzliche Probleme einer philosophischen Geschichte der Philosophie*, Basel: Schwabe.
Braun (1973): Lucien Braun, *Histoire de l'histoire de la philosophie*, Paris: Ophrys.
Braun (1985): Lucien Braun, *Théorie de l'histoire de la philosophie*, Strasbourg: Centre de Documentation en Histoire de la Philosophie.
Catana (2008): Leo Catana, *The Historiographical Concept "system of Philosophy": Its Origin, Nature, Influence, and Legitimacy*, Leiden: Brill.
Flasch (2005): Kurt Flasch, *Philosophie hat Geschichte*, vol. 2, *Theorie der Philosophiehistorie*. Frankfurt a. M.: Klostermann.
Geldsetzer (1968): Lutz Geldsetzer, *Die Philosophie der Philosophiegeschichte im 19. Jahrhundert: zur Wissenschaftstheorie der Philosophiegeschichtsschreibung und -betrachtung*, Meisenheim: A. Hain.
Gracia (1992): Jorge J. E. Gracia, *Philosophy and its history: issues in philosophical historiography*, Albany: State University of New York Press.
Hampe (2014): Michael Hampe, *Die Lehren der Philosophie. Eine Kritik*, Frankfurt a. M: Suhrkamp.
Holland (1985): Alan J. Holland, *Philosophy, its History and Historiography*, Dordrecht: Reidel.

Inglis (1998): John Inglis, *Spheres of Philosophical Inquiry and the Historiography of Medieval Philosophy*, Leiden: Brill.

Kang (1998): Jung-Min Kang, *Philosophische Philosophiegeschichte: Studien zur allgemeinen Methodologie der Philosophiegeschichtsschreibung mit besonderer Berücksichtigung der Philosophie der Philosophiegeschichte*, Konstanz: Hartung-Gorre.

Laerke, Smith a. Schliesser (2013): Mogens Laerke, Justin E. H. Smith and Eric Schliesser, *Philosophy and Its History: Aims and Methods in the Study of Early Modern Philosophy*, Oxford: University Press.

Mansfeld (1990): Jaap Mansfeld, *Studies in the historiography of Greek philosophy*, Assen: Van Gorcum.

Michalski (2010): Mark Michalski, *Der Gang des deutschen Denkens: Versuche und Programme nationaler Philosophiegeschichtsschreibung von der Aufklärung bis ins 20. Jahrhundert*, Würzburg: Königshausen & Neumann.

Passmore (1965): John Arthur Passmore, *The Historiography of the history of philosophy*, 's-Gravenhage: Mouton.

Rée, Ayers a. Westoby (1978): Jonathan Rée, Michael Ayers and Adam Westoby: *Philosophy and its past*, New Jersey: Humanities Press.

Rorty, Schneewind a. Skinner (1984): Richard Rorty, Jerome B. Schneewind and Quentin Skinner, *Philosophy in history: essays on the historiography of philosophy*, Cambridge [Massachusetts]: Cambridge University Press.

Sandkühler (1991): Hans-Jörg Sandkühler, *Geschichtlichkeit der Philosophie: Theorie, Methodologie und Methode der Historiographie der Philosophie*, Frankfurt a. M. et al.: P. Lang.

Schröpfer (1987): Horst Schröpfer, *Philosophiehistorisches Denken und seine Historiographie im Übergang von der deutschen Aufklärung zur klassischen deutschen Philosophie*, Jena: Universitäts Verlag.

Windelband (1916): Wilhelm Windelband, *Lehrbuch der Geschichte der Philosophie*, 7th edition, Tübingen: Mohr (Siebeck).

Zweerde (1997): Evert van der Zweerde, *Soviet historiography of philosophy: istoriko-filosofskaja nauka*, Boston: Kluwer Academic Publishers.

Gerald Hartung
Philosophical Historiography in the 19th century: A Provisional Typology

In memory of Klaus Christian Köhnke
(1953–2013)

In recent decades, scholarship has not taken much interest in the historiography of philosophy. But the question of how to write the history of philosophy is by no means trivial. However in academic philosophy it has become unfashionable to concede to the history of philosophy and its synthetic power a rank equal to that of systematic philosophy and its analytic concision. Some have gone so far as to wholly renounce the historical perspective in philosophy altogether. Meanwhile a popular philosophical historiography has conquered bookshops and bestseller lists. What I want to emphasize is the following: we have a flourishing practice of philosophical historiography but we lack a serious consideration of the principles according to which we proceed in this and of the standards which we employ. Consideration of this point raises many questions such as: does philosophy, like other disciplines, have its own history? Or is philosophical history part of a general scientific or cultural history? Has philosophical historiography its own methods or does it borrow its methods from other historical sciences?

To approach these issues, I want to look back at the 19th century, a century in which German philosophy took on the task of developing a methodologically reflective history of philosophy. Kant coined the expression "a philosophical history of philosophy" and with this provided a guiding idea: philosophical historiography is not a historical but a philosophical sub-discipline; it does not historicise its subject but approaches it philosophically. But what does this mean? For Kant reason is the principle of a philosophising historiography of philosophy and for Hegel the unity of reason is the principle for the historical representation of different philosophical schools of thought.

I will consider this view in the first part of this essay. I will examine philosophical history and its domain as well as looking at how philosophical historiography emerges from Hegel's shadow. In the second part I will consider the radical changes philosophical historiography underwent in the middle of the 19th century and place it in the horizon of scientific and cultural history. The headline for these changes could read: from the hypothesis of a "unity of the whole" to the search for a "relationship of the parts." In conclusion, I will sketch the situation in the years around 1900 by considering the case of Rudolf Eucken, a man who counted in his time as one of the most well-known national and international historians of philosophy and who endeavoured—like his contemporary Wilhelm Windelband—to find a new approach to the history of philosophy. Finally I will venture an answer to the question of what we today can learn from the historiography of philosophy in the 19th century.

1 Philosophical historiography in the first half of the 19th century – a historico-systematic construction

The 18th century had as yet no concept of a general philosophical historiography which understands the history of philosophy as the historical unfolding of philosophical positions from the work dedicated to the concept of philosophy.[1] Philosophical historiography in those times is certainly a scholarly subject, even if it is to large extent eclectic. The thought that first leads to a programme of reflective historiography is that historiography requires its own independent method because the concept and the history of philosophy do not stand in a stable relationship but must create their own relation and cohesion.[2]

1.1 Philosophical historiography and its domain

Philosophical historiography develops in several steps. Even at the beginning of the 19th century philosophical historiography still meant the depiction of a person and work in their context. Paradigmatic of this approach is Wilhelm Gottlieb Tennemann's twelve volume *Geschichte der Philosophie* (1798–1819). The beginning of such editorial activity as the edition of Plato proposed by Friedrich Schlegel and carried out by Friedrich Schleiermacher and the edition of Aristotle's works realized by August Brandis and Immanuel Becker brought the progenitors of philosophy to presence anew.[3] With this there is the possibility of depicting the history of philosophy as a linear process of the development of currents of thought (see in this regard August Heinrich Ritter's *Geschichte der Philosophie*

---

1 Compare the larger context in Braun's study (1990).
2 Compare Gilbert (1965), 320–339.
3 Compare Hartung (2006), 290–309.

[The History of Philosophy], 12 volumes, Hamburg 1829–1853) or as a dialectical process integrating philosophical currents as anticipatory of a philosophical system (Georg Wilhelm Friedrich Hegel: *Vorlesungen zur Geschichte der Philosophie* [Lectures on the History of Philosophy], Berlin) or the further possibility of depicting it as a continual unfolding of categorical determinations of thinking which underlie all changes on the surface of philosophical systems (Friedrich Adolf Trendelenburg: *Geschichte der Kategorienlehre* [History of the Theory of the Categories], Berlin 1846).

A further differentiation comes into play here, namely that philosophical history divides into two realms: a history of ancient philosophy and a history of recent and contemporary philosophy.[4] The history of ancient philosophy itself subdivides into various schools, on the one side Christian August Brandis as a representative of the Schelling school (see his *Handbuch der Geschichte der griechischen Philosophie* [Handbook of the History of Greek Philosophy], 2 volumes, Berlin 1835 and 1866), on another, Hegel's disciple Franz Biese (see his *Die Philosophie des Aristoteles, in ihrem inneren Zusammenhang, mit besonderer Berücksichtigung des philosophischen Sprachgebrauchs, ausdessen Schriften entwickelt* [Aristotle's philosophy, developed from his writings in its internal coherence with particular consideration of its use of philosophical language], volume 1, Berlin 1835), on another, Friedrich Karl Albert Schwegler as representative of the Tübinger School (*Geschichte der griechischen Philosophie* [History of Greek Philosophy], Tübingen 1859) and, towering far above the others, Eduard Zeller (*Die Philosophie der Griechen – Eine Untersuchung über Charakter, Gang und Hauptmomente ihrer Entwicklung* [The Philosophy of the Greeks —An Investigation of its Character, Course and Key Elements], 3 volumes, Tübingen1844–1852).[5]

On the other hand, the history of recent and contemporary philosophy is either the depiction of developments inside systematic philosophy, as with Karl Ludwig Michelet (see his *Geschichte der letzten Systeme der Philosophie in Deutschland, von Kant bis Hegel* [History of the Recent Systems of Philosophy in Germany from Kant to Hegel], 2 volumes, Berlin 1837/1838) and is consequently what the young Hegelians called "partisan," or it is a critical revision thereof as is the case with Immanuel Hermann Fichte (*Beiträge zu einer Charakteristik der neueren Philosophie zur Vermittlung ihrer Gegensätze, oder kritische Geschichte derselben von Descartes und Locke bis auf Hegel* [Contributions to a Characteristic of the Recent Philosophy to mediate its Oppositions, or a Critical History of the same from Descartes and Locke to Hegel], Sulzbach 1829) and Her-

---

4 Compare Schneider (1999), 327–340.
5 Compare Mann (1996), 165–195 and in particular the essays in Hartung (2010).

mann Ulrici (*Das Grundprinzip der Philosophie kritisch und spekulativ entwickelt* [The Basic Principle of Philosophy Critically and Speculatively Developed], volume 1, Leipzig 1845). It can also provide a superior depiction thereof, as is the case in Albert Schwegler's succinct *Geschichte der Philosophie im Umriß. Ein Leitfaden zur Uebersicht* [The History of Philosophy in Outline. An overlook] (1848) and in Kuno Fischer's large scale *Geschichte der neueren Philosophie* [History of Recent Philosophy] (8 volumes, 1852–1893).[6]

1.2 Philosophical historiography in the shadow of Hegel

In systematic regard, philosophical historiography in the 19th century develops in the shadow of the philosophizing historiography of philosophy initiated by Kant. It no longer gathers together what is lying at the wayside in a scholarly eclectic manner. Rather, only that which can be integrated into a progressive history of thought is considered historically valid. In this sense the great systematic philosophies, especially that of Hegel, advance the historicizing of philosophical theories by means of their integration into a system. Henceforth, philosophical thinkers and their theories are only of interest insofar as they are part of a (re)constructed history of the development of a philosophical system in which the history of philosophy finds its completion.[7]

On the basis of the Hegelian use of history by philosophy, by the middle of the 19th century the approach of a "scientific depiction" of the history of philosophy spreads and itself divides into two distinct fields. On the one hand, it became possible to depict the history of philosophy in a manner that is largely free from bias, as is the case in Johann Eduard Erdmann's *Versuch einer wissenschaftlichen Darstellung der Geschichte der neueren Philosophie* [Attempt at a Scientific Representation of the History of Recent Philosophy] (3 volumes, Leipzig 1836–1853). On the other, it is possible the present the history of philosophy as part of a general scientific history as in Eduard Zeller's *Geschichte der deutschen Philosophie* [History of German Philosophy] (München 1873) which was published as the thirteenth volume of a general history of the sciences in Germany: *Geschichte der Wissenschaften in Deutschland – Neuere Zeit*, [History of the Sciences in Germany—Recent Times] which was organized by the historical commission of the Royal Academy of the Sciences in Bavaria.

---

6 Compare for the context of this Köhnke's excellent study: Köhnke (1993).
7 Compare Forster (2012), 866–904; Rosen (2007), 122–154.

At the same time as the above projects, the first textbook of the history of philosophy is created; Friedrich Ueberweg's *Grundriß der Geschichte der Philosophie von Thales bis auf die Gegenwart* ([Outline of the History of Philosophy from Thales to the Present], 2 volumes, Berlin 1862 and 1864; the standard textbook for the history of philosophy up to its 12th edition in 1927). What had been initiated at the beginning of the 19th century is accomplished by the *Ueberweg*, as it was popularly known: philosophy receives its own exclusive disciplinary history. The sciences emancipate themselves from philosophy and, as the philosophical historian Trendelenburg puts it, went "happily on their own peculiar ways,"[8] a move which philosophy reflects in such new formations as epistemology (neo-Kantianism) and the theory of science (neo-Aristotelianism).[9] At the same time, a philosophical historiography develops in which philosophy as a scientific discipline with its own evolution is depicted as independent of the sciences.

2 Philosophical historiography in the second half of the 19th century – in the horizon of scientific and cultural history

Whoever wants to write the history of philosophy in more than just an eclectic manner requires an ordering principle. In the wake of Kant and Hegel there is the opportunity for an *a priori* form of construction according to which the history of the disciplines is a progressive whole that leads from a mythical to a scientific understanding of philosophy as metaphysics. This Kantian-Hegelian myth, as Michael Foster calls it, had a large number of followers in the 19th and earlier 20th century. These include the above mentioned histories of Zeller, Erdmann, Fischer and others—and even Ernst Cassirer's "problem-historical" studies on the problem of knowledge in the early twentieth century are still impacted by this tradition. Writing the history of the discipline as a progressive history is without doubt the central element of philosophical historiography until well into the second half of the nineteenth century. It is here that we can locate the connection between the scientific discipline of history as practiced by Ranke and Droysen and their shared ideological background.[10] However, while the

---

[8] Compare Trendelenburg (1840), VI.
[9] Compare Hartung (2011), 450–455.
[10] Compare Gadamer (1986), 177–179.

unity of the whole and the structural coherence of a progressive whole are presupposed, it remained wholly unclear to the method of philosophical historiography how the idea of the whole shows itself in the representation of the relation of the parts. This is by no means a minor issue. In as far as the 19th century historiography is professionalized, becoming philologically accurate with Zeller and contextually aware with Windelband, a heavy emphasis is placed on the depiction of historical relation and coherence. Subsequently, discourse about the unity of the whole degenerates into a mere rhetorical flourish.

2.1 After 1940: from the Hypothesis of a "unity of the whole" to the search for a "relation of the parts"

Much has already been written about Hegel's "brilliant achievement" (Dilthey) in historiography, speculation and empiricism, an achievement which mediates a vision of the whole as well as of the relatedness of the parts. We know that Hegel's historiography, also[11] his philosophy as science, is based on facts but we know as well that he is not primarily concerned with real history but rather with the development of historical consciousness. Furthermore, we know that in Hegel historical consciousness receives an apotheosis: the objective spirit and that which is objectified in it as historical knowledge is, in the last instance, stripped of all relativity and is transformed into absolute knowing. In an eschatological perspective all knowledge objectified in history is merely provisional. Hence, the art of the historian and also the philosophical historian are vital for distinguishing between the merely provisional historical moment from the eternal. According to Hegel, this is the task of critical historiography.

The "brilliant" element of this construction relies on the one hand on its rigorous implementation by Hegel but on the other—and this seems paradoxical at first—on the fact that the constructive principle still functions even if we relinquish the eternal as the measure of the temporal. In this case we are dealing with a historical consciousness that is objectified on the respective levels of its development and is related not to an end of history but to other, preceding, possibly following, simultaneous and also non-simultaneous levels of objectification whose relation and coherence is guaranteed through a continual progression.[12] A critical historical science—and a corresponding critical philosophical historiography—exists in this turn away from Hegel and towards the task of no

---

11 Compare Hartung (2006), 382–396 and the bibliographical references.
12 Fundamental to this is Trendelenburg's treatise in Trendelenburg (1855), 1–30.

longer being able to simply affirm the unity of history (including philosophical history) but of having to uncover or construct that which variously related historical facts have in common. It must excavate a general picture from the debris of historical data. The later Dilthey agrees:

> We look back at the immeasurable field of debris of religious traditions, of metaphysical claims, of demonstrated systems: the human spirit had through many centuries attempted avenues of all kinds for scientifically establishing, poetically depicting or religiously proclaiming the coherence of things. Subsequently, the methodico-critical science of history explores every fragment, every remnant of this long work of our species.[13]

Even now Paul Ricoeur's study *Histoire et Verité* (1955) contains pioneering reflections on questions concerning how fragments of historical knowledge are joined into coherence.[14]

Dilthey's is a fair-minded and honest effort dedicated to the fragments and to a hope that we will recognize coherence in the details of historical data if we only meet the latter with analytic care and sufficient endurance. It is not just an immanent historical theology (Hegelianism) that should be avoided but also a fictionalism (Nietzsche, Mauthner). We hear in the background here Nietzsche's loud laughter at those who speak of historical facts:

> *Facta!* Yes *facta ficta!*—a historian does not have to do with what actually happened but only with supposed events: only these have exerted their influence. [...] His topic, so-called world-history, are opinions about supposed acts and their alleged motives, which in turn give rise to opinions and acts, whose reality immediately evaporates again [...]. All historians recount things which have never existed except in the imagination.[15]

However, the representatives of philosophical historiography between Hegel and Dilthey in the 19th century are by no means prepared to go in this direction. While continuing to work in the vein of Hegel appears scarcely possible to them, they still think that they can push through to an overall view of philosophical history by way of an empirical analysis of data pertaining to philosophical history. This becomes clear, for instance, in the case of Albert Schwegler whose *Geschichte der Philosophie im Umriß* [History of Philosophy in Outline] (1848) is one of the most widely read and printed philosophical histories of the 19th century. In the spirit of Hegel, Schwegler describes a sequence of thinkers and of schools of thought. However he maintains the dissimilarities of the successive "philoso-

---

13 Dilthey (1968), 75–118, specifically: 76. Compare Rodi (2003).
14 Ricoeur (1974), compare Hartung (2010b), 311–331.
15 Nietzsche (1988), 224–225.

phies of the time" ["Zeitphilosophieen"] which develop in the light of the progress in the empirical sciences and can only advance in "interaction" with these: "the history of philosophy has to depict the content, the sequence and the internal cohesion of these philosophies of the time."[16] Schwegler adheres firmly to the thought of the unity of philosophy in its historical development and claims that "the individual philosophical systems emergent in history constitute an organic movement, a rationally, internally structured system."[17] In his view, these ideas were first formulated—and unduly exaggerated—by Hegel. Hegel's theory that the historical succession of philosophical systems coincides with the logical categories in the system of logic is—as Schwegler emphasizes—neither legitimate in principle nor actually carried through by history. Hegel errs in principle because history is not a thoroughly rational coherence or an "arithmetical problem." What is historically given is that which is factually given and this cannot be constructed as an *a priori* nor can it be integrated into a schema. And Hegel also errs with regard to the question of the form of representing history. The history of philosophy proceeds analytically. It proceeds from the concrete to the abstract, from consideration to thinking and releases the abstract from its concrete embedding in cultural and religious conditions. For Hegel, on the contrary, the beginning is the abstract construction which only subsequently penetrates into the concrete material of the empirically given.

Hegel's double error in construction causes the philosophical historians of the second half of the 19th century to assume an uncomfortable position with regard to his work, namely, that they make reference to a model they strongly caution against. Paul Ricoeur later speaks of an unavoidable "*tentation hégélienne*".[18] According to Schwegler philosophical historiography is not a synthetic work of construction but instead consists in analytically penetrating the abundance of empirical data. Here a basic feature of philosophical historiography in the wake of Schleiermacher appears, embracing August Heinrich Ritter, Karl Reinhold von Köstlin, Eduard Zeller and leading right up to Wilhelm Dilthey and Paul Ricoeur: the individual moments of history are conceded priority over every claim to generality or to the generic.

In this way, what Hegel had forced together falls apart with Schwegler: the claim to the unity of philosophy in its disciplinary development and the analysis of the cohesion of its individual parts. In the face of this, the task of the philosophical historian becomes increasingly complex.

---

16 Schwegler (1870), 2.
17 Schwegler (1870), 2.
18 Ricoeur (1985), 350–364.

> History often moves in serpentine traces, in apparent regressions; philosophy has not infrequently forsaken again a wide and already fruitful field to become settled on a small strip of land [...]; now millennia of failed attempts were expended only to produce a negative result, now an abundance of philosophical ideas presses into the space of one human lifetime [...][19]

The price of this confounding complexity is the unity of philosophy in its historical development becoming a regulative idea for the researcher or an ideal model for the philosophical historian.

This consequence becomes obvious in the case of Eduard Zeller, who in his *Grundriss der Geschichte der Griechischen Philosophie* [Survey of the History of Greek Philosophy] (1883) had also emphasized the interaction of individual philosophical horizons of experience and made up of these systems, a totality of historical developments imagined as an ideal. According to his conception, this mutual causation cannot be understood through an *a priori* construction of historical facts but only in a "purely historical way, on the basis of historical accounts".[20] Like Zeller, we as philosophical historians always begin with individuals, which we analyse individually (for instance Plato's philosophy). We then proceed to that which is associated with the individual phenomena (for instance pre- and post-Platonic philosophy). Finally, we test these analyses against our idea of the whole (for instance the development of philosophy into a scientific system), which we also have to continually revise.

Three types of factors must be taken into account: "the general state of education of the time and the people; the influence of earlier systems on the later; the idiosyncrasies of the individual philosophies."[21] The art of philosophical historiography depends, in Zeller's view, on the capacity to let these factors remain in tension rather than one-sidedly emphasizing one over others. Only then can an "image of the course of history and the relatedness of appearances" emerge.[22]

In summary, we can say that philosophical historiography in the wake of Hegel is a thinking of relations which historical analysis supposedly uncovers so as to depict them. This procedure is methodologically reflective and requires that the philosophical historian withdraw his own perspective. The price for the loss of a universal perspective, as assumed by Hegel, must not be the confession of any random, merely particular perspective. The generation of scholars who wrote between 1840 and 1860 remain bound to a universal-historical standpoint even if it fades into a regulative idea of philosophical historiography.

---

19 Schwegler (1870), 4–5.
20 Zeller (1886), 3.
21 Zeller (1886), 3.
22 Zeller .(1886), 5.

This clearly changes in the second half of the century. On the borders of academic philosophy, philosophical history reconnects with the social and political questions of its times. It is less such prominent and polemical speakers as Karl Marx, who suspects all philosophy of ideology, who introduces the principle of perspectival thinking into philosophical historiography. Much rather, this task is realised by authors such as Carl Biedermann, who in 1942 publishes his treatise *Die deutsche Philosophie von Kant bis auf unsere Zeit, ihre wissenschaftliche Entwicklung und ihre Stellung zu den politischen und socialen Verhältnissen der Gegenwart* [German Philosophy from Kant to our Time, its Scientific Development and its Position in the Social and Political Conditions of the Present] sets the trend, and Friedrich Albert Lange, who presents his *Geschichte des Materialismus und Kritik seiner Bedeutung in der Gegenwart* [History of Materialism and Critique of its Meaning in the Present] in 1866, as well as Theobald Ziegler whose study *Die geistigen und sozialen Strömungen des neunzehnten Jahrhunderts* [The Intellectual and Social Currents of the 19th Century] appears in 1899.[23] Here, we have an engaged philosophical historiography. Theobald Ziegler made this clear in his introduction to the above-mentioned work:

> I do not stand above the whole but in the midst thereof at a certain location, from which I can only see and trace what reaches this place. [...] Furthermore I assume a determinate perspective insofar as I judge, weigh and execute. That is, as much as I strive towards objectivity, this is not possible without the strongest if also unwanted parade of my subjectivity.[24]

Philosophical historiography becomes partisan, even if, Ziegler claims, it does not represent any certain individual party and, if necessary, it risks falling out with each and every party. This danger shows itself with stark clarity in the second half of the 19th century. Now the chance of a methodological reflective historiography such as that of figures like Schwegler and Zeller is squandered away. I do not wish to claim that a *histoire engagée* cannot produce remarkable results, particularly as it can be written in a very dynamic and exciting fashion, as is evident in Ziegler's work. But the loss not only of a trans-partisan perspective but also of a trans-partisan epistemological interest is deeply distressing. It reveals its consequences especially in the ideologically fostered popular philosophy around 1900.

To conclude this lecture I will turn to a philosophical historian whose work in philosophical historiography is aimed at dealing with this issue by overcoming the perspectival nature of philosophical historiography through the accept-

---

23 Biedermann (1842); Lange (1896).
24 Ziegler (1911), 4.

ance of its inevitability. This is the primary concern of Rudolf Eucken's philosophical-historical work (although, in this regard Wilhelm Dilthey and especially Wilhelm Windelband are equally valid in my opinion).

2.2 Around 1900: The problem of life as the principle of philosophical historiography in Rudolf Eucken's philosophy

In the late 1860s and the 1870s Rudolf Eucken appeared on the philosophical stage with studies on Aristotelian philosophy and works on a theory of philosophical historiography. These include his *Geschichte und Kritik der Grundbegriffe der Gegenwart* [History and Critique of Contemporary Fundamental Concepts] (Leipzig 1878. Second edition: *Die Grundbegriffe der Gegenwart. Historisch und kritisch entwickelt* [The Contemporary Fundamental Concepts. Historically and Critically Developed] Leipzig 1893), his *Geschichte der philosophischen Terminologie im Umriss* [An Outline of the History of Philosophical Terminology] (Leipzig 1879) and a series of treatises that were edited and published as *Beiträge zur Einführung in die Geschichte der Philosophie* [Contributions to the Introduction of the History of Philosophy] (Second edition: Leipzig 1906). Eucken was awarded the Nobel prize for literature in 1908. He was as popular a philosophical writer then as he is underestimated today. However, a look at Eucken's work is very revealing if we want to understand how philosophical historiography in the years around 1900 readied itself for meeting the demands of modernity.

In the following I will emphasize only two aspects of his work. One is Eucken's analysis of philosophical partisanship and the other is his reconstruction of philosophical history against the background of modern humanity's problem of life, whose perpetual striving for the renewal of its power and affirmation of its creative force is to be portrayed.

Eucken recognizes the topic of partisanship as the basic problem of the new philosophical history and philosophical historiography.[25] In the 19th century, as the result of the collapse of the great systems, the history of philosophy retroactively paints a picture of a continual struggle, a struggle which clearly dominates the scene most especially at its peak and turning point. Two elements, according to Eucken, are necessary for the formation of partisanship in philosophy. First the conflict between the parties must represent different sides and levels in the matter itself—for without a factual basis we would be dealing with mere "cli-

---

25 Eucken (1906a), 126–156.

ques" says Eucken. Second, "in the particular historical situation one opposition has to rise above all others, has to be adopted by the people, at the same time gathering and dividing spirits."[26]

Eucken sketches a series of such gathering and turning points in philosophical history but concentrates largely on the modern age. Descartes, Kant and Hegel are paradigmatic of philosophy's capacity to radically and irreversibly alter our perspective on reality. They set us a task that we cannot evade because they inquire into our "basic relation to reality."[27] In its specific context, this means the dependence or independence of the sphere of the mind regarding physical-universal and psychological-individual processes. This, for Eucken, is the "problem of life" for our time and philosophy has the task of articulating it. "Evidently, we don't struggle for the meaning of a commonly given reality but rather for the shaping of reality itself. As such we must place greatest emphasis on how humans realise their own lives and how they understand it."[28]

The second point concerns the struggle for the shaping of reality in which we must lead our lives. In Eucken's view, this is the fundamental topic of contemporary philosophical historiography.[29] Professionalized philosophical historiography has at its disposal "all the tools of a highly developed historical and philosophical research [...]; it teaches us to see appearances more precisely and individually; it thus changes the image of the whole and grants us much greater access to the full and pure factuality of the matter."[30] On the technical level of a Schwegler and a Zeller the question of the value of philosophical historiography for one's own life arises. It is necessary to ask "what the recollection of the collective striving of the past promises us in terms of knowledge of the truth."[31] In his own time, after the collapse of the systems of idealism, Eucken sees the danger of a complete dissolution of the relation between historical data such that the appropriation of history becomes subjected to the power of merely subjective moods and opinions (Nietzsche is a good example of this). To escape this danger we must designate a principle of appropriating historical data or, to put it otherwise: we must, as Eucken emphasizes, understand the history of philosophy as a struggle for principles of its own representability.

Eucken's famous study Die Lebensanschauungen der grossen Denker. Eine Entwicklungsgeschichte des Lebensproblems der Menschheit von Plato bis zur

---

26 Eucken (1906a), 130.
27 Eucken (1906a), 136.
28 Eucken (1906a), 139–140.
29 Eucken (1906b), 157–192.
30 Eucken (1906b), 157–8.
31 Eucken (1906b), 158.

Gegenwart [The Outlooks of Great Thinkers. A Developmental History of Humanity's Problems of Life from Plato to the Present] (1890) is his chief philosophical-historical work. Although once widely read, going in the twenty-five years between its initial appearance and the outbreak of the First World War through more than ten editions and being translated numerous times, today it is scarcely taken seriously at all. However, this book contains an interesting hypothesis. Eucken lays out strict conditions under which philosophical historiography can grow beyond a mere progressive history (the Hegelianism of the people is finished, in Eucken's view), can exceed purpose-bound developmental history (Eucken despised Darwinism) and a working out of philological scholarship (Eucken, unlike Zeller, is no philologist), and can become more than just the expression of partisan engagements (see above). It is only more than all these, Eucken claims, when it thematizes a basic problem, emphasizes its variations in other times and contexts and lets a "coherence" be grasped over and above historical, cultural, social—in brief, partisan conflicts. Only then does it become a genuine "problem of life".

The problem of life in the present, says Eucken, concerns the unstable relationship of human beings to their living reality (both with regard to nature and society). "So long as we are just part of events we lack a distanced perspective from which we can objectify the contemporary disproportioned relationship between human beings and reality." Eucken holds the "turn to realism"[32] in the 19th century responsible for this. The three main realist movements are positivism, the theory of evolution and social democratic sociology. Their analytic achievements are unquestionable but they stop at the observation of individual aspects of nature and society and they neglect the question of the structural cohesion of our reality.

The disproportionate character of human existence is causally related to the phenomena of social life, industrialization, the division of labour and metropolitan life. This indicates a missing cohesiveness in the social and cultural life of human beings. In Eucken's view philosophical analysis shows that the problem of subjective and objective spirit, the question of what constitutes individual life and what stabilizes trans-individual life, is not treated appropriately. The "relationship of the parts" of social and spiritual life is not found but first wrested from the analysis of social and spiritual phenomena and a particularity of a perspective is only gradually discarded. Two things follow from this. First, as concerns the systematic regard, contemporary philosophy is a philosophy of life and culture. Second, with regard to history, we are faced with the task of deter-

---

32 Eucken (1912), 484–486.

mining in the present the historical deposits of knowledge which we need to appropriate for the future viability of our ways of life. Philosophical historiography serves the purpose of pointing out how to appropriate knowledge in the light of the "living present"[33] and to cooperate in the formation of culture as objective spirit. Today we speak, especially from the point of view of educational philosophy, of philosophical historiography as providing orientational knowledge (Steenblock).

3 In conclusion: three hypotheses

If we summarize the results of the preceding sketch of facets of the 19th century historiography of philosophy, we can set down the following hypotheses:
1. Philosophical historiography is a philosophical sub-discipline and it remains committed to the ideal of a "philosophizing history of philosophy". In particular, the thought of progress (beginning with Hegel) and the necessary critique of this must be considered as the historical-philosophical heritage of philosophical historiography.
2. Philosophical historiography has its own subject matter only to a limited extent. It intersects at many points with other disciplines. In methodological regard it stands in debate with social-, cultural- and scientific historiography.
3. Philosophical historiography gains special relevance where ever it manages to connect current problems with traditional reserves of knowledge. In this sense the philosophical historiography of the 19th century is not exclusively monumental, antiquarian or critical, as in Nietzsche's typology, but it faces life.

In conclusion, I still owe an answer to the question of what we can learn from the philosophical historiography of the 19th century. This answer, like the typologies of the history of philosophy themselves, can only be provisional: The above-mentioned hypotheses make clear that philosophical historiography today cannot be written without a systematic guideline, nor without an embedding in scientific- and cultural history nor without making explicit a context of problems.

---

33 Eucken (1912), 3.

Bibliography

Biedermann (1842): Carl Biedermann, *Die deutsche Philosophie von Kant bis auf unsre Zeit, ihre wissenschaftliche Entwicklung und ihre Stellung zu den politischen und socialen Verhältnissen der Gegenwart*, vol. 1 and 2, Leipzig: Verlag von Mayer und Wigand.
Braun (1990): Lucien Braun, *Geschichte der Philosophiegeschichte*, Darmstadt: Wissenschaftliche Buchgesellschaft.
Dilthey (1968): Wilhelm Dilthey, "Die Typen der Weltanschauung und ihre Ausbildung in den metaphysischen Systemen", in: Wilhelm Dilthey, *Gesammelte Schriften*, vol. 8, Stuttgart / Göttingen: Vandenhoeck, 75–118.
Eucken (1906a): Rudolf Eucken, "Parteien und Parteiennamen in der Philosophie", in: Rudolf Eucken, *Beiträge zur Einführung in die Geschichte der Philosophie*, 2nd edition, Leipzig: Verlag der Dürr'schen Buchhandlung, 126–156.
Eucken (1906b): Rudolf Eucken, "Gedanken und Anregungen zur Geschichte der Philosophie", in: Rudolf Eucken, *Beiträge zur Einführung in die Geschichte der Philosophie*. 2nd edition, Leipzig: Verlag der Dürr'schen Buchhandlung, 157–192.
Eucken (1912): Rudolf Eucken, *Die Lebensanschauungen der grossen Denker. Eine Entwicklungsgeschichte des Lebensproblems der Menschheit von Plato bis zur Gegenwart*, 10th edition, Leipzig: Verlag von Veit & Co.
Forster (2012): Michael Forster, "The History of Philosophy", in: Allen W. Wood et al. (Eds.), *The Cambridge History of Philosophy in the Nineteenth Century (1790–1870)*, Cambridge: Cambridge University Press, 866–904.
Gadamer (1986): Hans Georg Gadamer, *Hermeneutik I. Wahrheit und Methode. Grundzüge einer philosophischen Hermeneutik*, in: Hans Georg Gadamer, *Gesammelte Werke*, vol. 1, Tübingen: Verlag Mohr-Siebeck.
Gilbert (1965): Felix Gilbert, "The Professionalization of History in the Nineteenth Century", in: John Higham et al. (Eds.), *History*, Princeton: Prentice Hall Inc, 320–339.
Hartung (2006): Gerald Hartung, "Noch eine Erbschaft Hegels. Der geistesgeschichtliche Kontext der Kulturphilosophie", in: *Philosophisches Jahrbuch der Görres-Gesellschaft* 113, Jg. 2. Hlbbd, Freiburg-München, 382–396.
Hartung (2006): Gerald Hartung, "Theorie der Wissenschaften und Weltanschauung. Aspekte der Aristoteles-Rezeption im 19. Jahrhundert", in: O. Höffe et al. (Eds.), *Zeitschrift für philosophische Forschung* 60/2, Frankfurt a. M., 290–309.
Hartung (2010): Gerald Hartung (Ed.), *Eduard Zeller. Philosophie- und Wissenschaftsgeschichte im 19. Jahrhundert*, Berlin: De Gruyter.
Hartung (2010): Gerald Hartung, "Abschied von der Geschichtsphilosophie? Paul Ricoeurs Geschichtsdenken im Kontext", in: B. Liebsch (Ed.), *Bezeugte Vergangenheit oder Versöhnendes Vergessen. Geschichtstheorie nach Paul Ricoeur* (Deutsche Zeitschrift für Philosophie. Sonderband 24), Berlin: Akademie Verlag, 311–331.
Hartung (2011): Gerald Hartung, "Aristoteles. V. Wirkung A. 1.7. 19. Jahrhundert", in: C. Rapp et al. (Eds.), *Aristoteles-Handbuch. Leben-Werk-Wirkung*, Stuttgart: Metzler Verlag, 450–455.
Köhnke (1993): Klaus Christian Köhnke, *Entstehung und Aufstieg des Neukantianismus. Die deutsche Universitätsphilosophie zwischen Idealismus und Positivismus*, Frankfurt a. M.: Suhrkamp.

Lange (1896): Friedrich Albert Lange, *Geschichte des Materialismus und Kritik seiner Bedeutung in der Gegenwart*, 2 volumes, 5th edition, Leipzig: Verlag von J. Baedeker.

Mann (1996): Wolfgang-Rainer Mann, "The Origins of the Modern Historiography of Ancient Philosophy", in: *History and Theory. Studies in the Philosophy of History*, volume 35, 165–195.

Nietzsche (1988): Friedrich Nietzsche, "Morgenröte", in: *Nietzsche. Kritische Studienausgabe*, vol. 3, Berlin / New York: Deutscher Taschenbuch-Verlag.

Ricoeur (1985): Paul Ricoeur, *Temps et récit*, volume 3 (Le temps raconté), Paris: Éditions du Seuil.

Ricoeur (1974): Paul Ricoeur, *Wahrheit und Geschichte*, Köln: Paul List Verlag.

Rodi (2003): Fridjof Rodi, *Das strukturierte Ganze. Studien zum Werk von Wilhelm Dilthey*, Weilerswist: Velbrück Wissenschaft.

Rosen (2007): Michael Rosen, "The History of Philosophy as Philosophy", in: Brian Leiter et al. (Eds.), *The Oxford Handbook of Continental Philosophy*, Oxford: Oxford University Press, 122–154.

Schneider (1999): Ulrich Johannes Schneider, *Philosophie und Universität – Historisierung der Vernunft im 19. Jahrhundert*, Hamburg: Meiner.

Schwegler (1870): Albert Schwegler, *Geschichte der Philosophie im Umriß. Ein Leitfaden zur Uebersicht*, 7th edition, Stuttgart: Verlag von Carl Conradi.

Trendelenburg (1840): Friedrich Adolph Trendelenburg, *Logische Untersuchungen*, vol. 1, Berlin: Bethge.

Trendelenburg (1855): Friedrich Adolf Trendelenburg, "Ueber den letzten Unterschied der philosophischen Systeme", in: Friedrich Adolf Trendelenburg, *Historische Beiträge zur Philosophie*, vol. 2, Vermischte Abhandlungen, Berlin: Bethge, 1–30.

Zeller (1886): Eduard Zeller, *Grundriss der Geschichte der Griechischen Philosophie*, 2nd edition, Leipzig: Fues's Verlag.

Ziegler (1911): Theobald Ziegler, *Die geistigen und sozialen Strömungen des neunzehnten Jahrhunderts* (Ungekürzte Volksausgabe), Berlin: Georg Bondi.

Gunter Scholtz
From Philosophical Historiography to Historical Philosophy

I

In contrast to the "philosophical" 18th century, the 19th century already called itself "historical", and the concept of "historical philosophy" seems to me characteristic of this. It is a peculiar expression and one that was certainly considered a paradox at the end of the 18th century, since philosophy and history were regarded to be antithetical, being mere synonyms for theory and experience. The concept of historical philosophy suggests, however, that history influences and changes philosophy.

The 18th century laid the foundation for the formation of this concept. Already the age of the Enlightenment took a keen interest in history. This focus was later called the beginning of historicism. I will restrict myself to three short theses:

Through its rationalistic optimism the Enlightenment—as historical Enlightenment—could provide a huge amount of historical knowledge, and thus also a history of philosophy. The historiographies of philosophy record and treat an impressive abundance of such literature from the 18th century.[1]

The Enlightenment, however, also *needed* history to legitimize its own, new point of view. To settle the issue of whether or not progress had been made not only in the natural sciences and technology but also in metaphysics, required knowledge of the history of philosophy.

The Enlightenment, then, *sparked* philosophical historiography as a countermovement, to compensate for its own one-sidedness and deficiencies. Something was missing. And thus, because of the decisive effect of Kant's criticism, Spinoza and Plato's metaphysical thinking received a previously unimagined topicality.

This new *philosophical* interest in the history of philosophy meant that paying attention to the past influenced the philosophy of the present in the form of legitimization and critique. The old was no longer merely being subjected to the judgment of newer views, but old or older philosophy was critically directed against the newer in the field. As a consequence, what was to be considered

---

[1] See the bibliographies in Braun (1990), 391–407, and Schneider (1990), 334–355.

as true philosophy was no longer determined by convention. This loss of convention through progress and Enlightenment becomes visible in the lively discussions about philosophical historiography and also in dictionaries at the end of the 18th century.[2] The older lexicons of philosophy such as those by Goclenius and Micraelius offer definitions that were always considered as binding. But in the 18th century, Georg Walch's handbook informs us in certain places only of what had earlier been thought and of what was now thought about a subject. This implies a higher degree of uncertainty, as compared to the established ways of traditional thinking. Earlier certainties became questionable due to new philosophies.

What philosophy is and should be now had to be worked out through productive philosophizing and through philosophical historiography. Hegel projected a philosophical system that claimed to integrate the truth the entirety of philosophical history had attained. His own philosophy was likewise put to the test of the history of philosophy and, simultaneously, history was interpreted in the light of his system. Whoever was sceptical of this connection could only attempt to find a relationship between philosophy and history characterized by mutual influence. In 1807 in Berlin, Schleiermacher began his lecture on the history of philosophy with the sentence: "Whoever wants to present the history of philosophy must possess philosophy and whoever wants to possess philosophy must understand it historically."[3] Kant could not yet have said this, for he saw the domain of philosophy as determined by the basic questions of reason. Schleiermacher's insight, however, proved to be so compelling in the face of historical knowledge that in 1907, Dilthey chose a very similar approach to determine the essence of philosophy.[4] For whoever excludes the history of philosophy defines only his own philosophy and whoever wants to write philosophy without the history pertaining to it does not even know its domain. Imre Lakatos, who had certainly read nothing of Schleiermacher or Dilthey, similarly related the *theory* of science to the *history* of science.[5]

At any rate, under the sign of historical consciousness, one's own philosophy and so-called systematic philosophy are confronted with the history of philosophy, and both the systematic and the historical are related and directed towards each other. Up to the middle of the 19th century, philosophers often did both, composing philosophical systems and writing philosophical historiography. They do this in full awareness and with philosophical justification. We

---

2 Geldsetzer (1968), 19–80.
3 Schleiermacher (1839), 15.
4 Dilthey (1982b), 339–346.
5 Lakatos (1974).

find examples of this not only in Schleiermacher and Hegel, but also in August Heinrich Ritter, Heinrich Moritz Chalybäus, Hermann Ulrici and many others.

II

But the balance between the historical and the systematic was soon endangered or rejected, and historical knowledge became dominant. There were two factors at work here: First, historical research was taken to be more scientific than drawing up philosophical systems by speculative reason independently of all experience. And second, it appeared only historical knowledge was able to do justice to reality's continual changes.

Already in the 19th century, in the midst of the age of system building, critique of systems began to emerge. All philosophers that were appointed to the newly-established University of Breslau in 1811[6] wanted to be original philosophers, but they expressly did not want to build systems. According to them, the basis for such an enterprise was missing and everything was in flux. They referred to Schelling, who had rightly relinquished systematization. In his thoughts on the university, written in 1810 but never completed and published, Wilhelm von Humboldt expressed himself as quite sceptical about pure speculative philosophy: it could, he claimed, "degenerate".[7] However, in his 1808 *Universitätsschrift* and in his 1810 inaugural address to the Academy, Schleiermacher publicly took the following position: philosophers, in their "petty passion" and "petty limitations", take only their own system as true, whereas unphilosophical observers find their fainthearted assessment that philosophy is not possible because of the "countless different figures" in philosophy and in the change of systems confirmed. What can a research institution such as the Academy do in this situation? Schleiermacher's answer is that it must neither serve a determinate system and thus partisan spirit nor may it facilitate contempt for philosophy, because the philosophical spirit is the basis of all vital research. According to Schleiermacher, the task of the Academy is therefore a "critical and historical examination of philosophy". This entails the following responsibilities: it assumes that all periods of philosophy contributed to the truth but were one-sided and it attempts to understand the individual figures as accurately as possible—both in their contemporary contexts and in their relations to one another, such that the earlier philosophies are often explained through the later and *vice*

---

[6] H. Steffens, L. Thilo, A. B. Kayßler, J. J. Rohovsky.
[7] Humboldt (1900), 363.

versa. It must emphasize in what respect and to what extent systems were one-sided and what remains to be done.⁸

According to Schleiermacher, this "critical and historical examination of philosophy", a combination of hermeneutics and critique, is the "most distinguished business of the philosophical class in an Academy of the Sciences". He had already taken to such a historical and critical examination in his comprehensive book *Grundlinien einer Kritik der bisherigen Sittenlehre* [*Outline of a Critique of Previous Moral Theory*] (1803), where he showed the one-sidedness of the historic configurations of ethics. Moreover, by mediating through a process of extraction, he showed what still had to be done to achieve an ethics that is worth its name. In this way this critical and historiographical approach is on the one hand *historiographical* in that it analyzes individual systems and their context and connections. On the other hand, it is also *philosophical* in that it liberates philosophy from one-sidedness and is thus able to bring it closer to truth. It is therefore able to counter both the one-sidedness of systems as well as the scepticism which appeals to the plurality of systems.

Schleiermacher opens up a field in the history of philosophy that Dilthey later called "historical research with a philosophical intent" and which connected philosophy with all the historical humanities. From 1809 to 1865, Schleiermacher's one-time student and colleague August Boeckh held influential introductory lectures on philology. He explained therein that philology contains all historical humanities because it strives for the reproduction of what is produced by humans, the recognition of what is known (*die Erkenntnis des Erkannten*). According to Boeckh, philology stands opposed to philosophy and it takes what is *handed down by history* as its starting point, whereas philosophy starts with *ideas*. Nevertheless, both disciplines approach each other. Boeckh claims that philology presupposes concepts and is directed towards ideas in history, and philosophy requires history so as to avoid one-sidedness and to reach reality at all. Because of the relatedness of the different areas there is a "point at which philosophy and philology coincide", the most obvious being the philosophy of history and the history of philosophy.⁹ Accordingly, the history of philosophy is a philological philosophy and the philosophy of history is a philosophical philology. Furthermore, since philology carries out historical work we could also aptly speak of a philosophical historiography and a historical philosophy.

Boeckh claims philosophy and philology to be of equal weight. However, his thinking affirms less the necessity of a philosophical "science of ideas" than the

---

8 Schleiermacher (2002a), 7f.
9 Boeckh (1966), 18.

great significance of the combination of philosophy and philology. Philosophical philology is directed towards a philosophy of history, which encompasses the entire development of human culture, of which the history of philosophy is only a part. The highest task of philological critique is to show how knowledge of the truth develops in the history of science and how knowledge of humanity develops within the entirety of cultural history.[10] One has the clear impression that according to Boeckh, philosophical philology—and thus also the history of philosophy—assumes the status pure philosophy used to hold. Philosophical philology has, as opposed to speculative philosophy, well-established and proven methods and it does not postulate and construct ideas but proves the effectiveness its ideas had in history. It is both more scientific and richer in content than pure, abstract philosophy. All historians that we today rank among the historicists (and so not only L. von Ranke) share this conception. Focusing on how "ideas" are effective in history[11], they nonetheless understand their historical work as a science of facts and consider their undertaking superior to merely constructive philosophy.

Also in philosophy did the balance soon incline towards the history of philosophy. As German academic philosophy before 1848 (the so-called *Vormärz*) was fragmented into various original systems and as "progressive system-building and the connected conceptual and linguistic confusion" was increasingly being recognized and bemoaned[12], Immanuel Hermann Fichte and Hermann Ulrici instigated the project of a common historiography of philosophy so as to reestablish agreement through a turn back to "historical objectivity". In their view, history (i.e. the historical philosophical tradition) is "the objective truth in which we live and are".[13] Although systems were still built and a "system of systems" was envisioned as a means of escaping isolation, the history of philosophy assumed the status of the only possible remaining mediator between fractious original philosophers.

III

Schleiermacher could have termed "the critical and historical activity of philosophy" which he recommended to the Academy also "historical philosophy", for it was still concerned with philosophical truth and true philosophy, although it

---

10 Boeckh (1966), 257.
11 See for example Jordan (1999), 116–126.
12 H. S. Lindemann cited by Scholtz (1995), 244.
13 Scholtz (1995), 247.

only dealt with the history of philosophy. His former friend Friedrich Schlegel had already made frequently use of this concept in his notes from 1797 to characterize his position. Thus he noted that all philosophical systems that are not historical are necessarily "lacking".[14] In his Jena lectures on transcendental philosophy from 1800 to 1801 he outlined his basic ideas as follows:

> One can take our philosophy as a *historical* one, as opposed to critical philosophy. But since a historical philosophy must be critical too, the historical is not in opposition to the critical because the latter is the superior to the other and comprises it.[15]

It is in this context that Schlegel makes clear why the historical and the philosophical can be happily united. First, the concept of history has changed. Knowledge consists in empiricism and theory, Schlegel says, and continues: "but the opposition is only relative. It is annulled [*aufgehoben*] by the mediator *history* (in a rigorous sense)."[16] History is no longer the reporting of factual truths, but a relating of empiricism and theory and therefore a theoretically reflected and processed empiricism. Accordingly, the historical treatment of philosophy permits a higher, that is to say an improved and more appropriate critique than Kant's *Critique of Pure Reason*, as this former, unlike Kant, has the multitude of existing systems in view and it also considers historical change. It is the new "philosophy of philosophy", as Schlegel puts it.[17]

This is still more clearly established in his 1805–1806 Cologne lecture course *Propädeutik und Logik*. The substance of thinking stems from three sources, from three "productive capacities", and thus three philosophies also originate from this. If one relies primarily on *sensibility*, one develops the "corrupt way of thinking" of empiricism, which devours everything of "higher mind". If one begins with the *imagination*, one ends up with enthusiasm and fancies. Therefore, true philosophy takes its substance from *memory*.

> Finally, those who want memory as their foundation, which, as a midway, is neither as restricted as sensibility nor as free and unconstrained as the imagination, may want to call this philosophy historical. And it is certain that only such historical philosophy would be perfectly instructive and fruitful for both science and life itself. However, such a philosophy has not yet been devised, let alone completed anywhere, since even the best philosophers have not sufficiently purged their systems from useless subtleties, inane formulas and abstractions.[18]

---

14 Schlegel (1962), 61.
15 Schlegel (1964a), 96. See also Bauer (1966).
16 Schlegel, in the place cited.
17 Schlegel (1964a), 94.
18 Schlegel (1964c), 256 f.

That means that purely systematic philosophy is abstract and empty, which is why the transition to historical philosophy is so necessary, because it takes heeds of historical change, which is made possible only by memory.

In 1804–5 Schlegel held his lectures concerning *Die Entwicklung der Philosophie* [*The Development of Philosophy*] which were posthumously published by Windischmann in 1836. In these lectures, Schlegel is true to his own thought and we can see in his history of philosophy the realization of his historical philosophy. He strives neither for a system nor a mere history of philosophy, but rather undertakes a critical reflection on the history of philosophy. Thus we read that "strictly speaking, there is no history of philosophy as such but [only] a *critique thereof*".[19] Schlegel explains that's because a critique that proceeds historically in no way presupposes a system.[20] Thus Schlegel abolishes the separation between system and history in his historical philosophy. However, in no way had he forsaken the orientation towards truth. Although he had literally said in his Jena lecture: "*all truth is relative*"[21], he did give an outline of the true philosophy. In a way similar to the later Dilthey, Schlegel's historical philosophy orients itself towards the plurality of systems by distinguishing between five general types: empiricism, materialism, scepticism, pantheism and idealism[22] and his characterization of these basic forms is reminiscent of Dilthey's later typology. In contrast to Dilthey, Schlegel shows the deficiencies of the systems and finally differentiates the truth of idealism from the other systems: idealism, according to Schlegel, derives everything from one spirit and this is the true, real philosophical way of philosophizing, which however does not reach a conclusion. Historical philosophy is therefore idealism or, to put it inversely, only idealism can think historically and take historical change into consideration.

Fittingly, Schlegel still closes his lecture with what we would call systematic philosophy, namely with a "psychology as a theory of consciousness" and a "theory of nature".[23] Here he develops the thoughts on which his whole philosophy rests. In his theory of knowledge, Schlegel explains that reason unites feeling, memory and intuitiveness and thereby arrives at a "view of the world" [*Wel-*

---

19 Schlegel (1964b), 111.
20 Schlegel (1964b), 111.—See the concept of critique in for example Schlegel (1975), 60: "One thinks of critique as a meditating part of history and philosophy which connects them both, in which both should be united to a new third element. They cannot thrive without philosophical spirit which is given to both, nor without historical knowledge. The philosophical clarification and testing of history and tradition is undisputedly critique; but it is also undisputable that every historical view of philosophy is also critique."
21 Schlegel (1964a), 94.
22 Schlegel (1964b), 115–153.
23 Schlegel (1964b), 324–408, 409–480.

tansicht]—but to a conception of the world as history, as universal becoming, and not as a static worldview, or a mere image.

> The world is infinite abundance in becoming, and insofar as this infinite abundance is only *one*, it is at the same time *infinite unity*.
>
> The aim of the understanding is the *view of the world [Weltansicht]*, world-wisdom, *history in one word*, and insofar as history includes all becoming, and truly there is in this highest standpoint only *one becoming*, only *one history* and all subdivisions are subsequent to this and relative to this.[24]

His history of philosophy thus shows that there is not and cannot be any complete and perfect philosophy and that the insight into the world as a process of becoming and as history, in which philosophy is embedded, is a necessary one. His formulation allows us to speak of a "historical world-view [*historische Weltanschauung*]".[25] It is insight into the world's being in permanent flux leads to historical philosophy in Schlegel. It has to be noted that Schlegel is the first who frequently makes use of the word "historicism" [*Historismus*].

IV

Schlegel's lectures *The Development of Philosophy* are historical philosophy and border on philosophy of history because philosophy is considered only as a part of *one* history. For methodological reasons, the transition from one discipline to another is also consciously being made. For if the context of a philosophical system is taken into account, one arrives at history as a whole anyway, and it is questionable whether one can or must interpret this too philosophically. Furthermore, this transition to the philosophy of history was also occasioned by changes in actual history. The generation of philosophers who, like Schlegel, thought and wrote in the years around 1800, saw themselves obliged to come to terms not only with the upheavals in philosophy brought about by Kant, but also with the disruptions in the entire human world: the changes in the political and social world due to the French revolution, of religion because of reformation and Enlightenment, of art because of the transition from Antiquity to Modernity, and the domination of nature due to the new sciences. Philosophy could not ignore these changes because as practical philosophy, philosophy of religion, aesthetics, philosophy of nature and philosophy of knowledge it was re-

---

24 Schlegel (1964b), 407.
25 See on the term Scholtz (2015).

lated to those areas of reality. At the same time, the development of philosophy was intertwined with these general historical changes. F. H. Jacobi even maintained that the history of humanity "does not originate from its ways of thinking but its ways of thinking originate from history",[26] something which might have been said already by J. G. Herder. As a result, philosophers felt compelled to connect the history of philosophy with the philosophy of history.

For such thinkers, the relation between the history of philosophy and philosophical world-history in Hegel was not sufficiently clarified. Hegel bases the history of art, religion and philosophy in "absolute spirit", whereas the history of the world is based in "objective spirit". It is not clear how these stand with regard to one another. Should art, religion and philosophy be said to run parallel to objective spirit? But that does not fit with Hegel's basic thoughts. Other authors have explicitly linked philosophy and the history of the world. I will restrict myself to three examples.

Friedrich Ast published his *Grundriss einer Geschichte der Philosophie* [*Outline of a History of Philosophy*] in 1807 and his *Entwurf einer Universalgeschichte* [*Sketch of a Universal History*] in 1810. He organized both of his writings according to the same principle: after the age of unity in the Orient, spirit divided into classical Greece and Christianity so as to proceed towards a higher unity in modernity. Here, philosophy becomes key to the whole development of humanity: it is considered the most important area of the history of the world, namely the "highest sphere of ideal history", which showed "the inner activity of the spirit" from which all else springs.[27] Accordingly, one cannot understand the history of the world without the history of philosophy.

In 1827, C. J. H. Windischmann made a similar connection. In his history of philosophy, he examines the "*history of the intelligence in the progress of the history of the world*" because "then an understanding of world-history in the mirror of intelligence is facilitated".[28] So the "epochs of world-history" manifest "philosophical principles".[29] To sum up the basic convictions of these positions, if philosophy shows a rational development, although being strongly connected with cultural and social history, history in its entirety must, in its main features, be rational.

We find a later example of this in Ch. J. Braniß, who conceptualizes his history of philosophy from 1842 as a philosophy of world-history, thereby wilfully opposing Hegel. According to Braniß, a "veritable historical conception of phi-

---

26 Jacobi (1819), 237, 241.
27 Ast (1807), 8f.
28 Windischmann (1827), IV.
29 Windischmann (1827), L.

losophy" [eine wahrhaft geschichtliche Auffassung der Philosophie] could only consist in "placing oneself in the middle of general historical life itself and becoming aware of its leading idea and therefore its inner purpose".³⁰ The "veritable historical conception" does not separate philosophy from general historical life and interprets the past in the light of present ideas. The history of philosophy elucidates the historical course of spirit, to which it owes its existence. In such a history of philosophy, ideas and general tendencies become much more decisive than individual authors. Braniß's historical conception of philosophy is thus still supported by a metaphysics.³¹

V

In the "historical philosophy" [geschichtliche Philosophie] by the later Schelling, the metaphysical interest is actually pre-dominant. Historical and metaphysical philosophy become one. From the end of the 18th century onwards, there was a turn within theology and jurisprudence towards positive religion and positive law, since the conceptions of reason were found to be abstract, empty and arbitrary. Schelling carries out a similar turn with this "positive philosophy", which deals with mythology and revelation, and in this considers itself obliged by the highest interests of the understanding spirit. Previous philosophy is merely "rational", i.e. it originates from human thinking and thus reaches neither the reality of God nor of human freedom and existing beings, and as such is "negative philosophy". This is supplemented by Schelling's "positive philosophy", which turns not to ideas, but to reality. This demands proof that not only the *idea* of God, but God *itself* "is an object of consciousness". And since "the demand is that divinity move not only into the consciousness of the individual but into the consciousness of humanity", it follows from this

> that this proof continuous with reality in its entirety and with the time of the human race in its entirety, that in this regard it is not a closed but a constant progressing, and extends well into the future of our race, just as it goes back into the past. In this sense especially, positive philosophy is historical philosophy [geschichtliche Philosophie].³²

---

30 Braniß (1842), 298.
31 Scholtz (1973), 73–92.
32 Schelling (1856), 571.

Positive, historical philosophy which interprets the consciousness of God combines "all true metaphysics" in itself.[33] The historically given traditions are, for Schelling, richer in content than rational philosophical systems (among which he groups the Hegelian). Schelling moulds his historical philosophy by considering all previous philosophy, and as such, his positive philosophy is also a critique of the history of philosophy.

He sees F. H. Jacobi as having already paved the way for his historical philosophy. Jacobi, "of all recent philosophers, [had] most vividly felt the need for a historical philosophy (in our sense)."[34] He "wanted historical philosophy" because he "had recognized the merely logical coherence of all earlier systems".[35] In his book on Spinoza, Jacobi had written: "[...] can a living philosophy ever be anything other than history? [...] Philosophy cannot create its material; this always lies in present or in past history."[36] In continuing these thoughts, Schelling no longer finds the most important basis and presupposition of philosophy in the history of philosophy but in positive, historical religion that as Christian religion already presents itself as a "historical" religion. The editor of Schelling's work, Manfred Schröter, finds the term so fitting for Schelling's works from the years 1821 to 1854 that he gave the subtitle *Schriften zur geschichtlichen Philosophie* [*Writings concerning Historical Philosophy*] to volume 5 of the jubilee edition.[37] Today, the term is almost exclusively associated with Schelling.[38]

That valorisation of the tradition over rational thinking makes Schelling's late philosophy attractive to the historical school of law. The conservative legal theorist F. J. Stahl takes Schelling's 1830 concept of historical philosophy as s foundation of his *Rechts- und Staatslehre* [*Theory of Law and the State*]. It is, according to Stahl, a "system of freedom" which understands the world as God's free deed and accepts historical changes, while rationalism subordinates all to its rigid concepts and laws.

> Historical philosophy [*geschichtliche Philosophie*]—this one word in the sense as employed by Schelling, is the most blessed achievement of science within our knowledge. For with this word, a place is prepared in philosophy for Christianity.[39]

---

33 Schelling (1858), 151, remark.
34 Schelling (1861), 168.
35 Schelling (1990), 61, 63.
36 Jacobi (1819), 234, 236.
37 See Schelling (1927).
38 See the still controversial interpretation of Schelling by Schulz (1955) and Hutter (1996).
39 Stahl (1830), 56, compare VIf. Already in 1797 the jurist J. A. L. Seidensticker, in his struggle against natural law in jurisprudence, saw only a "historical philosophy" as acceptable. Anonym (1797), 82: "One cannot be content with the letter of the law. We must raise ourselves to general

VI

At the end of the 19th century, being dominated by the empirical sciences and also by historiographical research, neither classical philosophy of history nor Schelling's new unification of philosophy and religious consciousness could be maintained. Hence the old constellation returned, namely the separation of philosophy from the history of philosophy which proceeds philologically. We find examples of this in neo-Kantianism and in the work of the later Eduard Zeller. Since, through historiographical research, insight into the historical contingency of philosophical thought and of all culture, and of the natural sciences too, had deepened and since nature in its development had also stepped into its view, "historical philosophy" emerged anew, but very differently. This newly emerged historical philosophy shares with Schelling's version only the view that the basis of philosophy is not itself philosophical and that philosophy rests on entirely different historical currents. I will briefly mention three representatives of this but have to keep my remarks to a minimum.

In *Menschliches Allzumenschliches* [*Human, all too Human*] (1878–86), Nietzsche launches a polemic against the traditional metaphysical philosophy which does not accept universal becoming, origination and decay in the natural and human world and opposes his historical philosophy to this:

> The lack of a historical sense [*historischem Sinn*] is the hereditary defect of all philosophers [...]. They do not want to learn that humanity has developed; that the capacity for knowledge too has developed [...]. But everything did develop; there are *no eternal matter of facts*: just as there are no absolute truths either.—Accordingly, *historical philosophizing* [*historisches Philosophiren*] is necessary from now on and with it the virtue of modesty.[40]

This is aimed at Schopenhauer in particular. With his conception of the alogical willing of the world, Schopenhauer had not only opposed the contemporary philosophy of spirit but also the link between philosophy and history. What's more, he had explicitly opposed "*historical philosophizing*". "For philosophy and therefore the understanding of the essence of life, one does not need history. It is ridiculous to want to make history a part of philosophy." The history of philosophy is only for the average mind which feels no desire for philosophy. "For we are of

---

principles but only those that can be abstracted from positive sources. We must throw ourselves into the arms of a philosophy, but only of a historical one, that means one that has before its eyes legislation in its legal determination, that lets itself be developed from positive sources, and that itself is part of the positive." See Thibaut (1817), 128 f.

40 Nietzsche (1967), 20 f (Aphor. 2). See Lanfranconi (2000).

the opinion that everyone who supposes that the essence of the world can be conceived somehow as *historical*, albeit ever so finely cloaked, is abysmally far from a philosophical knowledge of the world [...]."[41]

In Nietzsche's view, Schopenhauer, with this turn from historical philosophizing, represents the entire metaphysical tradition which has not come to terms with eternal becoming. Still, he remains close to Schopenhauer. For this principle of the willing of the world was a natural principle and Nietzsche's historical philosophy is, as he said, "no longer to be thought of as separate from natural science".[42] Nietzsche's new historical philosophy not only takes on Heraclitus' principle of permanent becoming. One of its unique characteristics is its link to Darwinism and its striving to be a kind of natural history in that it proceeds genealogically, leading the human world back to the natural phenomena and shows that "the most exquisite colours" of human culture "are derived from low, even despised substances".[43] Human history is understandable only when set against the background of natural history.

Dilthey did not, to the best of my knowledge, use the concept of historical philosophy, but he asked to do justice to the "historicity of consciousness" in philosophy. In his 1907 treatise *Das Wesen der Philosophie* [*The Essence of Philosophy*], he presents his typology of world-views and distinguishes three established basic forms, which recur in the history of philosophy in different variations: naturalism, the idealism of freedom and objective idealism.

> Just as the botanist classifies plants and researches the law of their growth so too the analyst of philosophy must seek out the types of world-views [*Weltanschauungen*] and recognize the lawfulness of their formation. Such a comparative examination raises the human spirit above confidence founded in its contingency to grasping truth itself in one of these world-views. Just as the great historiographers' objectivity does not seek to master [i.e. confirm or refute] the ideals of the individual times, so the philosopher must grasp the examining consciousnesses itself, which subjects objects to itself, historically-comparatively and thus assume a position over them all. For then the historicity of consciousness completes itself in it.[44]

This strange proposition can only be understood in context. Dilthey explains that the definition of the essence of philosophy necessarily demands the move from a systematic to a "historical standpoint". In this way the different philosophies, which originate in definite situations, are "understood in their necessity", and

---

41 Schopenhauer (1911), 322.
42 Nietzsche (1967), 19 (Aphor. 1).
43 Nietzsche (1967), 19 (Aphor. 1).
44 Dilthey (1982b), 380.

this constitutes "the superiority of this standpoint". At the same time, we achieve the insight that all systems are bound by their context and a definite perspective and that no single metaphysics can make a general claim to truth. While all productive philosophy lives in the hope of achieving something lasting which won't be lost in history, historical consciousness lives "in the embracing of all times and it becomes aware of the relativity and transience of everything done by individuals." Dilthey adds: "This contradiction is the pain present philosophy silently suffers"—for historical knowledge that has been achieved cannot be removed. The solution lies in the attitude of the philosopher. "His work must know itself as part of the historical nexus, a nexus in which he consciously realizes a contingency."[45] That means: *without* historical consciousness the philosopher only knows "a fraction of reality", *with* historical consciousness, however, he becomes conscious of his own finitude. It only remains to consciously bear this finitude, this limitation and contingency in the trust that the historical coherence of objective spirit is meaningful. The sovereign gaze at the history of philosophy in its entirety, which orders metaphysics by coldly compares its different types, leads, in a manner analogous to Nietzsche, to the modesty to see one's own thinking as only a small part of an expanding whole. The humanities lay bare this constantly changing whole in all its diversity. Dilthey calls this result the "historical world-view" [*historische Weltanschauung*].[46]

Dilthey's friend, Count Paul Yorck von Wartenburg, avoided the expression "historical world-view" probably because it meant again fixing a firm image where there are only forces in action. Yorck's whole thinking is directed against determining, distancing, aestheticizing, against objective observation and comparison of historical phenomena, against every "externally [oriented] manner" of consideration that is satisfied with so-called facts. Thus it is directed against metaphysics as well as against the dominance of natural-scientific modes of examination. All of these lose sight of the "historicity" of humanity, its being determined by history, and its actual life. Yorck's philosophy is avowedly a historical philosophy, and for him there cannot be another kind. This is because the philosophizing person lives in a specific historical context and thinking, feeling and wanting are all shaped by tradition, which has to be clarified. The idea to catapult oneself to a meta-historical standpoint by mental effort is an illusion. Already the language and concepts which the philosopher employs indicate his "belonging" [*Zugehörigkeit*] to a certain tradition. And this is not just a bar-

---

[45] Dilthey (1982b), 363f.
[46] Dilthey (1982a), 9. This is a *Weltanschauung* (world-view) that Dilthey did not take into his theory of world-views. Unlike the others it solves no vital enigmas. But there are good reasons for thinking it corresponds with objective idealism. See Scholtz (2015).

rier, but also the way in which history itself can be understood and dealt with. For (and here we are reminded of Schlegel): "All true living history, not merely that which glimmers with the semblance of life, is criticism."[47] The precondition of philosophizing is real, historical life—not an *a priori*, pure reason. A famous statement from York in a letter to Dilthey, which Heidegger quotes in *Being and Time*, suffices to support this:

> Because to philosophize is to live, there is, in my opinion (do not be alarmed!), a philosophy of history—but who would be able to write it?—Certainly it is not the sort of thing it has hitherto been taken to be, or the sort that has so far been attempted; you have declared yourself incontrovertibly against all that. Up until now, the question has been formulated in a way which is false, even impossible; but this is not the only way of formulating it. Thus there is no longer any actual philosophizing that would not be historical. The separation between systematic philosophy and historical presentation is essentially incorrect.[48]

This is not the place for a discussion of Yorck, but I aim to make clear why his thought exerted fascination and helped to further develop hermeneutic philosophy. At least this much can be noted: for Yorck, the main question is not whether one needs history and the history of philosophy. Rather, his thesis is that they can't be avoided since we're already within their sphere of influence. History without philosophy remains mute, at a distance, antiquarian—and systematics without history is empty, constructed, contrived, and removed from life and without content. Under the presupposition of their separateness, neither present nor past thinking are understandable or fruitful. Historical philosophy, however, is the elucidation of the present situation in context of history as a field of forces which are active over long periods of time.

Nietzsche's, Dilthey's and Yorck's historical philosophies were thus very different from each other. However, there are certain common denominators which can be summarized as follows:

Historical philosophy at the end of the 19th century bids a final farewell to the idea of a system. Dilthey presented ever new versions of his system only in his lectures. His friend Yorck von Wartenburg wholly gave up the idea of a system and wrote in 1887: "in the case of the inner historicity of self-consciousness, a systematics separated from history is methodologically inadequate."[49] Given its peculiar situation, philosophy can only reflect the current of history in which it is located. The ever-changing abundance of knowledge makes a system-

---

47 Dilthey (1923), 19: Count Yorck to Dilthey, 9. Mai 1881.
48 Dilthey (1923), 251: Count York to Dilthey, 11. II. 84.
49 Dilthey (1923), 69: Count Yorck to Dilthey, 4.12.1887.

atic ordering of philosophical principles difficult, since with the growth of knowledge all principles become questionable. Therefore, as Nietzsche brusquely puts it in *Götzen-Dämmerung* [*Twilight of the Idols*] (1889), "the will to a system is a lack of honesty."[50] In the same year, Wilhelm Wundt writes: "That philosophical systems are over once and for all is considered as a settled truth in many circles today."[51]

Nietzsche, Dilthey and Yorck also depart from idealistic philosophy of history. Instead, they emphasize or accept permanent historical change in all regions of culture and society. However, they sketch new interpretative frameworks, so as to orient themselves in these changes and to render the present comprehensible. These interpretative frameworks take the shape of something like a history which considered philosophically, or a new philosophy of history. One thinks of Nietzsche's confrontation of modern-Socratic civilization with antiquarian-tragic culture, of Dilthey's model of the differentiation the spheres of culture and of Yorck's contrasting the "positions of consciousness" in pagan Antiquity and in Christianity.

We see something similar in the metaphysics from which these thinkers turn. This too is not wholly abandoned without any replacement. Rather, one needs a theory which can explain the permanent change of all things and help us endure it. And hence, one ends up adopting constants nonetheless. Nietzsche orients himself towards Heraclitus' metaphysics of eternal becoming and finds a constant in the will to power. In Dilthey's philosophy, the concept of life increasingly becomes a final quasi-metaphysical principle on which everything is founded, and Yorck is very outspoken on how one ought to respond to the changes of history: by a religious relation to transcendence.

Henceforth, the history of philosophy is seldom isolated as the pure history of a discipline but is almost always examined within the context of culture and concrete realizations of life, and often the history of religion and science are considered to be more important than the history of philosophy because they have a greater influence. The relationship of these authors to tradition and the history of philosophy, however, vary considerably. In Nietzsche, it takes the form of an unmasking and of a universal critique of culture, whereas Yorck aims stabilizing of the tradition. Dilthey takes an intermediate position, at least with regard to metaphysical systems: although they will never become scientific, they are justified as an authentic expression of life. However, according to all three authors, the history of philosophy is—as Schlegel demanded—critique, never mere historical

---

50 Nietzsche (1969), 57.
51 Wundt (1889), III.

science. This critique is seen as a living examination of the past in the face of the present.[52]

If the historical has not yet been separated from the systematic (or more recently, the analytic) in German universities, we owe this to insights won in the 19th century.

Bibliography

Anonym (1797): [Johann Anton Ludwig Seidensticker], *Geist der juristischen Literatur von dem Jahre 1796*, Göttingen: J.Ch. Dieterich.
Ast (1807): Friedrich Ast, *Grundriss einer Geschichte der Philosophie*, Landshut: J. Thomann.
Ast (1810): Friedrich Ast, *Entwurf der Universalgeschichte*, zweite, vermehrte und verbesserte Auflage, Landshut: J. Thomann.
Ast (1825): Friedrich Ast, *Grundriss der Geschichte der Philosophie*, zweite, vermehrte und verbesserte Auflage, Landshut: J. Thomann.
Bauer (1966): Günther Bauer, *Der absolute Idealismus als Voraussetzung einer historischen Philosophie. Ein Versuch über die Philosophie des jungen Friedrich Schlegel*, Dissertation: München [o. V.].
Boeckh (1966): August Boeckh, *Enzyklopädie und Methodenlehre der philologischen Wissenschaften*, ed. by E. Bratuschek, *Erster Hauptteil: Formale Theorie der philologischen Wissenschaft*, Darmstadt: Wissenschaftliche Buchgesellschaft.
Braniß (1842): Christlieb Julius Braniß, *Uebersicht des Entwicklungsganges der Philosophie in der alten und mittleren Zeit* (*Geschichte der Philosophie seit Kant. Erster Theil, Einleitung*), Breslau: J. Max.
Braun (1990): Lucien Braun, *Geschichte der Philosophiegeschichte*, Darmstadt: Wissenschaftliche Buchgesellschaft.
Dilthey (1923): *Briefwechsel zwischen Wilhelm Dilthey und dem Grafen Paul Yorck v. Wartenburg 1877–1897*, Halle (Saale): M. Niemeyer.
Dilthey (1982a): Wilhelm Dilthey, "Rede zum siebzigsten Geburtstag" (1903), in: Wilhelm Dilthey, *Gesammelte Schriften*, vol. 5, *Die geistige Welt. Einleitung in die Philosophie des Lebens*, 7th edition, Stuttgart: B.G. Teubner, 7–9.

---

[52] This is particularly evident in their relation to Heraclitus. In the 19th century, the historical century, Heraclitus' thinking was the favourite philosophy of the philosophers that constantly argued and understood themselves historically. Schleiermacher published the first great treatise on Heraclitus, Hegel explained that there was no sentence of Heraclitus that he had not absorbed into his logic, F. Lassalle published a two volume study of Heraclitus, Count Yorck of Wartenburg wrote a relevant but incomplete treatise on, and lastingly Nietzsche criticized the whole metaphysical tradition with the help of Heraclitean metaphysics. It is as if one needed, before the experience of too much change and too much that was new, the solace of a very old theory that assures that it had always been so and was never otherwise.

Dilthey (1982b): Wilhelm Dilthey, *Das Wesen der Philosophie* (1907), in: Wilhelm Dilthey, *Gesammelte Schriften*, vol. 5, *Die geistige Welt. Einleitung in die Philosophie des Lebens*, 7th edition, Stuttgart: B.G. Teubner, 339–416.

Geldsetzer (1968): Lutz Geldsetzer, *Die Philosophie der Philosophiegeschichte im 19. Jahrhundert. Zur Wissenschaftstheorie der Philosophiegeschichtsschreibung und -betrachtung*, Meisenheim a. Gl.: A. Hain.

Humboldt (1900): Wilhelm von Humboldt, "Über die innere und äussere Organisation der höheren wissenschaftlichen Anstalten in Berlin" (1809/10), in: Adolf Harnack, *Geschichte der Königlich Preussischen Akademie der Wissenschaften zu Berlin*, vol. 2, Berlin: Reichsdruckerei, 361–367.

Hutter (1996): Axel Hutter, *Geschichtliche Vernunft. Die Weiterführung der Kantischen Vernunftkritik in der Spätphilosophie Schellings*, Frankfurt a. M.: Suhrkamp.

Jacobi (1819): Friedrich Heinrich Jacobi, *Ueber die Lehre des Spinoza, in Briefen an den Herrn Moses Mendessohn*, in: Friedrich Heinrich Jacobi, *Werke*, vol. 4, 1. Abt., Leipzig: G. Fleischer.

Jordan (1999): Stefan Jordan, *Geschichtstheorie in der ersten Hälfte des 19. Jahrhunderts. Die Schwellenzeit zwischen Pragmatismus und klassischem Historismus*. Frankfurt a. M. / New York: Campus.

Lanfranconi (2000): Aldo Lanfranconi, *Nietzsches historische Philosophie*, Stuttgart / Bad Cannstatt: Frommann-Holzboog.

Lakatos (1974): Imre Lakatos, "Die Geschichte der Wissenschaft und ihre rationalen Rekonstruktionen", in: Imre Lakatos a. Alan Musgrave (Eds.), *Kritik und Erkenntnisfortschritt*, Braunschweig: Vieweg, 271–311.

Nietzsche (1967): Friedrich Nietzsche, *Menschliches, Allzumenschliches I*, in: Friedrich Nietzsche, *Werke. Kritische Gesamtausgabe*, 4. Abt., vol. 2, ed. by Giorgio Colli a. Mazzino Montinari, Berlin: De Gruyter.

Nietzsche (1969): Friedrich Nietzsche, *Götzen-Dämmerung*, in: Friedrich Nietzsche, *Werke. Kritische Gesamtausgabe*, 6. Abt., vol. 3, ed. by Giorgio Colli a. Mazzino Montinari, Berlin: De Gruyter, 49–154.

Schelling (1856): Friedrich Wilhelm Joseph Schelling, *Einleitung in die Philosophie der Mythologie*, in: Friedrich Wilhelm Joseph Schelling, *Sämmtliche Werke*, 2. Abt., vol. 1, Stuttgart / Augsburg: J.G. Cotta.

Schelling (1858): Friedrich Wilhelm Joseph Schelling, *Philosophie der Offenbarung*, in: Friedrich Wilhelm Joseph Schelling, *Sämmtliche Werke*, 2. Abt., vol. 3, Stuttgart / Augsburg: J.G. Cotta.

Schelling (1861): Friedrich Wilhelm Joseph Schelling, "Zur Geschichte der neueren Philosophie", 1. Abt., vol. 10, in: Friedrich Wilhelm Joseph Schelling, *Sämmtliche Werke*, 2. Abt., vol. 3, Stuttgart / Augsburg: J.G. Cotta, 1–200.

Schelling (1927): Friedrich Wilhelm Joseph Schelling, *Werke*, ed. by Manfred Schröter, vol. 5, *Fünfter Hauptband: Schriften zur geschichtlichen Philosophie 1821–1854*, München: C.H. Beck.

Schelling (1990): Friedrich Wilhelm Joseph Schelling, *System der Weltalter. Münchener Vorlesung 1827/28, in einer Nachschrift von Ernst von Lasaulx*, ed. by Siegbert Peetz, Frankfurt a. M.: Klostermann.

Schlegel (1975): Friedrich Schlegel, "Lessings Gedanken und Meinungen" [1804], in: *Kritische Friedrich-Schlegel-Ausgabe* (= KFSA) vol. 3, *Charakteristiken und Kritiken (1802–1829)*, ed. by H. Eichner, München / Paderborn / Wien: F. Schöningh, 46–102.

Schlegel (1962): Friedrich Schlegel, *Philosophische Lehrjahre 1796–1828*, ed. by Ernst Behler, KFSA vol. 18, München / Paderborn / Wien: F. Schöningh.
Schlegel (1964a): Friedrich Schlegel, *Transcendentalphilosophie (1800–1801)*, KFSA vol. 12: *Philosophische Vorlesungen* [1800–1807], ed. by Jean-Jacques Anstett, München / Paderborn / Wien: F. Schöningh, 1–105.
Schlegel (1964b): Friedrich Schlegel, *Die Entwicklung der Philosophie in zwölf Büchern* [1804–1805], KFSA vol. 12, *Philosophische Vorlesungen (1800–1807)*, ed. by Jean-Jacques Anstett, München / Paderborn / Wien: F. Schöningh, 107–480.
Schlegel (1964c): Friedrich Schlegel, *Propädeutik und Logik* [Köln 1805–1806], KFSA vol. 13: *Philosophische Vorlesungen* [1800–1807], hg. Jean-Jacques Anstett, München / Paderborn / Wien: F. Schöningh, 177–384.
Schleiermacher (1839): Friedrich Schleiermacher, *Geschichte der Philosophie*, ed. by Heinrich Ritter, in: Friedrich Schleiermacher, *Sämmtliche Werke*, 3. Abt. vol. 4/1, Berlin: G. Reimer.
Schleiermacher (2002a): Friedrich Schleiermacher, "Antrittsvortrag" [1810], in: Friedrich Schleiermacher, *Kritische Gesamtausgabe* I. Abt. vol. 11, ed. by Martin Rössler, Berlin: De Gruyter, 1–7.
Schneider (1990): Ulrich Johannes Schneider, *Die Vergangenheit des Geistes. Eine Archäologie der Philosophiegeschichte*, Frankfurt a. M.: Suhrkamp.
Scholtz (1973): Gunter Scholtz, *"Historismus" als spekulative Geschichtsphilosophie: Christlieb Julius Braniß (1792–1873)*, Frankfurt a. M.: Klostermann.
Scholtz (1995): Gunter Scholtz, "Metaphysik und Politik im Spätidealismus", in: Walter Jaeschke (Ed.), *Philosophie und Literatur im Vormärz. Der Streit um die Romantik (1820–1854) (Philosophisch-literarische Streitsachen 4)*, Hamburg: Meiner, 235–259.
Scholtz (2015): Gunter Scholtz, "Weltanschauung", in: *Schlüsselbegriffe der Philosophie des 19. Jahrhunderts* (Sonderband des Archivs für Begriffsgeschichte), Hamburg: Meiner.
Schopenhauer (1911): Arthur Schopenhauer, *Die Welt als Wille und Vorstellung*, in: Arthur Schopenhauer, *Sämtliche Werke*, vol. 1, ed. by Paul Deussen, München: Piper.
Schulz (1955): Walter Schulz, *Die Vollendung des deutschen Idealismus in der Spätphilosophie Schellings*, Stuttgart / Köln: Kohlhammer.
Stahl (1830): Friedrich Julius Stahl, *Die Philosophie des Rechts nach geschichtlicher Ansicht*, vol. 1, Heidelberg: J.C.B. Mohr.
Thibaut (1817): Anton Friedrich Justus Thibaut, *Versuche über einzelne Theile der Theorie des Rechts*. Zweite verbesserte Ausgabe, vol. 1, Jena: J.M. Mauke und Sohn.
Windischmann (1827): Carl Joseph Hieronymus Windischmann, *Die Philosophie im Fortgang der Weltgeschichte. Erster Theil: Die Grundlagen der Philosophie im Morgenland. Erste Abtheilung*, Bonn: Adolph Marcus.
Wundt (1889): Wilhelm Wundt, *System der Philosophie*, Leipzig: W. Engelmann.

Emil Angehrn
On the Meaning of the History of Philosophy

1 Philosophy and its History

Philosophy has a history. Or, to put it more accurately, we can say that philosophy is *in* history and it *has* a history. Both elements constitute its historicity. It is, in its entirety as well as in every respective concrete form, *in* history, part of a comprehensive, temporal and factual history that precedes and exceeds it; and it *has* a history—its own history, that determines its character and its course. Philosophy shares this characteristic with other intellectual and cultural formations, with music, religion, the nation, football—in which both of these aspects of historicity also always exert their influence. These too are all historically situated and happen *as* history. Its particular history is part of a general history, the history of the collective, of the epoch, of culture, of humanity and, in other respects, of nature, of being.

1.1 Philosophy's Relatedness to History

Nevertheless, the realization that philosophy has a history is no triviality. This is because philosophy is historical and has a history in ways that differ from those of medicine or Baroque music (let alone the glaciers). Philosophy is a cultural formation that is essentially historical and this in the sense that it is not only factically rooted in history and historically conditioned but further in that it is constitutively related to its history. This is first of all a descriptive, distinctive characteristic of philosophy which conspicuously sets it apart from other sciences and cultural forms. A glance at philosophical research as well as at teaching, the conference calendar, publishing brochures, libraries and course catalogues sufficiently demonstrates this. Next to systematic themes and research questions of applied ethics up to ontology we find a many-sided pre-occupation with the history of philosophy as well as with individual authors and movements, epochs and with the history of philosophy as a whole. This kind of relatedness to history appears to be an essential characteristic of philosophy. However, it is an ambivalent and controversial basic feature of philosophizing. Historicity conflicts with philosophy's claim to truth, a claim which aims at a trans-historical knowledge that is not bound by the conditions of time. The separation of genesis and validity should uncouple the validity of an insight from its factical genesis. From the beginning philosophy maintains itself in opposition to relativism, to which belongs a return to subjective suppositions as well as to historiographical contextualization and to genealogical foundations. The tension between the claim to truth and consciousness of historicity appears to be inherent in prominent philosophical positions. The split manifests itself in the self-understanding of philosophy as well as in the external judgment of it. Respect and contempt for the historiographical stand immediately opposed in the conflict between purely systematic and historical-philological work. This conflict plays itself out between the apparent self-evidence of broad and highly elaborated historiographical research on the one hand and the critical rejection of classical readings as well as an equally differentiated conceptual-systematic discussion on the other.

It is a controversy that cannot simply be resolved by taking a strategic position for one or the other side. Even if this fundamental relatedness to history designates a controversial situation, it nonetheless stands for a distinctive and basic feature of philosophy that cannot be struck out unless one wants to engage in an arbitrary redefinition of the discipline. Philosophy, as a way of thinking that evolved historically and was shaped throughout its development by culture, *is* characterized by a strong relatedness to its history. It constitutes the overarching framework and lies at the basis of a common language within which philosophers negotiate their themes, articulate their hypotheses and contest opposing concepts; allowing for diversification and dissent, it makes possible a coherent expert discourse. The history of philosophy, as Wilfred Sellars says, forms the *lingua franca* of philosophy.[1]

1.2 The Continuity of Philosophy

At the same time, the relatedness to history is not only a controversial basic feature of philosophy but above all one that requires elucidation. This relatedness remains to be clarified, just as much as the question in which sense it is a constitutive element of philosophy. The historiography of philosophy is not external to philosophy; it does not occur as an auxiliary discipline, an external, optional supplement such as, for example, the way in which medical history is related to medical research. Rather, in classical concepts it becomes an integral part of philosophy itself (see, for example, Hegel). Externally its coherence manifests in the fact that the historiography of philosophy doesn't appear primarily in historio-

---

[1] Sellars (1967), 1.

graphical research or in the historiography of ideas in cultural studies. It is not studied primarily by historians but by philosophers. Philosophy writes its own history and does not hand it over to the professional expertise of historiographers. Likewise, the history of philosophy is read, interpreted and appropriated by philosophy itself. The historiography of philosophy stands for a specific reflexivity of philosophy, which relates in a specific way to itself in its relation to history. Elucidating this self-relatedness is an essential part of explicating the historiography of philosophy as well as of philosophy itself.

First of all a general characteristic must be identified which is associated with this self-relatedness in the medium of history. It can be located in the unusual continuity of philosophy. Even if the history of philosophy, as other cultural fields, is characterised by breaks, innovative new beginnings, diversions and losses, it is a fact that Western philosophy, which originated in Greece, is distinguished from other cultural creations through a progressive series of connections and references perpetuated through the epochs. It belongs not only to the oldest and most prestigious creations of this exceptionally creative epoch, in which many forms of European culture, artworks and sciences have their origin. Above all it is characterised by a unique kind of retrocursive relatedness both to earlier positions as well as to the beginning of the discipline and its history as a whole. The philosophers of late Antiquity, the Middle Ages and of the modern and contemporary eras work out their views and acquire their self-understanding by entering into dialogue with earlier authors and grappling with their own pre-history, a pre-history that they partly inherit and partly write anew, critically revise or dismiss. The pre-eminent meaning of the origin, namely the powerful impression Plato and Aristotle made on philosophical discourse is quite different to that made by the histories of Thucydides and Herodotus's on historiography or that made by Greek sculpture on the fine arts. The beginning not only had actual effects in subsequent history but it remains as that to which philosophy in the present attaches itself to or pushes off from. The communicative community in which every science develops in the case of philosophy expands from a synchronic to a diachronic dialogue with earlier generations.

1.3 The Historicity of Spirit

Why this is so remains to be clarified. The substantial, philosophical hypothesis which corresponds to these external characteristics of philosophy's relatedness to history and the continuity of philosophical discourse is that of the hypothesis of a fundamental historicity of thinking. In a pronounced fashion Hegel had worked this out in such a way that he doesn't read it as a form of temporal relativism but as an immanent historicity of reason. The historicity of reason and the rationality of history are contradictory indications, within this immanent intertwinement of philosophical thought and its history. The hypothesis of reason in history is obviously a strong one and rich in presuppositions, which Hegel believes to be the only *a priori* to a philosophical theory of history. But this is not merely a precondition, he thinks, but a demonstrandum and a result of the accomplished and material meaning of world-history, at the same time. Historical knowledge had to prove that history happened rationally. It is a basic hypothesis that is also, in Hegel, affected by the immanent tension between historicity and the claim to truth. It is the ambivalence of a form of thinking and reflection that developed in time and appears with the claim to the highest knowledge since its beginnings.

In this context, the history of philosophy is up for debate in two respects. To draw on a conventional German conceptual distinction, even though it tends not to be used consistently, it concerns the "history" [*"Geschichte"*] and the "historiography" [*"Historie"*] of philosophy respectively. What is at stake here is the temporal development of the matter itself, of philosophical thinking, as well as its representation and reflective recollection. Both are essential for an understanding of the historicity of philosophy, and both became object of philosophical theories. These theories are interested in the way in which thought essentially develops in time, is based on what preceded it, takes this in and alters it, progressing according to laws or through ruptures and unpredictable innovations. But it also concerns how philosophy itself is retrocursively related to its past, how this past is recollected and interpreted, the latter being the function of the historiography of philosophy [*Philosophiehistorie*] for philosophy. When I referred to 'meaning of the history of philosophy' in the title of this paper, this formulation points in both of these directions. On the one hand, it can be understood as the question concerning how far the development of thought possesses an immanent meaning, a teleological tendency[2] and on the other it can be understood as the question of what meaning and function the historiography of philosophy has *for* philosophy. The focal point of the following considerations is the second reading. I will not focus on considerations on the course of philosophical thinking throughout the ages but rather on questions concerning the logic and function of the recollection of philosophy. It concerns, schematically, the meaning of the historiography [*Historie*] and not of the history [*Geschichte*] of philosophy.

However it should be noted that the two analytically distinct aspects—"history" and "historiography"—cannot really be detached from one another. This applies to both the history of worldly events as well as to the history of ideas. History is not

---

[2] One such direction of questioning comes to fruition in Stekeler-Weithofer (2006).

simply the objective course and totality of past facts. It is a course of events in so far as it is of concern for the "subject" in question, is important and present to it, if it is reflected by him and appropriated through him. By means of the unity of both aspects a distinction can be made between what is commonly called history (human history) and objectively occurring processes in nature (the "history" of the Alps or of the universe). Also for philosophical-historical reflection the reciprocal interference of both sides is important and to some degree it constitutes the very point of conceptual history. History becomes human history only insofar as humans become aware of it, grasp it and insofar as it becomes controllable through reason, at least ideally. According to Marx we only speak of real history when people take destiny into their own hands and themselves determine the conditions of life.[3] Hegel envisions an even more radical entanglement of both sides when he situates the philosophy of history itself historically, claiming that the possibility of understanding history rationally is itself a result of the world-historical process of liberation. Firstmodern humanity is able to translate the rational claim of nature into the human world and to recognize the immanent *ratio* in the wealth of human productions. Both the philosophy of history [*Geschichtsphilosophie*] as well as the history of philosophy [*Philosophiegeschichte*] have, in this sense, their genuine place in the present.

2 The Writing and Reading of History

Before we further explore the function of the historiography of philosophy, the more fundamental question concerning its logic arises: in what forms and in accordance with what criteria does philosophy turn to its past and recollect its history? The logic of the historiography of philosophy, in this regard, embraces the logic of writing as well as that of reading, the construction as well as the reception of the history of thought—a unique entwining, which is based on the fact that that the historiography of philosophy on its part too is based on reading and practices a kind of reading. Similarly the question of the meaning of the history of philosophy encompasses the concerns of both side. Only a few aspects concerning the history of philosophy will be mentioned in the following.

---

3 Marx (1968), 546, 544, 570.

2.1 The Object of the Historiography of Philosophy

First, the historiography of philosophy is confronted with the question of what its object is. More accurately it concerns the extensional question of what is to be counted as within the field of philosophy and its history. Normally the delimitation of a subject area pre-necessitates an undisputed definition of philosophy that decides to what extent a history of philosophy ought to consider poetry, medicine, law and theology, the natural sciences and myths. Classical german lexicons such as the *Grundriss der Geschichte der Philosophie* or the *Historische Wörterbuch der Philosophie* suggest different demarcations. Rather than adhering to the confines of academic disciplines and publications, Kurt Flasch suggests to focus on the argumentative substance of texts and to work with an open concept of philosophy that is to be tested concretely.[4] At the same time the level on which philosophical thinking is or should be historically reconstructed is up for discussion. Historiographical studies are concerned with individual works and authors, with the development of concepts and problems, with currents, schools and epochs even including a comprehensive history of Western (or even human) thinking; and the approaches to this can be comparative, systematic or narrative-synthetic. A particular range, which the historical understanding of past philosophy covers, is that between intellectual work of individuals on the one hand and the "objective", trans-individual development of philosophical thought on the other. In this regard, Dieter Henrich[5] distinguishes between the history of the genesis of significant works on the basis of drafts, revisions and editions which have become accessible in the past two centuries and which were not available before and the genesis of the philosophical insights of their authors, on the other hand, which evolve through the typical stages of the perception of a deficit and of a problem, of absorbing new perspectives in their relevance for the immanent theory and their relatedness to life, their lengthy elaboration, differentiation and review. According to Henrich, "constellation research" complements the study of the genesis of works. It integrates the individual work and the author into a network of contemporary and historical discourses and it traces the reciprocal challenges, suggestions, adaptions and disassociations in their entanglement. On the whole a genuine intertwining of inner and outer perspectives belongs to such reconstructions and it inscribes the individual conception in a comprehensive development and, inversely, brings claims to objective knowl-

---

4 Flasch (2005), 17–19.
5 Henrich (2011), 8.

edge to bear on the historical position. For the epistemology of historiography, both are associated with open questions.

2.2 The Unity and Diversity of Philosophy

What is in question is the extent to which we are concerned with one and the same way of thinking, with one and the same project in exploring diverse developments. It is a question that analogously confronts the attempt to integrate a scattered sequence of events and settings into a regional, national or even human history. Historiographical philosophical construction too has to take into consideration breaks, innovations that are not merely derived from the preceding and paths that lead nowhere as well as developments and continuations related thereto, without refuting one by the other. On a structural as well as diachronic level it is confronted with the dichotomy of reference and distance, unity and heterogeneity. The balance between discontinuity and continuity is a question for concrete historiographical-philological research. The antagonistic and polemical character has been understood as an almost essential feature of philosophy as developing in conflict, a character that even becomes apparent to historiographical perception: for philosophical thinking maintains itself essentially in conflict with other, earlier views.[6] However, connections between problems are also striking and the formation of schools and traditions right up to the periodization and classification of epochs belongs constitutively to the historiographical form of philosophy. Their definition remains a construction that is to be solidified or criticised within substantive work. Here the basic problem of diversity affects not only the synthesizing needed for attaining a unified form or narrative. It is, in its virulence, a provocation to the truth claims of philosophy. Such a plurality raises the question of how the conflict between systems is compatible with the claims to knowledge made by philosophy. This problem establishes an obstacle for philosophy's self-understanding in that it demands that the plurality of positions be treated along the lines of works of art and styles or understands philosophies as co-existing worldviews. Philosophy remains, even in temporal and spatial dispersal, *one* project of thought that is distinguished through its overriding will to knowledge and a singular internal relatedness.

---

[6] Gueroult (1956), 47 f.

2.3 Historiographical Understanding

Finally the question arises as to the kind of theoretical attention to history. In what way is the historiography of philosophy to engage the specific claim to truth of its object? The following answer suggests itself: it relates discursively-argumentatively to the concerned philosophy, whose claim to validity it takes seriously and discusses critically. Thus it is taken into account that, as a philosophical discipline, it belongs to the discursive continuum of its object. Another perspective is offered by the literary-historical approach in which the genesis, the statements and the character of philosophical documents are explained from the outside; in a similar way a psychological or sociological reading can extrapolate the contingency of past views instead of their internal validity. Viewed abstractly, here conceptual-systematic and external-historiographical perspectives are juxtaposed. However remaining in such dichotomies appears unsatisfactory for a historiographical understanding of philosophy. The historiography of philosophy cannot restrict itself to oscillating between either temporal relativism or truth independent of time, between anticipating the unfamiliar and a translation of the unfamiliar into the familiar. It operates in the in-between, in mediation between resisting both historical relativism and schematic de-historization. Its basis is the insight into the fundamental historicity of past as well as current knowledge. Historical contextualization does not mean the refutation of preceding opinions or even a suspension of the truth-claims of knowledge. According to Kurt Flasch "[C]ontingent conditions of genesis" do not refute an argument but "position it"; generally historiographical philosophy moves neither in trans-temporal nor in merely local formations but in rules and forms of thinking that are marked by a "medium duration and extension of validity".[7] What is important in the historiographical analysis of ideas is to work out both the rational intelligibility of the formation of ideas and how it is comprehensible by external factors. It is precisely when positions are taken seriously in their truth claims that they can also be historiographically situated through critical judgment and can be interlinked with a certain perception of history.

Where this is the case ideas of a directed, teleological development, even rational progress, which Hegel saw as is inherent in history, can be registered. Still such "historization" does not necessarily need to be carried out with the sense of an emphatic supposition of rationality, much less be expanded to a putative overall course of *the* history of thought. Even "weaker" ways of reading, ways which are less rich in presuppositions, provide a genuine historiographical intel-

---

[7] Flasch (2005), 51, 70.

ligibility that illuminates both the individual work and the standpoint of current thinking. Such readings can emphasize the connections and interrelations of historical concepts and thereby not only span different times and spaces but take into consideration connections in their different modalities of receptions and criticisms, traditions and projects, variations and further continuations. Beyond the alternative of disillusionment and legitimation such reconstruction provides a historiographical knowledge that has not only object-related relevance. Historiographical philosophical consideration concerns philosophy's own reflectiveness. Philosophy becomes self-aware in its reflection on its history[8]. To clarify the form and content of this hypothesis, it must be considered within the horizon of the general question of the function of historiographical philosophy.

3 The Meaning of the Relatedness to History

Why should it not be possible to engage in philosophy in a strictly subject related manner, independently of historiographical references? What is the central importance, the possibly indispensible function of the historiography of philosophy, its own non-contingent interest in its history? Not only the actual writing of the history of philosophy are at stake here but also the different forms of the relatedness to history in philosophical work, from a cursory reference to historiographical positions, schools and trends in a thematic context, the reconstruction of works, theoretical coherences and traditions right up to the philosophical interpretation of ways of thinking as a whole. Obviously, the form and frequency of such references vary greatly in the course of epochs, but seen as a whole, one can speak of a growth in historiographical reflections of thinking, even if this growth is not continual or linear. However, this does not mean that that its motive and necessity would become in equal measure more clear and precise. It seems to me pointless to attempt to subsume the different kinds of interest in the historiography of philosophy under *one* guiding idea. I propose to distinguish the external relation to the historiography of philosophy (III.1) from the internal, constitutive relatedness to history of philosophy and to differentiate the latter according to three approaches. (III.2-III.4).[9]

---

8 Such is a leading thesis of Stekeler-Weithofer (2006, 229) and Flasch (2005, 72); see III.4 below.
9 The following draws partly on observations in Angehrn (2002).

3.1 History as a Quarry of Ideas

The most unproblematic interpretation, at least to a certain extent, considers the history of philosophy, as Hegel put it, as a "stock of opinions".[10] History is a fund of theories, ways of apprehending, concepts and arguments, that current work in philosophy and representatives of the subject can draw upon by virtue of their professional competence. Current debates can rely on historiographical examples for the purposes of illustration, for the exploration of a thematic field and the testing of solutions: in earlier theories explanations of concepts, argumentative strategies, *aporiai* and suggestions for solutions were explored which present work can draw upon and can gain a sense of direction from, concerning certain difficulties and prospects of certain ways of thinking.

Likewise, the history of philosophy can become a privileged medium of initiation and teaching. While the introduction to technology and the natural sciences occurs through praxis and the appropriation of basic principles, which both are also essential for philosophy, the latter further proceeds via a familiarisation with classical texts and discussions. Likewise, this ties communication to a common frame of reference which the formulation that historiography is the *lingua franca* of philosophy indicates. The resorting to and command over shared references (authors and concepts) is the precondition of any engagement, examination or debate in systematic discourse.

All this describes characteristics which explicate the manifest and close connection between philosophy and the history of philosophy. Historiography as a resource and a frame of reference sustains and regulates philosophical work. But it is a bond that, so to speak, which remains external and does not determine the philosophical way of thinking in its core. It remains to clarify in what sense philosophy draws upon past theories and positions not only as material or as an external frame but in the sense that it appropriates them as its own inner substance and in how far history forms a dimension of its own, forms a medium in which it situates itself and takes place as itself. To this end, we can distinguish three perspectives.

3.2 Historical Foundation and Argumentative Discourse

Philosophy is intertwined in a narrower way with history where historiographical reflection touches upon the question of truth. The truth of past as well as present

---

[10] Hegel (1970), 28–36.

thinking stands in question here. In a negative form this nexus strikes us as historiographical relativizing: facing the fact of its origination in the past, the diversity and mutability of thinking amounts to a calling into question, or at least to an indication of the contingency of one's own standpoint. Historicism is the basis of relativism and, further, every doctrine that wants to present itself as having an absolute claim to validity seeks to situate itself outside of history or to construe history as a development that is completed with its own appearance and which is external to the validity of its results. That philosophy has a history initially appears to be a suspension of its own truth. Hence what suggests itself here is an attempt to posit the self-authorization of reason as an abstraction from history, for example through a methodological doubt as the forgetting of all tradition.[11]

This contrasts with the opposed idea of the relatedness to history functioning as an authentication of philosophy, as a legitimating "proof of origin".[12] This can be the case with varying degrees of stringency. In the most general way insertion into a history, the connection to predecessors and the appeal to authorities constitutes a mode of legitimation in both practical and theoretical respects. Such a basic "tradition oriented" justification is familiar from the life-world and is established in both a science-theoretical and hermeneutically regards, but nonetheless can be still questioned. Its problematic adheres to philosophy in the contrast between emphatic truth and the constitutive relatedness to tradition. One answer to this *aporia* is presented by the philosophical-historical self-assurance of thinking which grasps the present as the destination of a history that comes to its truth and its conclusion in it. An exemplary implementation of this is achieved in Hegel's reading of history as an affirmative self-explication and legitimation of spirit. History as the occurrence of truth and the philosophy of history as theodicy are the conceptual stamp of such a foundation. But even in weaker versions the founding upon history can be articulated. Such can be seen in Aristotle's endeavour to support his own theories by appealing to the *consensus hominum et temporum*. A minimal premise of such types of argumentation is represented in the unity of history: the fact, that the progress of philosophical thought in the change of themes and dogmas is also understood as *one* development, in which the scattered voices are related in criticism and continuation. But what is essential for the potential for truth of such connections is that this is carried out as an argument and discussion with history that is oriented towards what is valid. What matters most centrally here is a discursive examination that is oriented to the matter itself, that includes past positions as well

---

11 See Beelmann (2001), 15.
12 Beelmann (2001), 15.

as contemporary statements in a dialogue rather than fixing them in a historicizing manner as facts and understanding them as certain convictions or as the results of developments. In such an attitude of a reflective historiography of philosophy, as distinguished from cultural-historical writing, past documents are interpreted in their claim to validity.

Not least is the insight into the historicity of knowledge of importance here, which does not intend a mere relativism. Rather it is aimed at integrating itself into a history and thus makes possible a discussion between different positions across times and spaces. It bridges the alleged incommensurability of divergent ways of understanding in that it opens them towards each other from out of overarching contexts. Thus it does not level down all claims to validity but on the contrary enables the discourse of legitimation and critical comparison. Historical consciousness is the pre-condition of a disclosing understanding as well as a rational and evaluating reference wherein the genetic reconstruction sustains critical examination of rational claims and, inversely the reflection on validity sustains the moment of the disclosing of meaning.

3.3 Remembrance and Continuation of Writing

The historiography of philosophy has, like cultural history in general, a purpose insofar as it participates in history: to keep the past alive and continue humanity's conversation into the future. Remembrance is a *leitmotif* of historical retrospection. In certain ways, this thrust of historiography approaches that which seems strangest to a philosophizing focused on the present: the retaining and cultivation of the by-gone for its own sake. It is the piety of preservation that Nietzsche attributed to what he calls the antiquarian historiographical attitude. Taken for itself it will not be primarily regarded as a constitutive moment of philosophizing. However it is thoroughly intertwined with the intrinsic motives of philosophical thinking. Philosophy shares in the dynamic of historicity, rooted in the fact that it can be addressed by the past and can respond to questions that the past directs at it. Derrida has emphasized that philosophical writing partakes of a duty to the past and relinquishes a debt to it: a debt towards the unsaid, the submerged and the displaced. Insofar as philosophy is confronted with this duty, it is interested in history for its own sake. By connecting to the past it discloses latent potentialities of the past that have not been voided and continues to write a history that was inherent in it but was not explicated. It continues a conversation whose historical radicality is not only related to the past but in equal measure reaches towards the future. As Rorty says, it is the highest task of philosophy to keep humanity's conversation from breaking off. When philosophy turns to its own history there is an irreducible interest not only in knowledge but in remembrance as such. In this, philosophy is both part of and an outstanding instance of historiographical culture as such.

3.4 The Historical Self-Understanding of Philosophy

In addition to discursive discussion and the remembering of tradition, historiography serves self-orientation and self-understanding. It is not only the truth of projects and concepts that is in question in the dialogue with the past; what is also of interest are its content and horizons of meaning, the directions of its questioning and its presuppositions. It is necessary to understand oneself in hindsight and to win clarity about one's activities and research. I want to specify this—deepest and most extensive—orientation of the interest in history from three angles.

On the one hand the historiographical perspective promotes better understanding insofar as it can elucidate the past evolution and the broader context of that understanding. This task is central in relation to thinking and the course of its development. We better understand a hypothesis, an argument, an intention when we trace the context of problems to which it responds, what experiences underlie them, and possibly in what ways it assimilated earlier formulations and attempts at solution which are hidden within it or only readable in traces. Historical analysis can reveal layers that remain concealed to direct descriptive access. This is true for the understanding of the other as well as the understanding of itself. Historical background and the genetic perspective allow a deeper understanding of cultural formations for both its subjects and for external observers.

On the other hand historical reflection serves not only a retrospective (self-) understanding but also prospective self-discovery. It is not only about an appropriate interpretation of a traditional teaching, but about ascertaining from the dialogue with the past what we are getting at in our own research and what we ask after in our work. Here the driving motivation is not the corroboration of the answer but the clarity of the question.

We find an eloquent testimony to such self-orientation through dialogue with the past in the earliest phase of philosophy. Aristotle's *Metaphysics*, a classical and fundamental work of the discipline named after it, does not propagate any speculation about first and last things. Rather the whole first book is devoted to determining what its concerns and objects are. The "science that it sought for"—as the guiding principle of the discussion—is gained via a pre-meditation of the highest, most eminent knowledge on the one hand and on the other through conversations with predecessors, with the Pre-Socratics and Plato. Their approaches are explored and elucidated so as to provide a twofold proof, namely that they all researched into first causes and principles and that this research operated within the framework of Aristotle's conceptualization of the four causes. From this the project of a first philosophy received its concretion and its historiographical attestation and authentication. The remark that the older thinkers worked on the project put forward by Aristotle but without expressly knowing it is revealing: First they dealt with what, with hindsight can be seen as their true concern, in a way that was "obscure", "stammering" and "unclear".[13] Philosophy gains a sense of its own path not by looking back at an initial foundational act but in conversation with a way of thinking that is still unsure of itself, a tentative beginning, that for its part first gains its clear orientation in extrapolation.

The opening book of the Aristotelian *Metaphysics* is exemplary insofar as it refers to the structural problem of beginning and first ascertains its goal while looking back at pre-history, out of which this self-ascertainment occurs. Such retrospection is essentially hermeneutical, intertwining understanding and communication, the exegesis of the origin and the act of beginning and self-orientation are intertwined. This consciousness of origin corresponds to a hermeneutic characteristic, which is likewise emphasised within deconstruction, insofar as it goes back to a tentative, underdetermined origin, not an underlying *Eidos* or an identifiable "primal foundation" which contains progress as a *telos* which is to be unfolded. Even without the support of a substantialist philosophy of history with firm original, developmental and purposive guidelines, historical reflection functions as the medium of self-understanding and self-discovery.

What the Aristotelian example illustrates with regard to the self-definition of philosophy can be analogously applied to particular themes and questions. Attention to history contains a hermeneutic-heuristic potential that aids communication about the content, the direction, the premises and the problems of certain questions. Questions concerning the immortality of the soul or the historicality of science, concerning the limits of the state or the legitimate grounds of subjective freedom are not, at all times, taken seriously as questions or even understood. Many leading concepts of philosophy are historically and culturally situated concepts in that they emerge and are worked out, modified and differentiated in a certain real and ideal historical framework and, as the case may be, fade and dissolve. To become conscious of its historicity belongs to the elucidation of its content and direction and impacts the negotiation of topics that have been treated in current discussions. Current philosophy does not simply realize itself from out of the present. It is not exhausted in the sum of current knowledge; its

---

[13] See Aristotle, Met. I.4, 985 a 5–18; I.7, 988 a 18–23; I.10, 993 a 12–17.

"state of the art" is grasped deficiently when cut off from history. Philosophical theories and their objects are, to a wide extent, historically impregnated and cannot be adequately grasped in their content and applied without explication of this historiographical density. Historiography is not only an external so to speak technical contribution to conceptual work but a way of penetrating into its material and self-orienting in one's own research.

A particular aspect of such communication is that in the historiographical look the external perspective acquires validity. History is the medium in which I encounter the strange but also the dimension in which I perceive myself from outside, from the other. In a particular way historiographical reflection is the medium of self-understanding where it is confronted with what was suppressed, marginalized or shut out in the history of thought, where it re-endows self-consciousness with what had been lost to it, what had been forgotten within it. In this sense Husserl's *Crisis* makes manifest the life-world as the forgotten fundament of meaning for science through historical retrospection. History works out the repressed of this history, becomes aware of what is other to this history itself. A form of thought can in the reconstruction of its genesis win an adequate understanding of its uniqueness, its determining motives and also its limits; philosophy can become aware of what, in its dominant form, was pushed back (non-European, female, non-academic philosophy) and of what remains unthought in its concepts (corporeality, nature, ontological difference). The relatedness to history is situated, in all of this, in the horizon of a self-enlightenment of philosophy—a deeper understanding of its self-definition as well as its motives, leading concepts and open questions.

4 Conclusion

History is the medium of self-knowledge. What humanity is, according to Dilthey, is recounted by history. What philosophy is, is revealed by its history; the historiography of philosophy as its reflexive recollection is the becoming self-conscious of philosophy, its accountability towards itself and its self-enlightenment. One can put the emphasis in this process more firmly on history or on historiography. Following a suggestion of Pirmin Stekeler-Weithofer, the course of philosophical thinking could be thought as a coherent developmental-process of the spirit in which initial open-endedness and ambivalences of the forms of human understanding are gradually resolved—not necessarily as a lawful and necessary higher development towards complete and perfect truth, but rather as a process of gradual self-clarification and disambiguation of thinking.[14] Correspondingly, the reflexive recollection of these processes can on its part be understood as a mode of self-knowledge and this, according to Kurt Flasch, can be understood as the motive and actual meaning of the historiography of philosophy.[15] Walter Jaeschke combines such self-knowledge with Hegel's paradigmatic claim about unity of philosophy and history of philosophy and reads this in terms of the reflexivity of philosophy. Philosophy has its truth, according to Hegel, ultimately in the absolute self-relation of thinking, as he lays out in the three conclusions at the end of the *Encyclopaedia* as three forms of philosophy's turning back to itself —to the forms of the absolute spirit, to the systematic representation of philosophical sciences and to the history of philosophy which, although to Jaeschke, there is no doubt that the last "historical form [is] comprehensive and fundamental."[16] The retrospective glance to the history of thinking, as a looking back to spirit's self-knowledge, is "if not the only, but the highest form of *noesis noeseos*."[17]

However, such self-relation does not necessarily need to be conceived in terms of a complete self-transparency of spirit in the Hegelian sense—an ideal that has become alien to today's thinking. Also quite independently of this it can stand as a vanishing-point in the reflexivity of spirit and its historical becoming conscious. Also what was for Hegel a further intertwinement between the history of spirit and its historiographical reflection remains at least as a question and as a task for current thinking, independently of Hegel's absolutization. According to Hegel it is itself a fact of history that the historiography of philosophy in the present has become possible and necessary: Only the modern subject which is able to grasp itself in the world is able at the same time and prompted to recognize itself in its thinking and willing. The genesis of the *historiography* of philosophy is itself an index of the progressive status of the *history* of philosophy, the historical self-explication of spirit; historical-reflectiveness belongs to the historicality of thinking. The question remains, to what extent this step to the becoming historical of thinking is irreversible. If post-metaphysical thinking raises the issue of the constructiveness of the world and its self, it remains to be seen to what extent its own history becomes increasingly present and easier to access—or slips away from it and becomes abstract, without interest for it.

---

14 Stekeler-Weithofer (2006), 229–231.
15 Flasch (2005), 72.
16 Jaeschke (2000), 500.
17 Jaeschke (2000), 501.

Bibliography

Angehrn (2002): Emil Angehrn, "Wozu Philosophiegeschichte?", in: Emil Angehrn and Bernard Baertschi (Eds.), *Philosophie und Philosophiegeschichte. La philosophie et son histoire*, studia philosophica vol. 61/2002, Bern / Stuttgart / Wien: Haupt, 37–65 (also in: Emil Angehrn, *Wege des Verstehens. Hermeneutik und Geschichtsdenken*, Würzburg: Königshausen & Neumann 2008, 111–134)

Beelmann (2001): Axel Beelmann, *Theoretische Philosophiegeschichte. Grundsätzliche Probleme einer philosophischen Geschichte der Philosophie*, Basel: Schwabe.

Flasch (2005): Kurt Flasch, *Theorie der Philosophiehistorie. Philosophie hat Geschichte*, vol. 2, Frankfurt a. M.: Klostermann.

Gueroult (1956): Martial Gueroult, "Le problème de la légitimité de l'histoire de la philosophie", in: E. Castelli et al., *La philosophie de l'histoire de la philosophie*, Paris: Vrin.

Hegel (1970): G.W.F. Hegel, *Vorlesungen über die Geschichte der Philosophie I*, in: G.W.F. Hegel, *Werke in zwanzig Bänden*, vol. 18, ed. by E. Moldenhauer and K.M. Michel, Frankfurt a. M.: Suhrkamp.

Henrich (2011): Dieter Henrich, *Werke im Werden. Über die Genesis philosophischer Einsichten*, München: Beck.

Marx (1968): Karl Marx, *Philosophisch-Ökonomische Manuskripte*, in: *Marx Engels Werke, Ergänzungsband I*, Berlin: Dietz.

Sellars (1967): Wilfrid Sellars, *Science and Metaphysics. Variations on Kantian Themes*, London: Routledge and Kegan Paul (1967) / Atascadero: Ridgeview (1992).

Stekeler-Weithofer (2006): Pirmin Stekeler-Weithofer, *Philosophiegeschichte (Grundthemen Philosophie)*, Berlin: De Gruyter.

Jaeschke (2000): Walter Jaeschke, "Philosophie und Philosophiegeschichte", in: Hermann Drüe et al., *Hegels 'Enzyklopädie der philosophischen Wissenschaften' (1830). Ein Kommentar zum Systemgrundriss*, Frankfurt a. M.: Suhrkamp, 487–533.

Martin Bondeli
The History of Philosophy as Progress towards a System of Reason

The history of philosophy is not a collection of opinions but a necessary coherence! The history of philosophy is a branch of philosophy in general and just like the latter it is an object of *a priori* reason!

Who are the representatives of such views? Immanuel Kant in a few places in his philosophical works, Karl Leonhard Reinhold in his essay *Ueber den Begriff der Geschichte der Philosophie* [Concerning the Concept of the History of Philosophy],[1] which was first published in 1791, as well as (undoubtedly) Georg Wilhelm Friedrich Hegel in texts stemming from the years 1820 and 1823 which belong to the introductory part of his *Vorlesungen über die Geschichte der Philosophie* [Lectures on the history of Philosophy].[2] These three thinkers were each in their own ways persuaded that real, scientific philosophy stands and falls with the representation of theoretical and practical rational knowledge brought to the form of a valid system. The history of philosophy, in this regard, is to be considered as nothing other than the progressive path to this system, a path which the philosophical spirit has travelled on since its beginnings in ancient Greece. Whoever writes the history of philosophy must reconstruct this path and select, analyse, arrange and link together the philosophical-historical material that has been handed down with this in view. It is thus necessary to bid farewell to a history of philosophy as a mere aggregate of materials, and especially to a history of philosophy in which accounts are given of the lives and doctrines of philosophers, of the adherents and adversaries of determinate philosophical schools—and even if the reasoning in such works is deep, critical, witty or morally edifying.

In the following I will discuss in detail Kant (I), Reinhold (II) and Hegel (III) with regard to their philosophical-historical claims made in relation to this conviction. After 1790 a concept of rational history of philosophy became dominant, a concept which Kant prepared, which Reinhold sharpened and strengthened conceptually and which Hegel ultimately concretized, adapted and expanded. This concept is characterized by clear continuities in the development of a fundamental philosophical-historical theme and remains largely unaffected by the changes that are typical for the path from Kant to Hegel, from a critical to an absolute thinking of reason.

---

[1] See Reinhold (1791). The essay also appeared slightly revised in 1796, see Reinhold (1796).
[2] See Hegel (1994), 1–108.

There is little doubt that philosophy in Germany, or at least its mainstream, after the era of Kant and Hegel, underwent an abrupt turn against the idealistic configuration as well as against the scientific contours of the Kantian critique of reason and post-Kantian systematic philosophy and that as a consequence the concept of the history of philosophy in this form of thinking lost acceptance.[3] This does not change the fact that from a certain systematic perspective one can certainly acknowledge the more general, exemplary function that this concept had on the history of philosophy beyond its epoch. We will consider this exemplary function in the conclusion (IV).

I

A discourse on the elevation of the history of philosophy to a branch of philosophy as a rational system must indicate Kant's role in this process. The philosopher from Königsberg had, as we know, more or less neglected the history of philosophy in his intellectual edifice and paid little attention to it in his teaching. Nonetheless Kant constitutes the starting point for a striking new direction and evaluation of the history of philosophy.

Pure reason, as Kant understands it, is not a form of thinking with a temporal and historical character but yet it is a form of thinking that is disclosed in the course of the history of philosophy and is thus already manifest at different historical stages. On the basis of this understanding, Kant gives a new emphasis to the systematic and methodological engagement with the history of philosophy. As can be seen in the section "The history of pure reason" at the end of the *Critique of Pure Reason*[4] as well as some of the philosophical-historical reflections[5]

---

3 See Geldsetzer (1968), Part I, Chapter 3 on this loss of acceptance. As Geldsetzer points out, the conceptual-methodological discussion concerning the history of philosophy recedes from the influence of Kant and Hegel around 1820, while the historiography of philosophy itself remains in thrall to Hegel's view for several decades. At the latest in 1870, with Eduard Zeller and Wilhelm Dilthey's approaches, it is reoriented in both the methodological and substantive regards.

4 See KrV A 852–856/ B 880–884.

5 See Kant (1942), 340–343.—Kant had apparently noted down these reflections, which only became known with the Academy Edition, in the middle of the 1790s. All in all, they summarize the results of the final section of the *Kritik der reinen Vernunft* on the idea of an a priori history of philosophy. That one finds mention in them of Georg Gustav Fülleborn (compare ibid., 343) suggests that Kant was familiar with the relevant essays from *Beyträgen zur Geschichte der Philosophie* [Contributions to the History of Philosophy] (ed. by Fülleborn, 12 Parts, Züllichau /Freystadt 1791–1799).

in the context of the prize essay[6] on the question that was posed by the Berlin Academy in 1791, namely, "What real progress has metaphysics in Germany made since the time of Leibniz and Wolff?", Kant assumes that there is, aside from the usual narrative history of philosophy, a "philosophical history of philosophy", that is to say a history of philosophy that is not "historically or empirically possible but rationally, that is, a priori".[7] He sees the assumption of such a philosophical history of philosophy as based on the fact that philosophizing in the determinate sequence of its historical unfolding shows "a gradual development of human reason", a development that could "not have occurred in an empirical manner".[8] In other words, the history of philosophy is not only the "history of opinions that contingently arise here or there" but also the history of unfolding reason, "developing from concepts."[9] Philosophical historiography with a claim to philosophy cannot restrict itself to just reproducing dates and materials in their natural order but rather it must also and above all conceptualise its object of study through "the nature of human reason as a philosophical archaeology".[10]

Kant does not indicate how he intends to classify history of philosophy in terms of the divisions of his architectonic of reason, whether it is to be located in the region of the metaphysics of nature or the metaphysics of morals, whether it is to be principally recognized as empirical or as pure philosophy or as a mixed form of both. He only mentions that the discipline in question has a "position" in the system of reason in its entirety that "must be filled in in the future."[11] In contrast Kant states in some detail how the history of philosophy is to be understood and treated from methodological points of view. Thus he makes clear, that, within the totality of what is considered the history of philosophy (dates, opinions, formations of systems and disputes between schools concerning the basic problems of philosophy) there is a general part which can be clearly identified as rational and a priori and thus not empirical, both in relation to its subject matter and also in relation to the procedure of reconstruction itself. The question of which a priori principles of reason are to be applied in this part must be addressed. When it comes to the division of history of philosophy, according to Kant in the prize essay, the a priori sequence of "dogmatism", "scepticism" and "criticism" can be taken as a starting point. Further there are clear indica-

---

6 Kant (1977).
7 Compare Kant (1942), 341.
8 Compare Kant (1942), 340.
9 Compare Kant (1942), 343.
10 Compare Kant (1942), 341.
11 KrV A 852/ B 880.

tions that this epistemologically relevant triad corresponds to the principal "three stages" of the previous history of metaphysics.[12] According to Kant in the section on "The history of pure reason" in the *Critique of Pure Reason*, when it comes to the evidence for progressions or "revolutions" in the history of philosophy, one is best advised to examine the matter in three a priori-systematic respects: firstly in regard to the "subject matter [*Gegenstand*]", that means, the material or intellectual nature of the objects [*Objekte*] of our rational knowledge, secondly in regard to the "origin", that means, the rational or empirical source of the insights of our reason, thirdly in regard to the "method", with which rational knowledge can be gained.[13] In his remarks on these three aspects Kant also mentions some ideal-typical schools or authors between the poles of idealism and materialism, rationalism and empiricism as well as naturalism and scientism. However, everything further, and above all the implementation of what was there programmatically outlined in this essay, should seemingly be reserved for his own later work or for work provided by his disciples.

Considered in the context of its historical development Kant's demand for a rational or an a priori history of philosophy marks not only a new beginning but also a striking counterpoint to the long dominant empiricist orientation of this discipline. In many of the well-known philosophical circles of the pre-Kantian era the history of philosophy was understood as a presentation of materials, even very insignificant materials, a presentation which was emphatically unchallenged or untouched by systematic constraints. The philosopher, historian and travel writer Christopher Meiners should be mentioned in this regard. The philosophical-historical works that Meiners published in the 1780s[14] testify to a breath-taking erudition and an unremitting drive to propagate and comment on doctrines of all kinds. However the reader schooled by Kant cannot help but complain that you can find almost everything in these works except a guiding thread. Meiners' philosophical-historical works (which were critically reviewed by, amongst others, Kant's disciple Christian Jacob Kraus[15]) are in their own way quite unique and ingenious, but undoubtedly also representative of a philosophical historiography that was surmounted by the standpoint of critical reason.

---

12 Kant (1977), 595.
13 Compare KrV A 852–856/ B 880–884.
14 Christoph Meiners, *Geschichte des Ursprungs, Fortgangs und Verfalls der Wissenschaften in Griechenland und Rom*, 2 volumes, Lemgo: Meyerische Buchhandlung 1781. Christoph Meiners, *Grundriß der Geschichte der Weltweisheit*, Lemgo: Meyerische Buchhandlung 1786.
15 See Landau (1991), 534–556.

II

What began with Kant as a reorientation in and sketch of ideas for the history of philosophy, was consolidated by his circle of followers into a new paradigm for this discipline. The Kantian Reinhold from Jena was the one who decisively advanced this cause. From 1789 he pursued under the title of "elementary philosophy" or "philosophy in general" the on-going project of a fundamental and philosophically unified restatement and revision of the Kantian critique of reason.[16] The establishment of comprehensive system of reason, of the entirety of pure and empirical, theoretical and practical philosophical knowledge, was planned. The history of philosophy, which Reinhold at this time also included in his teaching repertoire[17], was to be conceived as part of this comprehensive system as well, as can be seen in the essay *Ueber den Begriff der Geschichte der Philosophie* [Concerning the Concept of the History of Philosophy]. The decisive systematic starting-point was, for Reinhold, neither Kant's triad of dogmatism, scepticism or criticism nor his methodological approach in the section on "The history of pure reason" but a philosophical and systematic concept which was to be determined in close connection with Kant's "scholastic concept" of philosophy, that is to say, the conception of "philosophy" as the "system of all philosophical knowledge".[18]

Reinhold is of the opinion that a kind of definition of the concept of the history of philosophy is required which, on its part, follows from the definition of "philosophy in itself". In this sense, for him "philosophy in the strictest sense of the word" is considered as "the *science of the determined correlation of things independent of experience*"[19] and the "history of philosophy" is considered as "*the represented sum total of the changes which the science of the necessary correlation of things, or fate, which the pursuit of such a science has experienced from its beginnings down to our own time.*"[20] The intention behind this conception consists in a consolidation and extension oriented by Kant's results. The innovations that occurred in Kant's work in relation to the history of philosophy should be brought to their highest and final point. Moreover a series of conclusions should be explicated from this point. It will accordingly be shown where the history of

---

16 On the individual aspects of Reinhold's fundamental and unified philosophical revision of Kant, see Bondeli (1995), 41–78.
17 On Reinhold's lectures on the history of philosophy, see Fuchs (1995), 171–173, 186f. Reinhold took Gurlitt (1786) as a guide in his lectures on the history of philosophy.
18 KrV A 838/ B 866.
19 Reinhold (1796), 217.
20 Reinhold (1796), 226.

philosophy is to be located within the philosophical system, what extent and which object this discipline has and, finally, which method of presentation should applied within it.

When it comes to its *localization* in the system of philosophy in general, for Reinhold it is certain that the history of philosophy has to be considered part of "experiential philosophy" and not of pure philosophy, if it is to focus on *changes* and the temporal *origination* of the science of the necessary correlation of things.[21] On the basis of the fact that the goal of philosophy is a science of *the necessary correlation of things independent of experience*, it also makes sense however that there is also a distinctive connection between the history of philosophy and pure philosophy. From this perspective the history of philosophy is more accurately considered as a philosophy of experience that not only, as every philosophy of experience, is subsumed by pure philosophy and thus depends on it systematically. It is also to be considered as a philosophy of experience in the process of approaching pure philosophy: in other words it strives towards pure philosophy.

As for its *scope* or *extent*, for Reinhold there is, in the light of the fact that a necessary correlation of those things under discussion exists (which one can characterize with Christian Wolff as logical and ontological things), strong evidence in favour of the hypothesis that the history of philosophy itself should mainly cover the path of the development of a system, which—in connection to the basic divisions into pure and empirical, theoretical and practical philosophy—is subdivided into the fields of *"logic"*, *"metaphysics"* (*"ontology"*, *"rational psychology"*, *"rational cosmology"* and *"rational theology"*), pure *"physics"* and pure *"morality"*.[22] In other words, based on his definitions Reinhold sees cause for broadly approving of the basic division of philosophy Kant had suggested in the architectonic chapter of the *Critique of Pure Reason*.[23] Moreover Reinhold considers it legitimate to narrow down the history of philosophy, especially as it should be a science of the correlation of "things in general" and of not particular things. Such a narrowing down disregards some natural, legal and humanities subjects that older and more recent historiographers of philosophy had included within it. Philosophical historiographers should worry as little about "the fate of *mathematics*, of *natural history*, of *rhetoric* and *poetics* as they should worry about the *art of medicine, jurisprudence* and *theology*."[24]

---

21 Compare Reinhold (1796), 225 f.
22 Compare Reinhold (1796), 222–225.
23 See KrV A 841 f./ B 869; A 845–847/ B 873–875.
24 Compare Reinhold (1796), 231.—Reinhold's argument needs a lot of clarification at this point. This is mainly due to the unclear use of the expression "things in general." As Reinhold develops

As Reinhold explains in a further deductive step, with regard to the *subject matter* of the history of philosophy, relevant insights emerge by a renewed but yet different consideration of the centrality of *change* or *emergence* pertaining to the science of the necessary correlation of things. The subject matter of the history of philosophy is the development of this science. That means that in this history a form of change or origination predominates which is to be understood as a progress to a goal or an ideal and thus, in the sense of a progressive teleology, it can be organized into steps, stages and levels. Reinhold characterizes the subject matter of the history of philosophy as the path to the discovery and increasing conceptual comprehension of the presupposed ideal. The subject matter of the history of philosophy consists in nothing other than the "human spirit, occupied with a single and determinate purpose, [namely] the endeavour to discover the correlation of things and to extend and to rectify its concept of this."[25] The subject matter of the history of philosophy is the "business of philosophizing reason" which has brought it to the "consideration of the correlation of things."[26]

If the subject matter of the history of philosophy is taken to be the evolution of the science of the necessary correlation of things, Reinhold also ultimately provides the *method* for putting this discipline into practice. The method must be appropriate to the subject matter. This means that the history of philosophy or—better in this context—the historiography of philosophy must not be limited to the consideration of individual things but must have the correlation of things in view. Further, this means that the task arises of subsuming materials into a form. The correlation of things is a complex of form and material. The historiographer of philosophy has to reconstruct this complex and must select, prepare, order and classify the given material to this end. Reinhold considers a history of philosophy that wears itself out in a "collection of biographies of famous philosophers", in accounts of "their teachings and opinions from their notes or the transcripts of others"[27], to be unsatisfactory. In this only the material for the discipline is provided: "Even the most accurate *historical* information on the teachings and opinions of philosophies give nothing more than the mere materials for

---

the issue, it is obvious that the subject matters of pure philosophy (logic, metaphysics, physics and morality) are meant. However this would then mean that not only the individual sciences or subjects of the type mentioned but also the empirical parts of pure philosophy, such as for example empirical psychology or philosophical anthropology, would not belong to the history of philosophy. In addition one would have to ask why mathematics is left out.

25 Reinhold (1796), 228f.
26 Compare Reinhold (1796), 245.
27 Reinhold (1796), 234.

the history of philosophy."²⁸ Whether the presentation of the form of the history of philosophy should also include biographical information of the respective philosophers is something that Reinhold denies in principle. Such information is in his opinion appropriate at best where it can help the interpretation of the teachings, where it, in others words, "can ascertain the influence of the psychological or moralistic character of a man, or of certain circumstances in his life-history on his philosophical system".²⁹ Also, according to Reinhold, all the works of a philosopher should not be named or listed in a history of philosophy but only those "which have made epochs in science, which have produced essential changes in the form of these sciences, and have determined its respective condition."³⁰

In how far and with what implications Reinhold, implemented his own definitional, systematic and methodological guidelines in his lectures on the history of philosophy is difficult to ascertain on the basis of source material today. It is however obvious from Reinhold's writings from 1791 that he worked, when carrying out historical-philosophical extrapolations and excurses, with patterns of thought [*Denkmustern*] that correlate with his reflections on the subject matter of the history of philosophy. Accordingly his own system of elementary philosophy is considered to be the goal of a path that philosophizing reason has taken, encountering striking theoretical-conceptual hypotheses since Plato and Aristotle. Thus, with a view to more recent times, Locke, Leibniz, Hume and Kant are repeatedly portrayed as four precursors who have successively helped the fact of consciousness (which is to be understood as the foundation of all philosophical knowledge) to a more complete determination.³¹ And in a later stage of his thinking also Reinhold describes the history of philosophy—oriented towards the level of his own philosophy—as the path to the discovery of the true foundation of philosophy.

---

[28] Reinhold (1796), 236.
[29] Reinhold (1796), 234 f.
[30] Reinhold (1796), 236.
[31] See Reinhold (2011), 19–21, 34–36, 39–41, 66 f., as well as Reinhold (2011), Introduction, LIX-IXXVII.

III

Kant and Reinhold's versions of a rational form of history of philosophy directly influenced the course of this discipline for the next three decades.[32] A highpoint in this framework is marked undoubtedly by the representative of German idealism who most intensively engaged with history of philosophy: Hegel, who first lectured on this subject in 1806 and then did so regularly from 1817 right up to his death in 1831. As distinct from Kant and the Kantians, with Hegel rather an absolute form of reason and no longer a critical reason that becomes the focal point and reason is no longer primarily a transcendental structure but rather has a dynamical-dialectical form. However on the systematic level a continual progress can be observed. Hegel thus did not only further develop Reinhold's idea of a principal and unified philosophical restatement of critical reason in an original way and realize his encyclopaedic rational system of logic and metaphysics along with it in impressive form, but in *Vorlesungen zur Geschichte der Philosophie* he had, interestingly, thought it through in a deeper manner and seen new facets of the discipline that Reinhold had also thematized in its systematic and methodological aspects.

Like Reinhold Hegel took it as self-evident that the history of philosophy should be a branch of systematic philosophy and not an ancillary or accessory structure and, furthermore, that this discovery had certain implications of a systematic and methodological nature. The similarities with Reinhold on this point are more than merely superficial. Not unlike Reinhold Hegel emphasizes that the conceptual understanding of the history of philosophy depends on that of philosophy in general, on philosophy as the "science of the necessary ideas, their essential correlations and system",[33] that the history of philosophy is more accurately seen as the time bound origination or emergence of this science. Against this background Hegel outlines a basic definition of the history of philosophy, which is kindred to Reinhold's proposed definition. It reads: "What this history represents to us, is the *series of noble minds*, the gallery of heroes of thinking reason, who with the power of *this reason* penetrated into the essence of things, nature and the spirit, into the essence of God and have prepared for us the highest

---

32 See here Geldsetzer (1965). In addition to Kant Reinhold, Hegel and the above mentioned Fülleborn at that time, among others, Wilhelm Georg Tennemann, Johann Christian August Grohmann, Georg Friedrich Daniel Goess and Traugott Wilhelm Krug also appear on the public scene with notable methodological reflections or contributions to the history of philosophy.
33 Hegel (1994), 13.

treasure, the *treasure of rational knowledge.*"³⁴ Like Reinhold Hegel takes it for given that, from the discussed basic definition of the history of philosophy "*consequences*" arise "for the way of dealing with this [subject]",³⁵ that is to say, for the method of presentation as well as guidelines concerning its scope. Among other things the "*concept* of *philosophy*" is supposed to disclose "what we have to gather from the endlessly varied material and the many aspects of the *spiritual* formation of peoples and distinguish as meaningful".³⁶ There is also conspicuous agreement with Reinhold in his polemic against the historiographer of philosophy who merely reproduces philosophical opinions. So for Hegel too, it is indisputable that a history of philosophy which wears itself out in a mere "gallery of *opinions*" would be unworthy of philosophy and its ideal of truth and, over and above this, would be a "superfluous and boring science".³⁷ Hegel does not speak of the consequences of this basic understanding of the history of philosophy for, for instance, the division of the system into logic, metaphysics and certain subdivisions of it, but rather of other consequences, related to the subject of the history of philosophy. Here Hegel ultimately takes decisive steps beyond Reinhold's explications. The thought, still articulated rather prosaically in Reinhold, of the human spirit which progresses in the form of philosophizing reason to the discoveries and to the perfecting of the current system of philosophy, returns in Hegel in a vitalized and enriched version, the latter especially with regard to the structure and organization of the progression.

Hegel attaches great importance to ensuring that the evolution of the history of philosophy to the present (and that means to his own philosophical system) is presented as a gallery of high-lights, and is framed, in an emphatic sense, as "development." Development should not be understood "as it stands", but in the sense of the dynamic, dialectical-organic guise of his own system of philosophy. "Philosophy", as Hegel stated in regard to his own understanding of philosophy, is a "system in development and so too is the history of philosophy".³⁸ More precisely, this means that one has to understand the prevailing form of development in the history of philosophy as corresponding to the structural features of his own system, as an interplay of continuity, fractured progress and totalization.³⁹ Development implies a link with the "sacred chain" of the

---

34 Hegel (1994), 5f.
35 Hegel (1994), 14.
36 Hegel (1994), 14.
37 Compare Hegel (1994), 18.
38 Hegel (1994), 25.
39 On the "economic-juridical", "nautical" and "religious" metaphorics that correspond to these three developmental moments in Hegel, see Bodei (1984), 80–83.

"tradition" and is accordingly unthinkable without the "legacy" of the fruits that previous generations have prepared for us. However development also includes "progress" in the sense of renewal and that is why it is not sufficiently understood without the accompanying will to discovery and daring "work" of our spirit, without an imaginative and creative producing.[40] Finally development means the ordering and availability of an "organic progressive whole"[41], of an "organic system, a totality, which contains a wealth of stages and moments within itself."[42] Without these totalizing moments, without a necessary balance of tradition and progress, remembrance and renewal, development would be without orientation, wandering about aimlessly.

Moreover, Hegel considers it appropriate to conceive the philosophical-historical course of development no longer as rudimentary steps but as a detailed progression of "periods" in which in this case too his own system acts as a measure. In this matter in particular Hegel employs the hypothesis of a unity of theological and historical orders. He claims "that the succession of philosophical systems in *history* is the *same* as the *succession* in the logical *derivation* of the conceptual *determination* of the idea."[43] What is implied here is the existence of a correspondence between the sequence of the major systems in the course of history on the one hand and on the other the sequence of the basic logical concepts, which are explicated in Hegel's own system of the science of logic.

Considered more closely, this hypothesis of the unity of logical and historical sequence is based on two preconditions, which are to be characterised as further peculiarities of Hegel's conception of the subject of the history of philosophy. Hegel not only assumes that his own system represents the peak of the course of development of the history of philosophy but also assumes that the essential systems of the history of philosophy, the principal treasures of this history, are preserved in his system. In addition Hegel operates with the assumption that there is an "inward" and an "outward" continuous development in the history of philosophy,[44] in brief, an inner and an outer history. The former is necessary or rational history, the latter history that exists contingently, in an "empirical form".[45] Only these two preconditions allow Hegel to establish the hypothesis

---

40 See Hegel (1994), 6f.
41 Hegel (1994), 14.
42 Hegel (1994), 24.
43 Hegel (1994), 27.
44 Hegel (1994), 24.
45 Hegel (1994), 27.—For Hegel "empirical" here means the same as "contingent" or "external". The empirical history of philosophy is considered to be the superficial or the trivial aspect of its

of the unity of logical and historical sequence. This hypothesis is only defensible under the condition that the history of philosophy has the contour of an inner history concentrated on essential results and that the main stages of this inner history are immanent to his own system. It is further understood from both these preconditions that Hegel at the same time defends his hypotheses with the qualification that from a certain point onwards, the historical sequence of systems also "*differs*" from the logical sequence of the conceptualisation of ideas.[46] If there is an external history of philosophy that is not immanent to his own system, then with regard to this external history, the question of the possible agreement between the sequences is irrelevant.

It is obvious that with these preconditions concerning the hypothesis of a unity of logical and historical sequence this hypothesis itself is at the same time not proven [*bewahrheitet*],[47] but that it can at best be maintained that the essential systems which are found in the history of philosophy are preserved [*aufbewahrt*] in the treasure house of ideas of Hegel's own system but not at a specific place. It is also necessary to acknowledge that the assumption that there is an inner, rational history of philosophy is only valid if this same history can be identified through experiential data.[48] The outer, empirical history could contribute nothing here: as the embodiment of the contingent, it runs counter to or is indifferent to that which is deemed the necessary inner history. It must therefore also be presumed that there is an empirical history of philosophy that is on a par with inner, rational history. Hegel's own remarks on this point remain underdetermined, but this does not prevent him, with this distinction of inner and outer history, from bringing an aspect of this issue to language which suggests a fruitful extension of the Kantian and the Reinholdian notion of a rational history of philosophy.

With the working out of an inner history, Hegel had transformed after his own fashion the progressive-teleological form of rational history of philosophy

---

rational course of development. In contrast Reinhold understands by empirical history of philosophy the movement of history that approaches the pure concept or ideal of philosophy.

46 Compare Hegel (1994), 27.

47 A proof [*Bewahrheitung*] of this can only be established by empirical means. Here Hegel had, apart from occasional attempts to indicate an assignment of the logical ideas from his system to philosophical-historical authors or forms of thinking, lets the matter rest with the notion that a task that has still to be fulfilled is that of providing proof of this [*eine Bewahrheitung in dieser Richtung zu erbringen*].

48 This foundation could be dispensed with, if the inner, rational history of philosophy was not merely characterized through the development of reason, but was at the same time realized by reason and thus would not be in need of any external object. But this obviously cannot be considered here.

that began with Kant and consolidated with Reinhold into a concrete and multifaceted form. But not only that. With the assumption of an outer history of philosophy Hegel had also broached the issue of there being, next to the inner history of philosophy another history of philosophy, a history that does not proceed in a linear fashion but rather depicts a cycle of arising and passing away, a history, in which the human spirit does not ascend to higher stages, but unfolds its individualities and thereby brings the idiosyncrasies of the current epoch to conceptualization, a history, that does not involve the peaceful accumulation of intellectual treasure but comes with struggles over its direction and conflict between schools, a history finally that not only knows an internal dynamic but also an external one, involved in the processes of the religious and political spirit. Philosophy, as Hegel summaries, has also "a history of its arising, dissemination, blossoming, degeneration, revival, a history of its teachers, promoters, and also fighters, and likewise of external relations, frequently to religion, sometimes also to the state."[49] Moreover, as Hegel concedes, the history of philosophy as outer history is in fact to a large extent what it should not be from the perspective of a historiographer working under a philosophical claim: a mere aggregate of opinions and curiosities. The fact that outer history is also familiar with a movement of the philosophizing spirit, that it, wholly in contrast to inner history as a gallery of heroes, manifests only a gallery of opinions, or in some cases, better, a "gallery of follies", cannot be ignored.[50] These attempts to reach towards several aspects of an outer or another history do not change the primacy of inner history of Hegel. This latter is and remains his opinion the real, philosophical history of philosophy. By delimiting outer history from inner in more than just a negative fashion and with more than a merely polemic intent, Hegel did some limited justice to outer history.

IV

The concept of a rational history, leading from Kant to Reinhold and Hegel itself now belongs (and has belonged for almost two hundred years) to the sediments of the philosophical spirit. This naturally raises the question of which aspects of this concept we should bid farewell to and which should be kept [*aufzubewahren*]. An answer to this question must, in my opinion, start with the considera-

---

49 Hegel (1994), 11.
50 Compare Hegel (1994), 15.

tion of what has actually become problematic about this concept and, respectively, the consideration of what was already problematic about it in its own time.

One could follow the neo-Kantian direction to the standpoint that it is the way and manner in which Hegel had developed the concept of a rational history of philosophy that is problematic. In keeping with his understanding of philosophy Hegel, with his contribution to the concept in question is no longer on the ground of critical reason, as Kant and Reinhold still are, according to the neo-Kantians. He had, in their view, presented this concept in the context of a new kind of absolute reason and furthermore went astray through unnecessary and, upon closer consideration, irredeemable proposals for concretisation, such as the thesis of the unity of the logical and the historical. A reorientation of Kant's critical reason as well as a restriction on empirically valid systematization and periodization thus become essential for every future reflection on the history of philosophy.

There is scarcely any doubt that Hegel understands rational knowledge not in the sense of a regulative idea, hypothesis or knowledge under moral-normative guidelines but in a stronger, constitutive form, without an explicit distinction between being and ought and that he suggests that history of philosophy is not in its core an empirical, rational science but a form of self-reflexive pure philosophy, the philosophy of philosophy. Thus, with reference to the relationship between conception and experience, he puts forward an understanding of a rational history of philosophy which is in need of revision and less open than that of Kant and Reinhold. However, a treatment of the problem which starts from a position of absolute reason cannot do. For there are problematic assumptions in Kant, Reinhold and Hegel in equal measure.

Critical and absolute reason differ in their response to the question of what validity and what capacity is attributable to reason in relation to experience. Kant and Reinhold's conception of reason on the one hand and Hegel's on the other also differ, as already indicated, with regard to the structural components of reason. In contrast, they all agree that reason in its historical dimension has exhibited a clear systematic orientation and a progressive-teleological form. As we have seen Kant (in a prototypical form) and Reinhold and Hegel (in a paradigmatic and highly differentiated fashion) put forward the idea that the history of philosophy should be seen as the progress of reason to a philosophy that exists in the form of a system of reason. They uphold this view, basically, with a claim to truth and exclusivity. It is to be assumed that only the one philosophy that extends beyond the borders of history and which leads to this form of the system is the true philosophy. In other words only in this and not in any other philosophy is there the progress of reason the progress to true knowledge.

This assumption is, of course, not undisputed. The conception of the progress of reason as a progress to true knowledge is proposed and handed down by philosophies since the beginning of the history of philosophy which did not set out a system but which held a rhapsodic, an aphoristic, a polemical-critical, a dialogic, a commentating form of philosophy to be appropriate. They are at the very least since modern philosophy part of the common understanding of philosophies that operate with conception of systems other to those of the era of Kant and Hegel. No matter how many different ideas concerning the extent, initial principle, unity, conceptual structure and foundational method of the system take shape in it, this era defends a classical definition of systems along the lines of Aristotle and Christian Wolff. It is a matter of rational knowledge in the entire region of natural, human and divine things; it is a matter of conceptualizing these things starting from the highest grounds, principles or as an arrangement of a priori representations, which is to be understood as the most important foundation, what is at stake here, is the reconstruction of these things in their context and their stages of development. True knowledge is accordingly understood as something that is dependent on this classical concept of a system. In other philosophical currents, such as in the theory of science in the 20th century, true knowledge, in contrast, is made conditional upon a definition of a certain system or theory, the object of which are individual facts or problems, represented as precisely as possible and in the form of a system of propositions. To this definition of a system or theory the desire to operate with most original grounds and most widely conceived interrelations plays no role. In addition, we have to keep in mind that since time immemorial there are philosophies with claims to truth or wisdom that balk at a subsumption under a progressive teleological form of reason of every kind. The tradition of a radical scepticism of reason should be remembered, where the fundamental issue is not the progress of reason but the discovery of the higher philosophical insights, obstructed by reason. Philosophies should be remembered which see their task—comparable to artistic creation—to be the unfolding of a divine principle or a spiritual-creative potential of humanity and which understand the history of philosophy as a series of individual contributions, bringing characteristics of an epoch to expression and contributing to a comprehensive unfolding of events. As far as the idea of teleology is of any importance to these philosophies, it is a matter of the telos of a continuous or regular happening of events, but not a telos that is associated with progress. If there is any talk of progress in this, it is only meant in the sense of the usual educational introduction to the respective understanding of philosophy.

In view of these concerns it should not be concluded that the concept of a rational form of history of philosophy associated with the names of Kant, Reinhold and Hegel fails entirely. However, it is self-evident that, this concept's claim to exclusivity represents a heavy mortgage. The progress of reason as progressing to true knowledge is not a privilege exclusive to the systematic philosophy of the era of Kant and Hegel or of systematic philosophy generally. In addition rational progress is not a mandatory criterion for philosophy. Without the claim to truth or wisdom philosophy is scarcely thinkable, but it can certainly be thought without the claim to the progress of reason. The claim to exclusivity could only be maintained if it could explain that the aforementioned different forms and traditions of philosophy do not suffice to meet their own standards and therefore are to be classified as species of false philosophy or as mere philodoxy. However when considered more closely such an undertaking has little chance of success. It is therefore to be accepted from the standpoint of said concept that there are other true philosophies and accordingly other true histories of philosophy. As we have ascertained, Hegel had taken a remarkable conceptual step in this direction in his reflections on the external or other history which accompanies the internal. But beyond Hegel's result it is crucial to think the other histories of philosophy as others that are of equal value and not as trivial histories.

A fundamental assumption, which is nonetheless necessary for Kant, Reinhold and Hegel's philosophical-historical insights, is, as already mentioned, the conviction that the history of philosophy is not to be regarded a kind of historical but as a philosophical discipline. The three authors hold that an understanding of what essentially philosophy and its history are is indispensible, they require a clarification of the subject matter and the method of this discipline. Their concept of a rational history of philosophy is, in this respect also, not unproblematic. In view of the different forms and traditions that the history of philosophy presents us, it makes little sense to start from a single relevant definition of philosophy and the history of philosophy as well as a single philosophical-historical subject matter. However, this univocity is a peculiarity rather than the general form of the entirety of the aforementioned demands. Thus there is particular reason to recognize the demands as valid above and beyond the respective context in which they concretised in the past. The fact that a plurality of diverse forms and traditions of philosophy has to be assumed does not exclude but confirms against a new backdrop that the essence of philosophy and the history of philosophy needs to be discussed, negotiated. Likewise, one must understand the history of philosophy as regards its subject matter not only as raw material but as the thematic object, as an aspect of the continuous movement of the philosophizing spirit.[51] For this requirement also applies when there are several and dis-

---

51 Talk of a philosophical spirit is perhaps not unproblematic, especially as the protagonists are more accurately seen as philosophers or philosophical schools or trends. Since the protag-

tinct movements, when these movements are understood as progress or merely as continuity. Thus, also the task of the historiographer of philosophy is of lasting significance. He must reconstruct the thematic object, the different movements. It is thus evident that the historiography of philosophy is carried out under the condition of reconstructing the various and distinct movements and thus cannot be restricted to a miscellany of philosophical opinions and disputes between schools. The historiographer should point out correlations, and point these out across the entire spectrum of philosophical forms and traditions. He should keep in view the progress in the course of different philosophical systems as well as the progress in the formulation and solution of individual philosophical problems, the progress of systems and solutions to problems as well as the continuity of philosophical motives and intentions.

It is not too much to maintain that Kant, Reinhold and Hegel's discussion of the concept of a rational history of philosophy, with regard to its list of fundamental demands, is of a more general relevance, transcending its own specific horizon. Whoever shares the view that the history of philosophy is a branch of philosophy or at least needs to be treated philosophically, will consider this list of requirements as exemplary today too.

Bibliography

Bodei (1984): Remo Bodei, "Die ‚Metaphysik der Zeit' in Hegels Geschichte der Philosophie", in: D. Henrich, R.-P. Horstmann (Eds.), *Hegels Logik der Philosophie. Religion und Philosophie in der Theorie des absoluten Geistes*, Stuttgart: Klett-Cotta, 79–98.

Bondeli (1995): Martin Bondeli, *Das Anfangsproblem bei Karl Leonhard Reinhold. Eine systematische und entwicklungsgeschichtliche Untersuchung zur Philosophie Reinholds in der Zeit von 1789 bis 1803*, Frankfurt a. M.: Klostermann.

Fuchs (1995): Gerhard W. Fuchs, *Karl Leonhard Reinhold – Illuminat und Philosoph. Eine Studie über den Zusammenhang seines Engagements als Freimaurer und Illuminat mit seinem Leben und philosophischen Wirken*, Frankfurt a. M. / Berlin et al.: Lang.

Geldsetzer (1968): Lutz Geldsetzer, *Die Philosophie der Philosophiegeschichte im 19. Jahrhundert. Zur Wissenschaftstheorie der Philosophiegeschichtsschreibung und -betrachtung*, Meisenheim am Glan: Anton Hain.

Geldsetzer (1965): Lutz Geldsetzer, "Der Methodenstreit in der Philosophiegeschichtsschreibung 1791–1820", in: *Kant-Studien* 56, 519–527.

Gurlitt (1786): Johannes Gurlitt, *Abriß der Geschichte der Philosophie*, Leipzig: Müllersche Buchhandlung.

---

onists interact, argue, learn from one another, correct and improve each other over long distances, this does not speak against assuming there is a coherent movement of the philosophical spirit.

Hegel (1994): Georg Wilhelm Friedrich Hegel, *Vorlesungen über die Geschichte der Philosophie. Teil 1. Einleitung in die Geschichte der Philosophie. Orientalische Philosophie*, in: Georg Wilhelm Friedrich Hegel: *Vorlesungen, Ausgewählte Manuskripte und Nachschriften*. vol. 6, ed. by P. Garniron and W. Jaeschke, Hamburg: Meiner.

Kant (1942): Immanuel Kant, *Gesammelte Schriften*, vol. XX, *Dritte Abteilung, Handschriftlicher Nachlass, Siebenter Band*, ed. by Königlich Preußische Akademie der Wissenschaften, Berlin: Reimer, De Gruyter.

Kant (1977): "Über die von der Königl. Akademie der Wissenschaften zu Berlin für das Jahr 1791 ausgesetzten Preisfrage: Welches sind die wirklichen Fortschritte, die die Metaphysik seit Leibnizens und Wolffs Zeit in Deutschland gemacht hat?", in: Immanuel Kant: *Werkausgabe*, vol. VI, ed. by W. Weischedel, Frankfurt a. M.: Suhrkamp, 583–676.

Kant (1998): Immanuel Kant, *Kritik der reinen Vernunft*. Nach der ersten und zweiten Originalausgabe, ed. by J. Timmermann. Hamburg: Meiner.

Landau (1991): Albert Landau (Ed.), *Rezensionen zur Kantischen Philosophie 1781–87*, Bebra: Landau.

Reinhold (1791): Karl Leonhard Reinhold, "Über den Begriff der Geschichte der Philosophie. Eine akademische Vorlesung", in: G. G. Fülleborn (Ed.), *Beyträge zur Geschichte der Philosophie, Erstes Stück*, Züllichau und Freystadt: Frommanische Buchhandlung, 5–35.

Reinhold (1796): Karl Leonhard Reinhold, "Ueber den Begriff der Geschichte der Philosophie", in: Karl Leonhard Reinhold, *Auswahl vermischter Schriften. Erster Theil*, Jena: Mauke, 207–245.

Reinhold (2011): Karl Leonhard Reinhold, *Ueber das Fundament des philosophischen Wissens nebst einigen Erläuterungen über die Theorie des Vorstellungsvermögens*, in: Karl Leonhard Reinhold, *Gesammelte Schriften. Kommentierte Ausgabe*, ed. by M. Bondeli, vol. 4, Basel: Schwabe.

Frederick Beiser
Two Traditions of Idealism

1 The Hegelian Heritage

Nowadays our concept of German idealism is firm and fixed. We seem to know very well who were the German idealists, and when their movement began and ended. Almost all of us would say that the movement lasted some fifty years, spanning the late eighteenth and early nineteenth centuries. It begins in 1781 with the publication of Kant's *Kritik der reinen Vernunft*, and it ends in 1831 with Hegel's death. The grand thinkers in this tradition are, most everyone would agree, Kant, Reinhold, Fichte, Schelling and Hegel. It is a controversial question whether we include the romantics in this tradition; but even if we do so, it only slightly alters the *dramatis personnae*. Kant, Reinhold, Fichte, Schelling and Hegel remain the major players, while the romantics are merely "transitional figures" or "minor players".

This concept of German idealism has a venerable history, which we can trace back to the early nineteenth century. Its major source was an eminent thinker in that tradition: Hegel himself. In his *Geschichte der Philosophie*,[1] which first appeared from 1833 to 1836, Hegel described the idealist tradition as a movement beginning with Kant, passing through Fichte and Schelling, and then culminating in himself. Hegel saw his own system as the grand synthesis of all that came before it. The romantics played a minor role in this self-aggrandizing tale of dialectical triumph—Hegel gave a page each to Friedrich Schlegel and Novalis—though they all fell under the patronizing rubric "*Hauptformen, die mit der Fichteschen Philosophie zusammenhängen.*"[2]

Hegel's account of the idealist tradition has been remarkably influential. It has indeed become the standard account, the prevailing paradigm. This is not least because it was reaffirmed later in the nineteenth century by two major philosophical historians, Johann Erdmann and Kuno Fischer,[3] who, not accidently, were Hegelians themselves. It was then revived in the twentieth century by Ri-

---
[1] Hegel (1971), 314–462.
[2] Hegel (1971), 415–419.
[3] Johann Erdmann, *Die Entwicklung der deutschen Spekulation seit Kant,* volume 5 of *Versuch einer wissenschaftlichen Darstellung der Geschichte der Philosophie* (Stuttgart: Frommann 1977), first published 1834; and Kuno Fischer, volumes V-VIII of his *Geschichte der neueren Philosophie* (Heidelberg: Winter 1872–1877).

chard Kroner and Frederick Copleston,[4] who, though not Hegelian, followed Erdmann's and Fischer's precedent. Recent histories of nineteenth century philosophy have, for the most part, followed in the Hegelian tradition.[5]

Although still the standard model, Hegel's account of the idealist tradition is very misleading and problematic. It is so for several reasons. First, it gives such short shrift to the romantics, to Hölderlin, Friedrich Schlegel and Novalis, who were major innovators in the development of absolute idealism.[6] Second, it leaves out Schopenhauer, who has always been regarded as an outsider but whose philosophy, in fundamental respects, falls squarely within the idealist tradition. To leave out Schopenhauer, to regard him as "a maverick", is a major historical mistake, given that he was, with no exaggeration, the most famous and influential philosopher in Germany in the second half of the nineteenth century. Third, it assumes that the idealist tradition came to an end with Hegel's death, though there were major idealist thinkers after Hegel. I refer here to the late idealist tradition of Adolf Trendelenburg (1802–72), Hermann Lotze (1816–81) and Eduard von Hartmann (1842–1906), which flourished in the second half of the nineteenth century. Of course, Hegel could not have known about these thinkers; but there is no excuse for us, because the late idealist tradition has been thematized long ago.[7] Such, however, has been the hold of the Hegelian model that most historians of idealism have simply ignored its existence.[8]

All these reasons are more than sufficient to abandon the Hegelian model. But here I want to add a fourth reason, one that has hitherto gone unnoticed in the literature on German idealism. Namely, the Hegelian model omits another entire tra-

---

[4] Richard Kroner, *Von Kant bis Hegel* (Tübingen: Mohr, 1921), 2 vols; and Frederick Copleston, volume 7 of *A History of Modern Philosophy: Fichte to Hegel* (New York: Doubleday 1963).
[5] See, for example, Solomon (1988), 23–72; Sandkühler (2005); O'Connor a. Mohr (2006); Bréhier (1932), 111–203.
[6] I have protested against this account of the romantics in the idealist tradition in: Beiser (2002), 10–11, 350–351. But here I will leave these issues aside. My inclusion of the romantics in the idealist tradition has been questioned by Manfred Frank. See Frank (2007), 15–19. I have replied to Frank in: Beiser (2014a). Recent work in the history of idealism is giving more recognition to the romantics. See, for example, the articles by Dieter Sturma and Charles Larmore in Ameriks (2000); and Jaeschke a. Arndt (2012), 191–308.
[7] See Lehmann (1953), 4–30. The theme has been reaffirmed in Röd (2004), 234–238. I have taken up the theme in: Beiser (2013).
[8] The only scholar, as far as I know, to anticipate my position is Kuno Fischer in Fischer (1862). Fischer contends that there were two Kantian traditions active in Jena in the late eighteenth and early nineteenth centuries, the "metaphysical" tradition of Reinhold, Fichte, Schelling and Hegel and the "anthropological" tradition of Fries. Fischer was on to something important. However, he does not mention Beneke at all, while he places Herbart in the "metaphysical" tradition. The anthropological tradition, on his reckoning, consists only in Fries and his followers.

dition of idealism, one that competed and was roughly contemporaneous with the tradition of Reinhold, Fichte, Schelling and Hegel. When Hegel wrote his history of philosophy, he left out of account three rival philosophers: Jakob Friedrich Fries (1773–1843), Johann Friedrich Herbart (1776–1841) and Friedrich Eduard Beneke (1798–1854). These three thinkers formed—so I will argue—an alternative idealist tradition to that of Reinhold, Fichte, Schelling and Hegel. So if we accept Hegel's account of German idealism, we capture only one half of the idealist topography from 1780 to 1830; we miss nothing less than the opposing or alternative half. Because this tradition has been virtually completely ignored in the standard Hegelian history, I refer to it as "the lost tradition".

It is one of the old saws of historiography that history is a tale told by its victors, and that its losers are either forgotten or remembered in ignomy. Nowhere is this more true than in philosophical history, and especially in the case of Hegel's version of it. Hegel's omission of Fries, Herbart and Beneke— whether deliberate or not—was highly strategic because it virtually wrote his competiton out of history. Hegel did mention Fries in a single paragraph, though only to belittle him; and he did not mention Herbart or Beneke at all, though both became major figures in the 1830s. It is no accident that Hegel was all too aware of these thinkers, who had been highly critical of him, and whom he viewed as dangerous rivals. Notoriously, he had vehemently denounced Fries in the preface to his *Philosophie des Rechts*; he referred to Herbart with contempt, refusing to respond to his criticisms; and he knew about, or had even connived in, the withdrawal of Beneke's *venia legendi* in 1822.[9]

Fries, Herbart and Beneke are three philosophers who have seldom been classed together and placed within a single tradition.[10] I wish to show here, how-

---

9 On Hegel's attack on Fries, see d'Hondt (1988), 83–99. On Hegel's attitude toward Herbart, see Hegel (1954), 330: Hegel to Keyserlingk, January 1831. Regarding the withdrawal of Beneke's *venia legendi*, it is widely accepted in Beneke scholarship that Hegel was indeed the culprit. For its part, as far as I know, Hegel scholarship has not discussued the Beneke affair. There is evidence for and against Hegel's role. The evidence for it, which is only circumstantial, is Hegel's willingness to use his influence on the government to silence his critics; thus he attempted to get the government to censure the *Hallesche Allgemeine Literaturzeitung* for its critique of his treatment of Fries in the preface to the *Philosophie des Rechts*. On this episode, see Rosenkranz (1844), 336–337. The evidence against it is that Hegel himself, at least in 1831, had nothing against Beneke's receiving a professorship in the Faculty of Philosophy in Berlin. See Beneke (1994), 189: Beneke to Altenstein, November 28, 1831. It could well have been, however, that Hegel had simply relented from his earlier stance.
10 Seldom though not never. In Bergmann (1893), 476–583, Julius Bergmann noted the important affinities between Fries, Herbart and Beneke as opponents of speculative idealism and devoted a whole chapter to them. And in Röd (2006), 182–226, Wolfgang Röd treats Fries, Herbart

ever, that there are many fundamental similarities between them, that they share so many attitudes, values and beliefs that one is justified in regarding them as a distinct tradition. They were united on many fronts, and first and foremost in their opposition against the "speculative idealism" of Reinhold, Fichte, Schelling and Hegel. They had in common an allegiance to Kant's transcendental idealism, a program for reforming epistemology through psychology, a mistrust of rationalism and speculative metaphysics, a belief in the methods of the empirical sciences, and a theory about the close connection between ethics and aesthetics.[11] Although they did not form an organized and self-conscious movement, they still knew one another, corresponded with one another, and on one occasion even attempted to collaborate.

2 The Clash of Traditions

So the general fact obscured by Hegel's history of philosophy is that there were two competing idealist traditions in Germany in the late eighteenth and early nineteenth centuries. To give them general names, there was the *rationalist-speculative* tradition of Reinhold, Fichte, Schelling and Hegel, and there was the *em-*

---

and Beneke together, though he adds Schopenhauer, who would have protested loudly from his grave to be placed in such company (he despised all of them). Röd maintains that Fries, Herbart and Beneke deviate too much from transcendental philosophy to be regarded as Kantians; he ignores the fact that all three regarded themselves as Kantian.

[11] It will be utter heresy to Herbart scholars to see him classified as a transcendental idealist. The standard reading of Herbart is that he is a realist opposed to all forms of idealism. Otto Flügel articulates this view when he writes in the very beginning of his book on Herbart: "Whoever knows only very little about Herbart still knows that he was a realist while his age mostly thought idealistically." (Flügel (1912), 1). For a similar reading, see Asmus (1972), 11–15. Attributions of realism to Herbart suffer, however, from vagueness and prove ultimately untenable. When one becomes more precise, it is questionable whether Herbart is any more realistic than Kant. It is true that Herbart believed in the existence of a reality that exists apart from and prior to our representations, but so did Kant; that reality is the thing-in-itself, for both Kant and Herbart. It is also true that Herbart believed that sensations are given; but so did Kant, at least on one plausible reading. Herbart stressed that we cannot assume that our representations give us direct or immediate knowledge of reality itself, and he accepted Kant's distinction between appearances and things-in-themselves. See his important statement in: Herbart (1814), 19. Herbart also explicitly postulated the existence of unknowable things-in-themselves. See Herbart (1806), §3, Anmerkung, 13–14. The idealism opposed by Herbart was the Platonic idealism of the speculative-rationalist tradition, the very idealism attacked by Kant in the *Prolegomena*. See the appendix or "Beylage" to his dissertation in: Herbart (1805), 51–63. The question of Herbart's realism needs much more detailed examination, which cannot be provided here. See Beiser (2014b), chapter 2.

piricist-psychological tradition of Fries, Herbart and Beneke. The existence of these competing traditions, and the point behind these labels, will become fully clear only when we consider the many points of conflict between them.[12] They were opposed in at least five fundamental ways, each of which deserves a little explanation.

2.1 Empirical versus Rational Methods

The rationalist-speculative tradition was "rationalist" insofar as Reinhold, Fichte, Schelling and Hegel believed in the powers of reason to construct a system of philosophy and to reach substantive conclusions through pure thinking alone. This neo-rationalism is especially apparent in Reinhold's *Elementarphilosophie*, which attempted to base philosophy on a single self-evident first principle, and in the program of Fichte's *Wissenschaftslehre*, which followed Reinhold's method. It was also evident in Schelling's *Naturphilosophie*, which would "construct" nature according to general a priori principles.

The empiricist-psychological tradition, however, questioned this belief in the powers of pure reason. Fries, Herbart and Beneke insisted that philosophy has to begin from experience, that all reasoning has to be based on facts of observation, and that philosophy should imitate the inductive methods of the empirical sciences. They saw the confidence in reason of the speculative tradition as a relapse into the bad old ways of pre-Kantian rationalism.

Fries, Herbart and Beneke sometimes formulated their complaint against the rationalist-speculative tradition along classical Baconian lines: philosophy should begin not with "the synthetic method", which proceeds from universal to particular, but with "the analytic method", which goes from particular to universal. They did not contest the value of the synthetic method, and they even stressed its role in the exposition and organization of knowledge; they insisted, however, that it should be employed only *after* the analytic method, which provides all the material of knowledge.

---

[12] The conflicts between these traditions became clear and self-conscious especially in some of the polemical writings of Fries, Herbart and Beneke. The most important of these are Fries' *Reinhold, Schelling und Fichte* (Leipzig: Reineicke 1803); Beneke's *Kant und die philosophische Ausgabe unserer Zeit* (Berlin: Mittler 1832); and the first volume of Herbart's *Allgemeine Metaphysik* (Königsberg Unzer 1828).

2.2 Conflicting Attitudes toward Empirical Science

Corresponding to this rationalist/empiricist dividing line, the two traditions had opposing attitudes toward the empirical sciences. For Fichte, Schelling and Hegel, philosophy is the master science which should provide a foundation for the empirical sciences and give each of them a place in the general system of knowledge. For Fries, Herbart and Beneke, however, philosophy should not lead the sciences but follow them. The empirical sciences are one and all autonomous, having the power to reach reliable results through their own methods independent of philosophy. While they maintain that psychology is the master science, because it follows the forms of knowing in all the other sciences, they insist that it too should follow an empirical method and be modelled around the other natural sciences.

These different attitudes toward the sciences become especially apparent in their opposing views of mathematics. Schelling and Hegel spurned the use of mathematics in their *Naturphilosophie*, and they saw the quantitative side of nature as its mere appearance. Fries and Herbart, however, agreed with Kant's maxim that there is only as much science in a discipline as there is mathematics in it. It was on these grounds that Fries employed mathematics in his *Naturphilosophie*, and that Herbart introduced it into psychology.[13]

2.3 Opposing Idealisms

The rationalist-speculative tradition rejected Kant's transcendental idealism in its original intended sense, i.e., the distinction between appearances and things-in-themselves, the limitation of knowledge to appearances, and the existence of the thing-in-itself. This is true whether we are talking about Fichte's "subjective idealism" or Schelling's and Hegel's "objective idealism". Both forms of idealism denied the distinction between appearances and things-in-themselves, and both attempted to eliminate the existence of the thing-in-itself in the Kantian sense as an unknowable object beyond experience.

In this respect, the empiricist-psychological tradition of Fries, Herbart and Beneke makes the most startling contrast to the rationalist-empiricist tradition. For Fries, Herbart and Beneke, the thing-in-itself is not a flaw but a merit of Kant's philosophy. They affirm the existence of the thing-in-itself as an unknowable entity in the original Kantian sense. This concept marks the inevitable limits

---

13 See Fries (1822) and Herbart (1824). Also see Herbart (1822).

of all human knowledge, which is conditioned by the human forms of sensibility and understanding. They accepted, therefore, Kant's transcendental idealism in its original sense, i.e., the limitation of knowledge to appearances and the distinction between appearances and things-in-themselves. Fries and Beneke saw Kant's Copernican Revolution as the culmination of the anthropolgical tradition of philosophy, according to which human nature is the measure of all things and we know only what conforms to it.

2.4 Conflicting Positions on Dualism

A favorite trope of the standard history is that idealism after Kant strives to overcome his notorious dualisms. Among these dualisms are those between understanding and sensibility, form and content, essence and existence. The idealist tradition from Fichte to Hegel has been called *"Einheitsphilosophie"* insofar as it attempted to find that point of unity in reason, nature or the ego which would overcome Kant's dualisms.

While this trope is perfectly accurate for the rationalist-speculative tradition, the very opposite is the case for the empiricist-psychological tradition. Fries, Herbart and Beneke were intent on upholding the Kantian dualisms because they marked inevitable limits upon human cognition. They served as limits within the realm of experience just as the thing-in-itself served to demarcate the entire boundary of human experience. They disapproved of the speculative tradition precisely because it attempted to transcend these limits.

2.5 Clash over Teleology

In Schelling and Hegel, the rationalist-speculative tradition develops in the direction of an objective or absolute idealism, according to which all reality manifests ideas and is governed by purposes. A crucial and controversial aspect of this metaphysics is that it strives to transcend Kant's regulative strictures about teleology. It attempts to give teleology a constitutive status, i.e., it assumes that nature and history *is* governed by ends, and that we should not just proceed in our enquiries *as if* it were so.

The empiricist-psychological tradition of Fries, Herbart and Beneke staunchly opposes this teleological metaphysics. Following Kant, it insists that we give a strictly regulative status to teleology, and that we must investigate everything in nature according to mechanical methods. It was on these grounds that Fries, Herbart and Beneke were opposed to Schelling's and Hegel's *Naturphilosophie*, whose teleological postulates they regarded as a violation of Kantian strictures on knowledge. By questioning the teleological concept of the world as a relic of an old metaphysics, Fries, Herbart and Beneke were able to uphold another crucial Kantian dualism: that between theoretical and practical reasons. They could find no norms or rules within nature itself; all were human creations, having their source in the human will and emotions.

3 The Contested Kantian Legacy

It is a striking and perplexing fact about these traditions that, despite all the differences between them, they shared a common Kantian legacy. Both invoked the name and authority of Kant; both claimed to represent "the spirit of the Kantian philosophy"; and both strived to complete the Kantian Copernican Revolution. The source of the differences between them lay indeed in their conflicting interpretations of Kant's main project.

The rationalist-speculative tradition understood Kant's philosophy as a foundationalist enterprise, as if it were Kant's aim to provide a basis for knowledge immune from skeptical doubt. Reinhold, Fichte and the early Schelling maintained that Kant's philosophy contains self-evident first principles—viz., the unity of apperception, the possibility of experience, intellectual intuition, the concept of representation—and that from them it is possible to derive, through rigorous deduction, the entire system of human knowledge. Although they admitted that Kant did not realize this project, they still held that it was implicit in his texts and that it was his ultimate design. Realizing that project was the aim of Reinhold's *Elementarphilosophie,* Fichte's *Wissenschaftslehre* and Schelling's *Vom Ich als Prinzip der Philosophie.*

Flatly contrary to this interpretation, the empiricist-psychological tradition understood Kant's transcendental philosophy as a psychological or anthropological project whose chief aim was to describe human psychology, the basic faculties and activities of the mind. In their view, Kant's aim was to realize the old Enlightenment project for a science of human nature or anthropology. Although they too conceded that Kant's exposition fell short of his intention, they still insisted that his chief goal was to make epistemology into psychology. A critical epistemology was for them first and foremost based on experience, so that its foundation lay in empirical psychology.

Kant's philosophy was meant to be a synthesis of empiricism and rationalism, an attempt to combine the strong points of each position. Each tradition, however, had taken hold of one side of Kant's legacy, putting his rationalist and empiricist aspects at odd with one another. Reinhold, Fichte, Schelling and Hegel had latched onto Kant's rationalist side. Hence they stressed his demands for systematic unity, for strict demonstration and conceptual rigor, and for a priori principles in the foundation of the sciences. Fries, Herbart and Beneke, however, had stressed Kant's empiricist side. They emphasized his demands that concepts get content from experience and that metaphysics stay within the limits of experience. Both traditions complained about the other side of Kant's philosophy, as if it should have no place in his system as a whole. Thus Reinhold, Fichte, Schelling and Hegel reviled Kant's empiricist side, which, allegedly, was responsible for his lack of systematic rigor, for his failure to justify his table of categories, and for the general lack of unity in his system. Fries, Herbart and Beneke, however, would grumble about Kant's rationalist side, which surfaced in the alleged "remnants of scholasticism" still lingering in his system, viz., his rickety faculty psychology, his rigid demonstrations and his artificial distinctions. In sum, if Kant was too much an empiricist for the rationalist-speculative tradition, he was too much of a rationalist for the empirical-psychological tradition.

In the battle over Kant's legacy, both traditions could put forward a strong case for why they alone were the true heirs. Fries, Herbart and Beneke could make several arguments. First, they could point out that they advocated Kant's transcendental idealism in its original form, especially its limitation of knowledge to appearances, its distinction between appearances and things-in-themselves, and its postulate of the thing-in-itself. Second, they could maintain that they alone upheld Kant's regulative constraints upon teleology, which had been violated by Schelling and Hegel. Third, they could add that, true to Kant's teaching, they banished all appeals to intellectual intuition, which had been re-invoked by Fichte, Schelling and the young Hegel. Fourth, they could note that they too dwelled in "the bathos of experience", that they followed Kant's warnings about remaining within the limits of experience while Fichte, Schelling and Hegel dared to go beyond them. Fifth, they could stress that they re-affirmed Kant's dualisms, more specifically, his dualisms between understanding and sensibility, essence and existence, practical and theoretical reason, which are central to and characteristic of his critical teachings.

The rationalist-speculative tradition could also provide a strong defense. In stressing the foundationalist side of Kant's philosophy, Reinhold, Fichte and Schelling were attempting to show how it could be a response to skepticism, which had been Kant's intention all along. For had not Kant said that he was aroused from his "dogmatic slumbers" by Hume? And had he not made it clear that it was his intention to reply to the Scot's skepticism? It was in Kant's transcendental deduction, Reinhold, Fichte, Schelling and Hegel claimed, that one could find the true spirit of the Kantian philosophy, for it was the plain purpose of that deduction to legitimate synthetic a priori knowledge against skepticism. The demands for rigorous reasoning, strict systematic form and a single first principle also seem sanctioned by Kant himself. For Kant had often insisted that reason is by its very nature systematic, that a system should be organized around a single idea and derive from one principle.[14] Fichte, Schelling and Hegel were well aware that they were revising and reformulating Kant, and that in some respects they were violating the letter of his philosophy, e.g., in abolishing the thing-in-itself, in appealing to intellectual intuition, and in casting aside regulative constraints on teleology. But for all these infractions of the Kantian letter, they could find reason enough in the Kantian spirit. After all, they were only trying to make Kant's philosophy consistent, to help him solve his problems from his premises. Since it transcends the limits of experience, the thing-in-itself is an untenable postulate. The concept of intellectual intuition, though contrary to the Kantian letter, is suggested and presupposed by Kant's teaching in several places: it is implicit in his theory of mathematical construction, in his conception of the self-awareness of our own cognitive activity, and in the fact of reason. And as for the regulative constraints upon teleology, Schelling and Hegel insisted that Kant himself had to infract them, for it is only by giving constitutive status to the idea of the organism that it is possible to overcome the Kantian dualisms, which otherwise pose an insuperable obstacle to explaining synthetic a priori knowledge.

Who, then, were the true heirs of Kant? Fortunately, we need not decide that question here. Since both sides have strong arguments, the question is probably irresolvable. Yet the battle was won—whether rightly or not—by the empiricist-psychological tradition. For, as we shall soon see, it was their arguments that were later adopted by the early neo-Kantian movement.

4 Reclaiming the Lost Tradition

At this point we might well concede that there was a lost tradition in post-Kantian philosophy. But we might well ask ourselves: Why bother with it? After all, who nowadays reads Fries, Herbart and Beneke? No one, it seems, but a few historians. Here, in this final section, I would like to say a few words in behalf of the lost and forgotten. There are good philosophical and historical reasons to remember them.

Those who think that Fries, Herder and Beneke are unimportant because no one bothers with them today fails to heed the first lesson of history: that we should not measure the significance of the past by what we remember today.

---

14 Kant, *KrV*, B 502, 673, 708, 862.

Though we have forgotten Fries, Herbart and Beneke, they were in fact very influential in the late nineteenth and early twentieth centuries. Take the case of Fries. His influence extended beyond the early 1800s and his life time. Few philosophers can claim two revivals in their name. But such is the case with Fries. In 1848, four years after his death, a Friesian school was formed in Jena under the leadership of Ernst Friedrich Apelt (1815–59), who had been a student of Fries. Among the members of that school were some of the most prominent scientists of the day, viz., the mathematician Oskar Schlömilch (1823–1901), the zollogist Heinrich Schmid (1799–1836), the botanist Matthias Schleiden (1804–1881), and the mathematician Karl Friedrich Gauss (1777–1855). The group formed a common journal, *Abhandlungen der Fries'schen Schule*, whose express purpose was to keep alive the spirit of the critical philosophy "as founded by Kant and developed by Fries."[15] Though the first Friesian school soon dispersed, a neo-Friesian school was formed in 1903 in Göttingen under the direction of Leonard Nelson (1882–1927). The group surrounding Nelson was equally distinguished, counting among its members the theologian Rudolf Otto (1869–1937), the psychiatrist Arthur Kronfeld (1886–1941) and the nobel prize winner Otto Meyerhoff (1884–1951).[16] In 1904 Nelson restarted the Friesian journal, rededicating it to "philosophy in the spirit of Kant as formulated by Fries".[17]

Apart from his influence, Fries is important in the history of philosophy for at least two reasons. First, for his critique of the rationalist-speculative tradition. Fries' 1804 *Reinhold, Fichte und Schelling* is a compelling and persuasive attack on the foundationalist methodology of Reinhold, Fichte and Schelling. No one saw more clearly than Fries the problems with this methodology; as a critique of foundationalism, his book can still be read with profit today. Second, for his pioneering role in psychologism. Fries was among the first philosophers to advance a psychological interpretation of Kant's philosophy, which interpreted epistemology essentially as an empirical theory of mental activities. Thanks partly to Fries' influence, this became the dominant interpretation of Kantian epistemology for decades—it was adopted by Hermann Helmholtz, Eduard Zeller, Jürgen Bona Meyer and Friedrich Lange later in the nineteenth century—and it was not questioned until the 1870s. Of course, to many philosophers nowadays, to say

---

15 E.F. Apelt, Heinrich Schmid a. Oskar Schlömilch (Eds.), *Abhandlungen der Fries'schen Schule* (Leipzig: Engelmann 1847–49), 2 volumes.
16 On the history of the neo-Friesian school, see Kronfeld (1920); and Blencke (1978).
17 Leonard Nelson, Gerhard Hessenberg a. Karl Kaiser (Eds.), *Abhandlungen der Fries'schen Schule, Neue Folge* (Göttingen: Vandenhoeck & Ruprecht 1907–1937), 6 volumes. On the purpose of the *Neue Folge*, see "Vorwort der alten Folge zugleich als Vorwort der neuen Folge" in volume I, vii-xii.

that Fries is important for advancing psychologism is like saying quacks selling snake oil are important in the history of medicine. Since the work of Husserl and Frege at the beginning of the twentieth century, "psychologism" has been regarded as a basic fallacy, the simple conflation of logical rules of inference with natural laws of thought. Because of his association with psychologism, Fries was widely discredited in the early twentieth century. Yet the time is long overdue, I believe, for a reappraisal of psychologism, which we can now see in more detached and objective terms than our forbears.[18] If we return to Fries earliest programmatic writings,[19] we can see that he never made the simple fallacies that his succesors often attributed to him. Fries never thought that knowing the causes and processes involved in thinking provided a justification for it; and he was careful to distinguish the *quid facti?* from the *quid juris?* His aim was not to provide a foundation for logic but to understand thinking as a mental process on the model of the natural sciences.[20] It is chiefly by going back to Fries, I would suggest, that we can best understand the motivation and rationale behind psychologism.

Now take the case of Herbart. Although he scarcely gets a mention in recent Anglophone histories of philosophy, he was one of the most influential philosophers of the nineteenth century.[21] There were Herbartians in philosophy throughout the German speaking world well into the twentieth century. A Herbartian journal, *Zeitschrift für exakte Philosophie*, was founded in 1860; and though it ended in 1875, it was rehabilitated in 1883. Two of Herbart's students, Franz Exner (1802–1853) and Karl Lott (1807–1874), taught Herbart's philosophy at Vienna, and virtually made it into "the official Austrian philosophy". One historian wrote of the Herbartian school: "In its methodological strictness, its moral earnestness and scientific sobriety, the Herbartian school excelled all other philosopher directions of the century."[22] Apart from his influence, Herbart is important in the history of philosophy for at least two reasons. First, along with Fries,

---

[18] For such a reappraisal, see Kusch (1995).
[19] See Fries early articles published in volume III (1798) of the *Psychologisches Magazin*. They are "Ueber das Verhältniß der empirischen Psychologie zur Metaphysik", 156–202; "Propadeutik einer allgemeinen empirischen Psychologie", 203–267; "Von der rationellen Seelenlehre", 268–293; "Abriß der Metaphysik der inneren Natur", 294–353; "Allgemeine Uebersicht der empirischen Erkentnisse des Gemüths", 354–402.
[20] In Fries (1837), 1–5, Fries is careful to distinguish *demonstrative* from *anthropological* logic; the former deals with the formal laws of inference and the latter with inference as an activity of the mind. It is absurd, Fries notes (p. 5), to prove the laws of logic on the basis of empirical psychology.
[21] On the Herbartian school, see Siebert (1898), 136–183.
[22] Siebert (1898), 136.

he led the charge against the rationalist methods of Fichte, Schelling and Hegel, formulating a conception of philosophy as the analysis of concepts and the resolution of problems. Second, he was a founder of modern psychology, stressing the importance of observation, experiment and measurement. His *Psychologie als empirische Wissenschaft* (1824) is one of the classic texts in the history of modern psychology.

Finally, there is the sad and more difficult case of Beneke. He had none of the influence of Fries or Herbart, and he had few disciples. This had much to do with his tragic life: deprived of his *venia legendi* in 1822, he had grave difficulty in finding an academic position; he never became an *Ordinarius* in Berlin, though he taught there for nearly three decades. Frustrated by his lack of recognition, Beneke (most probably) committed suicide in 1854. A very prolific author, most of his work was devoted to the development of empirical psychology, and much of it is very dated because of later advances in that discipline. Yet Beneke's early epistemological writings are interesting for their radical empiricism and naturalism.[23] And one product of his pen—the one that cost him his academic career—is still very much worth reading: his *Grundlegung zur Physik der Sitten*, which is an existentialist ethic *avant la lettre* and an interesting critique of Kant's moral philosophy.[24]

Quite apart from the contributions of its individual authors, there is another reason we should not forget the lost tradition. The main reason to remember it today concerns its founding role in one of the most important and influential philosophical movements of the late nineteenth and early twentieth centuries: neo-Kantianism. Whoever were the true heirs of Kant, the battle for the Kantian legacy was ultimately won by Fries, Herbart and Beneke. Whatever the merits of their case, history decided in their favor. For it was their arguments that were later adopted by the early neo-Kantian movement. Their criticisms of the speculative-rationalist tradition laid the foundations for the neo-Kantian position decades later. The first generation of neo-Kantians in the 1860s—Kuno Fischer, Otto Liebmann, Eduard Zeller, Jürgen Bona Meyer and Friedrich Lange—reacted against the neo-rationalism of Schelling and Hegel's metaphysics much along the lines of Fries, Herbart and Beneke decades earlier. The neo-Kantians were writing in an age even more dominated by the empirical sciences, and to them it seemed all the more necessary that philosophy give up its pretensions to legislate for the sciences; its only feasible task seemed to be examination of the underlying "logic" of the sciences, i.e., their methods, presuppositions

---

23 Beneke (1820a) and Beneke (1820b).
24 See Beneke (1822).

and standards of truth. The position of the empiricist-psychological tradition, which aligned philosophy more closely with the empirical sciences, therefore seemed prescient, providing the best advice for philosophy to go forward in a more scientific age.

These neo-Kantians also adopted other basic contentions of the empiricist-psychological tradition: that Kant's philosophy should be interpreted in psychological terms; that philosophy should remain within the limits of experience; that Kant's concept of teleology should remain regulative; that it is necessary to accept Kant's dualisms between understanding and sensibility, essence and existence, as inherent limits of the human understanding. So Fries, Herbart and Beneke can well be regarded as the founders and fathers of neo-Kantianism. It was mainly in the neo-Kantian movement that their legacy lived on in the late nineteenth and early twentieth centuries.

Though the lost tradition paved the way for neo-Kantianism, its powerful influence has been scarcely recognized. Some neo-Kantians acknowledged the importance of Fries,[25] but later scholars of neo-Kantianism have virtually ignored him. Recent works on neo-Kantianism by-and-large ignore the figures of the lost tradition.[26] There are at least two reasons for such neglect. First, there was the reaction against the psychological interpretation of Kant in the 1870s and 1880s by the later neo-Kantians, especially Windelband and Cohen. The argument that Kant's transcendental philosophy is epistemology and not psychology made it seem legitimate to leave out of account a whole tradition of interpretation that had stressed the psychological aspect of Kant's project. For this reason, it is common in neo-Kantian scholarship to limit the movement to the Southwestern and Marburg schools alone; even the Friesian school has been largely ignored. Second, though it has been widely recognized that neo-Kantianism arose from a rejection of the methods and metaphysics of absolute idealism, they date that reaction much too late, placing it in the 1840s after the collapse of

---

[25] Thus Hermann Cohen and Jürgen Bona Meyer acknowledged Fries importance in the development of the psychological interpretation of Kant. See Cohen (1871), 125; and Bona Meyer (1870), 9–22. Otto Liebmann devoted an entire chapter each to Fries and Herbart in Liebmann (1865), 111–156.

[26] Among these works are Hans-Ludwig Ollig, *Der Neukantianismus* (Stuttgart: Metzler, 1979); Thomas E. Willey, *Back to Kant* (Detroit: Wayne State University Press, 1978); Klaus Christian Köhnke, *Entstehung und Aufstieg des Neukantianismus* (Frankfurt a. M.: Suhrkamp, 1986); Ulrich Sieg, *Aufstieg und Niedergang des Marburger Neukantianismus* (Würzburg: Königshausen & Neumann, 1994); L.W. Beck, "Neo-Kantianism" in *The Encyclopedia of Philosophy* (New York: MacMillan, 1967), V, 468–473; and H. Holzhey, "Neukantianismus" in *Historisches Wörterbuch der Philosophie* (Basel: Schwabe, 1984), VI, 747–754. Though Köhnke has a valuable chapter on Beneke, he does not discuss Fries or Herbart.

Hegel's metaphysics. It is important to realize, however, that the reaction against sepculative idealism took place much earlier, and indeed for very Kantian reasons. It arose as early as the 1790s when Fries and Herbart criticized the methods and metaphysics of Fichte's and Schelling's idealism.

Not the least reason to remember the lost tradition is that our philosophical affinities and allegiances are more with it than with the speculative-rationalist tradition. Few philosophers today are willing to adopt the a priori methodology or foundationalist program of Reinhold, Fichte and Schelling, still less the dialectical method of Hegel. Our reaction to the metaphysical excesses and methodological extravagence of speculative idealism are very much like those of Fries, Herbart and Beneke in the early nineteenth century. Our conception of philosophy as an analytic, problem-solving enterprise, rather than as a foundationalist, system-bulding project, is also very close to that of the lost tradition. Our view about the relationship between philosophy and the sciences is no less that of Fries, Herbart and Beneke, who preached that philosophy should learn from the sciences rather than trying to provide a foundation for them. It is not too much to say that the great turn against the metaphysics and methodology of speculative idealism, which was so important for the development of positivism and analytic philosophy, had its sources in the lost tradition, in the early critiques of Fries, Herbart and Beneke.

It is should be a maxim that all good philosophy is self-critical, i.e., aware of its basic assumptions and values. This means, though, that philosophy should be self-conscious of its past, which is the source of its assumptions and values. For just this reason, we should not forget the lost tradition, which has been very much part of our past. Our task as philosophers and historians should to re-discover that tradition and make it lost no more. But need I add: we have scarcely begun?

Bibliography

Asmus (1972): Walter Asmus, *Herbart in seiner und in unserer Zeit*, Essen: Neue deutsche Schule Verlagsgesellschaft.
Ameriks (2000): Karl Ameriks, *The Cambridge Companion to German Idealism*, Cambridge: Cambridge University Press.
Beiser (2002): Frederick Beiser, *German Idealism*, Cambridge MA: Harvard University Press.
Beiser (2013): Frederick Beiser, *Late German Idealism: Trendelenburg & Lotze*, Oxford: Oxford University Press.
Beiser (2014a): Frederick Beiser, "Romanticism and Idealism", in: Dalia Nassar (Ed.), *The Relevance of Romanticism. Essays on German Romantic Philosophy*, Oxford: Oxford University Press, 30–46.

Beiser (2014b): Frederick Beiser, *The Genesis of Neo-Kantianism. 1796–1880*, Oxford: Oxford University Press.

Beneke (1820a): Friedrich Eduard Beneke, *Erkenntnißlehre nach dem Bewußtsein der reinen Vernunft in ihren Grundzügen*, Jena: Frommann.

Beneke (1820b): Friedrich Eduard Beneke, *Erfahrungsseelenlehre als Grundlage alles Wissens, in ihren Hauptzügen dargestellt*, Berlin: Mittler.

Beneke (1822): Friedrich Eduard Beneke, *Grundlegung zur Physik der Sitten. Ein Gegenstück zu Kants Grundlegung zur Metaphysik der Sitten*, Berlin: Mittler.

Beneke (1994): Friedrich Beneke, *Ungedruckte Briefe*, ed. by Renato Pettoello and Nikola Barelmann, Aalen: Scientia Verlag.

Bergmann (1983): Julius Bergmann, *Geschichte der Philosophie*, vol. II: *Die deutsche Philosophie von Kant bis Beneke*, Berlin: Mittler.

Blencke (1978): Erna Blencke, "Zur Geschichte der neuen Fries'schen Schule und der Jakob Friedrich Fries-Gesellschaft", *Archiv für Geschichte der Philosophie* 60, 199–208.

Bona Meyer (1870): Jürgen Bona Meyer, *Kants Psychologie dargestellt und erörtert*, Berlin: Hertz.

Bréhier (1932): Emile Bréhier, *The History of Philosophy*, vol. 6, *The Nineteenth Century*, Chicago: University of Chicago Press.

Cohen (1871): Hermann Cohen, *Kants Theorie der Erfahrung*, Berlin: Dümmler.

Fischer (1862): Kuno Fischer, *Die beiden Kantischen Schulen in Jena*, reprinted in *Akademische Reden*, Stuttgart: Cotta.

Flügel (1912): Otto Flügel, *Herbarts Lehren und Leben*, 2nd edition, Leipzig: Teubner.

Frank (2007): Manfred Frank, *Auswege aus dem Deutschen Idealismus*, Frankfurt a. M.: Suhrkamp.

Fries (1822): Jakob Friedrich Fries, *Die mathematische Naturphilosophie nach philosophischer Methode bearbeitet*, Heidelberg: Mohr und Winter.

Fries (1837): Jakob Friedrich Fries, *System der Logik*, Heidelberg: Winter.

Hegel (1954), G. W. F. Hegel, *Briefe von und an Hegel*, ed. by Johannes Hoffmeister, Volume III. Hamburg: Meiner.

Hegel (1971): G.W.F. Hegel, *Vorlesungen über die Geschichte der Philosophie III*, in: G.W.F. Hegel, *Werke in zwanzig Bänden*, vol. 20, ed. by Karl Michel and Eva Moldenhauer, Frankfurt a. M.: Suhrkamp.

Herbart (1805): Johann Friedrich Herbart, *De platonici systematis fundamento commentatio*, Göttingen: Roewer.

Herbart (1806): Johann Friedrich Herbart, *Hauptpunckte der Metaphysik*, Göttingen: J.C. Baier.

Herbart (1814): Johann Friedrich Herbart, *Ueber meinen Streit mit der Modephilosophie dieser Zeit*, Königsberg: Unzer.

Herbart (1822): Johann Friedrich Herbart, *Ueber die Möglichkeit und Nothwendigkeit Mathematik auf Psychologie anzuwenden*, Königsberg: Bornträger.

Herbart (1824): Johann Friedrich Herbart, *Psychologie als Wissenschaft neu gegründet auf Erfahrung, Metaphysik und Mathematik*, Königsberg: Unzer.

D'Hondt (1988): Jacques d'Hondt, *Hegel in his Time, Berlin, 1818–1831*, Lewiston N.Y.: Broadview Press.

Jaeschke a. Arndt (2012): Walter Jaeschke and Andreas Arndt, *Die Klassische Deutsche Philosophie nach Kant*, München: Beck.

Kronfeld (1920): Arthur Kronfeld, "Geleitworte zum zehnjährigen Bestehen der neue Friesschen Schule", in: Arthur Kronfeld, *Das Wesen der psychiatrischen Erkenntnis*, Berlin: Springer, 46–65.

Kusch (1995): Martin Kusch, *Psychologism*, London: Routledge.

Lehmann (1953): Gerhard Lehmann, *Geschichte der Philosophie*, vol. IX, *Die Philosophie des neunzehnten Jahrhunderts II*, Berlin: De Gruyter.

Liebmann (1865): Otto Liebmann, *Kant und die Epigonen*, Stuttgart: Schober.

O'Connor a. Mohr (2006): Brian O'Connor and Georg Mohr (Eds.), *German Idealism: An Anthology and Guide*, Edinburg: Edinburg University Press.

Röd (2004): Wolfgang Röd, *Geschichte der Philosophie*, vol. XII, *Die Philosophie des ausgehenden 19. und des 20. Jahrhunderts*, München: Beck.

Röd (2006): Wolfgang Röd, *Geschichte der Philosophie*, vol. IX,1: *Die Philosophie der Neuzeit 3*, München: Beck.

Rosenkranz (1844): Karl Rosenkranz, *G.W.F. Hegels Leben*, Berlin: Duncker & Humblot.

Sandkühler (2005): Hans Jörg Sandkühler (Ed.), *Handbuch Deutscher Idealismus*, Stuttgart: Metzler.

Siebert (1898): Otto Siebert, *Geschichte der neueren deutschen Philosophie seit Hegel*, Göttingen: Vandenhoeck & Ruprecht.

Solomon (1988): Robert C. Solomon, *Continental Philosophy since 1750*, Oxford: Oxford University Press.

Valentin Pluder
The End of the Story, the End of History

I Jakob Friedrich Fries

The last chapter of the last volume of Jakob Friedrich Fries' 1840 *Geschichte der Philosophie* [*History of Philosophy*] is entitled *Das Ende der Geschichte der Philosophie—The End of the History of Philosophy*. This title is accurate in a double sense. On the one hand it designates the actual end of Fries' historical narrative and so of the *historia rerum gestarum*. Fries' concluding chapter is thus one of the more detailed examples of the genre of concluding words or remarks in the 19th century in which the respective author, following after many hundred pages of rigorous philosophical history, gives a personal estimation of history *in toto*. On the other hand the concluding chapter of Fries' *Geschichte der Philosophie* is also consistent with the book's project on conceptual grounds. Already the title of his book indicates that the narrative history of philosophy therein is represented *according to the progress of its scientific development*. And to describe a process as a progressive development, it is necessary to have an idea of the goal of this process. The goal, of course, need not be the end of the process, but it may be its end.

However, Fries does not merely narrate a history that has a beginning and a defined end. He is convinced, above all, that the history of philosophy itself, and so the *res gestae*, is a progressive development, that has a defined beginning (with the ancient Greeks) and a defined end.

Fries does not place this end of philosophy described at the end of his *History* in a distant and possibly unattainable future. In doing so, he sharply distinguishes his work from popular concluding words of then contemporary historians of philosophy. In the last lines of such voluminous books we often find the hope expressed that philosophers would not keep producing new conceptual variations one after the other to all eternity but that they will eventually (albeit it in the distant future) come to a more or less undisputed conclusion. But the weight of the previously recorded divergent positions of diverse philosophers makes many authors pull back, retreating and making concessions to get back to safe ground. A goal or end of philosophy is thus hoped for in such works that can be neither attained nor determined as finally valid, which is not particularly philosophical.[1] The writing of voluminous histories of philosophy seems

---

[1] Examples of the image of an 'infinite approach' are Weiller (1813), 262; Lichtenfels (1836), 223; Bauer (1863), 374; compare also Ast (1829), 1–3; Schneidewind (1825), 28.

to have not infrequently the effect of threatening to make the progressive or developmental character, maybe even *all* order in history, disappear. Dilthey, for example, was plagued by the nightmare of the "frightful anarchy of thinking".[2] For if not at least a view of one approximate beginning and one approximate end emerges immanently out of philosophy, then the history of philosophy cannot in and of itself be understood as a development. This shows then, ultimately, that no philosophical concept whatsoever of the history of philosophy is available. Order then will be created arbitrarily and wilfully with criteria that lie beyond philosophy, such as, for example, in a particular, chronological sequence.

None of these problems bother Jakob Fries. In the year 1840 he looks back onto the end of the history of philosophy and, from a raised standpoint, can comfortably consider the course of history through to its successfully completion. The end of the history of philosophy had, after all, already been reached more than half a century ago with Kant's critical philosophy[3]:

> Philosophy is a science, which contains a system of necessary truths for the human spirit. A history of such a science can only exist up to the point at which we reach a secure, complete and perspicuous statement of these truths. Once this goal is reached, a tranquil state of ownership sets in that permits no further historical development. We have now attained to this quiet state of ownership with regard to pure philosophy through the entirety of the Kantian teaching [...].[4]

Thus, the end of the history of philosophy is achieved here in the mode of completion.[5] And the genesis of this completion is a historical one. The validity of the completed philosophy is not historical although a long course through the history of philosophy was needed in order to finally form a "true science of philosophy".[6] The validity of this philosophy is not, however, bound to a historical context but is meta-historical: it was true already before the beginning of its genesis with the ancient Greeks and it endures as such, at least so long as there is a human mind.[7] Accordingly it would be actually more precise to speak of a

---

[2] Dilthey (1931), 218–224.
[3] That this too is a position that needs at least an explanation according to Kant's own self-understanding is a point that will not be examined here.
[4] Fries (1840), 717.
[5] However later Fries pulls back a little, writing "the end of the history of philosophy should be brought about by the solid scientific education of pure philosophy [...]" (Fries (1840), 719).
[6] Fries (1840), 715.
[7] Fries also understands this in that he speaks of a meta-historical form of philosophy that he contrasts with the particular and incomplete historical form up to Kant. Compare Fries (1837), 9.

pre-history of philosophy or of a history of the genesis of philosophy as philosophy in its state of completeness is beyond history, no longer has a history.

Fries sees philosophy as completed with Kant. Hence he must measure all philosophy before Kant by its relationship to Kant.[8] Accordingly the true philosophers *before* Kant are anonymous Kantians and the non-Kantians *after* Kant are not philosophers at all. In his *Geschichte der Philosophie*, Fries shows himself to be rigorous in this regard. It is true that the main text does not end with Kant but is entitled *Kant's school*. Indeed it should have more appropriately been named *Kant's students* or *Kant's only student*, because the only student who is allowed to speak at length there, who identifies 'defects' in Kant's theory and who proposes 'improvements', is Jakob Friedrich Fries. Other than him, only Ernst Reinhold is mentioned, although only in a footnote which explains why there is no further mention made of him.[9] The so-called philosophers after Kant—namely, Karl Leonard Reinhold, Schulze, Jacobi, Fichte, Schelling, Hegel and Herbart – are, according to the actual history of philosophy, dealt with in an addendum which bears the title: "recent great regressions".

What brings the history of philosophy to its end? The completion of philosophy is reached through Kant's insight into its limitations:

> all humanity's knowledge remains piecemeal; only the faith that is alive in love raises us to completeness. Therefore what is now required is firstly a clear determination of the realms of our knowledge and their bounds, secondly the elevation of faith to perfection beyond all knowledge, thirdly the proof, that faith is only alive in love. The first the Kantian theory achieves through the establishment of the system of the categories and their mathematical schematism; the second through the establishment of the system of ideas of the absolute, the third through the theory of the primacy of practical reason.[10]

These insights form the core of "pure philosophy". It is "[…] a solid system of necessary truths, like pure mathematics."[11] To pure philosophy Fries furthermore adds an applied philosophy. While pure philosophy is perfected as a meta-historical truth, applied philosophy (that is, natural philosophy, philosophical political science, psychology, philosophy of religion, etc[12]) remains an inexhaustible

---

8 Compare Fries (1837), 3.
9 Fries (1840), 590.
10 Fries (1840), 717. Compare also 718: "No one can dispute that these categories with their transcendental schema are bound to the conditions for the possibility of experience in our knowledge and with this contain the law and the limits of all our scientific explanations."
11 Fries (1840), 725.
12 Fries (1840), 221 f.

field of tasks for philosophers after Kant because of its entanglement with the empirical sciences.[13]

The end of the history of philosophy declared by Fries is therefore based on the assumption of a development, that "corresponding to the nature of the human spirit",[14] lawfully and necessarily[15] takes its course through history and ends in Kant with the final elevation of pure philosophy to science. While the genesis of scientific philosophy is a historical one, the content of scientific philosophy is considered meta-historical. It remains unbesmirched by its genesis and the various preceding historical forms of philosophy have no inherent worth. They are only deficient representations of the one truth and in the light of the "true science of philosophy" they fade away without a trace.

II Johann Christian August Grohmann

The perfection and completion of philosophy means simultaneously the end of the history that leads to this perfection and completion. Although this needs no explanation the claim that the history of philosophy should be the end of philosophy does. In 1797 in his text *Über den Begriff der Geschichte der Philosophie* [*Concerning the Concept of the History of Philosophy*] Johann Christian August Grohmann comes to just this conclusion: "The history of philosophy is the end of all philosophizing."[16] One thinks spontaneously of the paralyzing effect of the dusty weight of philosophical ideas and arguments that have accumulated over the centuries. Scarcely anyone is well-advised to re-read a few thousand pages of the history of philosophy if any new philosophical thought is to emerge. In fact this insight is also common among the philosophical historians of the 19th century. Thus Johann Eduard Erdmann complains at great length at the end of *Grundriss der Geschichte der Philosophie* [*Outline of the History of Philosophy*] (1866), that philosophy will busy itself only with history and the authentic engagement with philosophical content is atrophying as a result. Erdmann sees the spirit of his time as entirely in the grip of this tendency:

> The fact of the matter which cannot be denied, that wherever there is still an interest in philosophical studies, there is, however no urge to philosophize, but the desire to see

---

13 This tendency, to restrict philosophy with its completion or its end to 'pure logic' or 'pure method' shows itself more frequently in the future.
14 Compare Fries (1837), 45.
15 Compare Fries (1837), 27.
16 Grohmann (1897), 101, also Grohmann(1898), 66, compare Geldsetzer (1968), 30.

how others philosophized. This is a parallel occurrence to the simultaneous phenomenon of literary historians replace the poets, and biographies replace great men.[17]

If, half a century earlier, Grohmann speaks of the end of philosophizing through the history of philosophy he has something quite different in mind. For with the term "history" Grohmann does not think of a chronological development as Fries does. History is *"istoria"* not in the sense of a linear sequence of acts and the recounting of these acts but a systematically ordered corpus of knowledge. Grohmann means by the term "history" therefore almost the opposite of what Fries understands to be "history". By way of illustration Grohmann refers to the "(natural) history of birds". In no way does he mean by this the evolution or the developmental history of birds from the dinosaurs to the late 18th century but rather he means the totality of all birds as systematically ordered according to genera and species on the basis of the criterion of similarity.[18]

Correspondingly the history of philosophy means the systematic ordering of all philosophies according to genera and species or, perhaps better, according to different types. For Grohmann, in this regard, the individual philosophical system constitutes the smallest unit. The question as to when a philosophical system enters into time is accordingly not relevant for its placement within the systematic as a whole. Temporal sequence is therefore no criterion for ordering, although it is the criterion of reality. That a system emerges at all at some point in time thus signals the reality of a philosophical system.[19] Hence what is at stake here is not an entirely unempirical deduction of all possible philosophies. However, reality is understood as a quality that does not pertain to systems in different quantities. Actual existence is expressed as an ordering criterion going hand in hand with temporal allocation.

How are the ordering criteria of Grohmann's history of philosophy constituted? The ordering criteria of a comprehensive general systematic of all philosophical systems must fulfil clear conditions. They are not allowed to be contingent or determined arbitrarily but must exist beyond history and hence be *a priori*. Groh-

---

[17] Erdmann (1866), 796. The last sentence of his book sounds again more conciliatory: "As against the complaint therefore, that philosophers have become historians, only being driven by the history of philosophy and no longer philosophize, [there is the claim that] the historian of philosophy himself fosters philosophizing, and so perhaps the same lance that once wounded can become healing" (Erdmann (1866)., 798). On the threat of philosophy being suffocated by its history, see also Hermann (1961), 5, 12.
[18] See Grohmann (1898), 34.
[19] Compare Geldsetzer (1968), 29 and Grohmann (1897), 53.

mann finds these criteria (without further elaborating this point) in "the first criteria determined within the imaginative capacity".[20]

The structure of the imaginative capacity forms therefore the fundamental basis for the ordering of all philosophical systems in types such as, for example, dogmatism, idealism, critical philosophy and so on, which can themselves be further subdivided.[21] As Grohmann defines it:

> The history of philosophy is the systematic representation of necessary existing systems of philosophy, as the science of the a priori in the imaginative capacity for determinate knowledge according to concepts, in as far as the system can be lead back to its first determinate grounds in the capacity for imagination and are possible according to them.[22]

This systematic of all manner of philosophical systems forms a closed unity. This unity is established on the common origin of the different types of philosophy in the *a priori* structures of the capacity for imagination. Were there not such a common origin, the different types of philosophical systems would not only stand next to one another without any mediation and there would also be no reason for assuming that *all* types were in fact accounted for. The claim that Grohmann stakes with his history of philosophy, however, is to have recorded all possible types of philosophical systems in his systematic.

Given that the envisioned systematic is based on the *a priori* structures of the capacity for imagination, the philosophy which discloses the structures of the capacity for imagination assumes a special role. For one thing it is, so to speak, the system of systems because it provides the fundamental basis on which the different types of philosophical systems can be set in a specific relation to one another in such a way that that they together form a closed unity. On the other hand, philosophy, as that which makes the systematic possible, stands outside of the systematic that forms the history of philosophy. For it is not traced back to a structure in the capacity for imagination. It precedes these structures because it discloses them as the precondition for the possibility of imagination in general.

Thus, it is again Kant's philosophy that also crowns Grohmann's history of philosophy. This time it is not because it, as the complete philosophy, renders all other philosophies obsolete but because it makes possible a survey of all the different philosophies and transforms them into an ordered totality. The *Critique of Pure Reason* raises the researcher to a standpoint that towers above all

---

20 Grohmann (1897), 42, compare Grohmann (1898), 65.
21 Compare Grohmann (1898), 41.
22 Grohmann (1897), 65.

other philosophies and thereby enables the systematic that Grohmann calls the "history of philosophy".[23]

The completion of the total systematic of all possible philosophical systems ends philosophizing also, at least insofar as concerns the development of new philosophies. Grohmann thus continues:

> The history of philosophy shows how and where once there is a silence and a standstill of all systems, so that no further ones can come, none can emerge any more, and that, if in the future times there is still controversy in philosophy, this can only concern old systems, that which has been there before, because any new material is lacking.[24]

The completion of the history of philosophy in Grohmann's sense is obviously at the same time the end of the history of philosophy as a development of new types in time. Nothing new can be discovered anymore because all that is possible has already been disclosed. At first glance Grohmann's approach appears to be not so different from that of Jakob Fries. Both believe that with Kant the last word in philosophy had been spoken and both hold these last words as valid over and beyond history. Both associate the end of the history of philosophy with the conversion of philosophy to science.[25]

Fries however lets each new philosophy on its path to science (at least in principle) cast its predecessor into oblivion. At the end of the history of philosophy there remains just one philosophy, Kant's philosophy. In Grohmann, in contrast, philosophies, at least in principle, do not succeed and replace one another. They remain static. The thought of development is missing. The conclusion instead is signalled by the philosophy that assumes all philosophies of all times into a definitive order and that, here too, is Kant's philosophy.

III Georg Wilhelm Friedrich Hegel

Besides Kant, Hegel is the philosopher who tends to be mentioned most frequently when the end of philosophy or the end of the history of philosophy in the 19th century is at issue.[26]

---

23 Grohmann (1897), 99.
24 Grohmann (1897), 102f., compare Geldsetzer (1968), 189.
25 Compare Grohmann (1898), 5.
26 Which is not to say that the supposed Hegelian position is argued for. Some examples of this are Schubarth a. Carganico (1829), 178; Reiff (1840), 253; Frantz (1844), 40; Müglich (1849), 62; Carnier (1836), 176.

The end of the history of philosophy which Hegel allegedly wanted to bring about himself is at odds with his insistence on a historicity of philosophy. If the question concerning the position of *Hegelian* philosophy in the history of philosophy is disregarded, then Hegel should not actually be the first but the last philosopher who is mentioned in connection with the end of the history of philosophy. For with Hegel it is not only the genesis of philosophy that is historical but also its validity.

Historicity of genesis means (as ever) that the development of philosophy is to be understood as a process in time. Within this process every subsequent step builds on the preceding step and findings previously made are transformed, assimilated or sublated, respectively.

Historicity of validity means (and this is new) that in principle every time has a philosophy that is valid for this time without restriction. As a consequence, on the one hand, at each point in time philosophy can be completed and on the other no philosophy is the completion of philosophy for all points in time, for ever—at least not as long as history itself has not come to its end.

The explanation for this does not need to resort to profound metaphysical considerations. It arises simply from Hegel's conception of philosophy. Philosophy "[...] is its time comprehended in thought."[27] If the times changes philosophy must change with them. If there is, then, history at all, neither philosophy nor the history of philosophy are at an end. Or put inversely, if it is true that with Hegel the history of philosophy is conclusively finished, then history itself must have ended sometime in the first third of the 19th century.

But why should anybody think this, especially in the face of the emphasis on the historicity of philosophy? The reason for this lies (in relation to Hegel's philosophy, not to history in its entirety) in the fact that Hegel in no way presents an open system, possibly one containing anticipatory moments, but rather brings his system to a closure that could hardly be more hermeneutical. The system is closed as a circle. The end returns consciously to the beginning. Considering that the consummation of this completion does not favour an individual position but rather is the unification of antagonistic positions, it appears not so remarkable that Hegel attracts the suspicion that he had wanted to claim for himself the conclusion of all philosophy. What, in the end, should be added to a thinking that has always already recognized and assumed into itself the opposing positions and draws confirmation even from that which contradicts it?

---

[27] Hegel (2009), 15. Compare also Hegel (1994), 48: "Every philosophy, precisely because it is the depiction of a particular stage of development, belongs to its times and is entangled in its *bounds*."

At the end of the Association of Friends Edition [*Freundesvereinsausgabe*] of *Vorlesungen über die Geschichte der Philosophie* [*Lectures on the History of Philosophy*] one can find those sentences, recorded by Griesheim: "This is now the position of the current time, and the sequence of spiritual configurations is thus for now closed [*geschlossen*]—and this history of philosophy is thus *concluded* [*beschlossen*]."[28]

Thus the union of historicity and the conclusion of philosophy in Hegel could be shown to be a variation of the thought of philosophy's completion.[29] Philosophy is only historical so long as it not only recognizes its own historicity but also understands the unity and inner coherence of different historical positions as the necessary road towards the richest and thus conclusive, that is, absolute knowledge. All that might come after Hegel are then varieties of what has been, not unlike Grohmann's position.

This anticipation of the future as the constant repetition of the past—standing still is not a Hegelian option—is however in contrast to the otherwise strictly retrospective orientation of Hegel's philosophy. Hegel never goes beyond his own standpoint towards the future. "It is just as foolish to imagine that any philosophy does beyond its current world as to imagine an individual leaps out of his time [...]."[30]

To the view that is rigorously directed to the past, one's own position is always the last in history. And a philosophy that thinks that it has taken up every past philosophy in its principle must understand itself as the absolute, but only "for now". In a trivial sense, every history of philosophy has an end in the present at the latest, but it does not follow from this that the future will not bring any new philosophies.

In fact new philosophies do not just narrate once again the histories of older philosophies. They do not just add another chapter to the end. New philosophies narrate their own history on the basis of new principles. The anticipation of new philosophies with new principles and new history is however, for Hegel, not knowledge but at best opinion that has no place in science and about which one should, therefore, not speak.

Hegel's position, which insists strictly on the historicity of the validity and genesis of philosophy, may also be interpreted in such a way that every present can be understood as the completion of its past, but that every completion of history ends, as soon as its present becomes past again.

---

[28] Hegel (1971), 461.
[29] This is also the view of Baumgartner (1995), 50.
[30] Hegel (2009), 15.

IV Friedrich Engels

Friedrich Engels was not only of the view that Hegel was himself convinced of having concluded the history of philosophy, but Engels was further convinced that this was in fact the case:

> With Hegel philosophy as such is finished; on the one hand because he comprehends its whole development in his system in the grandest manner, on the other because he, even if unconsciously, shows us the way out of this labyrinth of systems to real, positive knowledge of the world.[31]

As is clear from this citation, the end of philosophy and with this also the end of the history of philosophy is not, for Engels, an occasion for mourning. The end is rather a milestone on the way to real knowledge.

First of all let us look at Engel's conception of Hegel's philosophy as he presents it in *Ludwig Feuerbach und der Ausgang der klassischen deutschen Philosophie* [*Ludwig Feuerbach and the End of Classical German Philosophy*]. Engels too refers to two seemingly antagonistic aspects of Hegelian philosophy: on the one hand the supposedly final determination of philosophy in a closed system and on the other its emphasis on qualitative, revolutionary development in thinking as in reality. Instead of attempting to mediate these two aspects Engels leaves them in opposition and declares the developmental character together with Hegel's dialectical method to be progressive and contrastingly the closed system to be reactionary.

This alone would be no reason to mention Engels together with the end of the history of philosophy in the 19th century. It is thinkable that Engels pleads simply for a continuance of philosophizing by Hegelian means after Hegel without having an end in view, knowing that there are no eternal truths and much less closed systems, but that it is always necessary to comprehend one's times ever more appropriately and ever anew.

In fact, the (according to Engels) progressive aspect of Hegel's philosophy does not find its expression in an improved philosophy. The thought of dialectical development becomes rather a form of science that itself should no longer be philosophy.

The desire to transform philosophy into science pervades, of course, at the very least the entirety of modern philosophical history right up to the present. For Fries and Grohmann this becoming scientific is completed by Kant. Hegel

---

31 Engels (1973), 270.

too characterizes his philosophy as scientific. For Engels however—and here he clearly differs from Fries, Grohmann and Hegel—the conversion of philosophy into science does not mean the improvement of philosophy but instead its end as philosophy and, with this, the end of the history of philosophy. For Engels the slogan does not read "Philosophy as science" but "Science instead of philosophy".

If we follow the argument in *Feuerbach*, the need to clarify facts in a philosophical manner is expression of a defect: anytime knowledge about actual facts, that is, not least empirically experiential conditions, is lacking, philosophy is required. Philosophy closes the gap in knowledge in an idealistic manner with fanciful speculation. Philosophical explanations become obsolete over the course of historical development with the increasing knowledge of actual conditions. Connections that had to be developed speculatively in earlier times can now be developed on the basis of empirical research. Science thus replaces philosophy. For example, speculative natural philosophy becomes natural science.

The notion that empirical science would replace philosophy once and for all and thus bring about its end can be found—albeit with a different emphasis—in the "bourgeois" philosophy of the 19th century. Already Joseph Marie Degérando's history of philosophy, which appeared in a translation by Tennemann in 1806, thus ends, with reference to Francis Bacon, in a detailed and elaborate defence of experiential philosophy. This was a conclusion that inspired the translator Tennemann to write a long commentary in which he makes clear that this would be far too simple. Even though Degérando is quite conciliatory, indeed, and does not advocate pure empiricism and obviously does not speak of the end of philosophy through empiricism, either. Instead he advocates the union of empirical and rational methods.[32] Wilhelm Busse, for example, is less squeamish and, referring to Trendelenburg, as a matter of fact, writes in 1848: "We eliminate philosophy because historical empiricism has come to the stage of its development where it is capable of doing so. The fact that philosophy is being eliminated proves that the end of philosophy has arrived."[33] Carl Vogt speaks of the "blessed death of natural philosophy"[34] and in 1869 Ludwig Büchner writes: "If religion, if Christianity is out of date for us, so the same applies in no less degree to real or speculative philosophy which unfortunately for a long time, especially in Germany, has exercised an injurious and debilitating influence on the free and true spirit of research."[35]

---

32 See Gérando (1806), 507–530.
33 Busse (1848), 55.
34 Vogt (1861), 4.
35 Büchner (1869), 338 f.

Engels, of course, wants to distance himself from bourgeois natural science and in particular from bourgeois materialism. He considers not only that which is empirically measurable and quantifiable but also the relations of things as well as people in their respective historical praxis to be actual reality.[36] The progressive aspect of Hegelian philosophy should have found an entry into dialectical materialism at exactly this point. It is relevant indeed to the question concerning the end of the history of philosophy: Engels assumes that spirit's historical forms of manifestation—including philosophy—are not random or arbitrary. Mediated through many stages, they are the expression of respective concrete relations in which humans live. Thus a feudal form of society brings forth different philosophies than a capitalistic one. Philosophy can therefore not be considered in isolation from the social context in which it emerges. What is more, actual historical development does not pertain to philosophy but social relations, namely the productive forces. Philosophy may even be—at times perhaps not inessential[37]—element of this history. However considered on its own it has no history in the sense of a determinate development from out of itself.

> The cloudy formations in the brains of humans are necessary sublimations of their material, empirically established processes of life that are tied to material conditions. Morality, religion, metaphysics and other ideologies and their corresponding forms of consciousness thus no longer retain the semblance of independence. They have no history, they have no development, but the humans who develop their material production and their material commerce, in changing them, change their reality as well as their thinking and the products of their thinking. It is not that consciousness determines life, but life determines consciousness.[38]

The end of history is not proclaimed by Engels and Marx because of the perfection of a development internal to philosophy. The end of philosophy is not even due to its conversion into science. Philosophical historiography must on the contrary come to its end because it has no equivalent in reality, because there is no real history of philosophy.

V Wilhelm Dilthey

Reflections on the end of the history of philosophy in the 19th century come to some degree together in both positive and in negative respects in Wilhelm Dilth-

---

36 Compare the first of Marx's theses on Feuerbach (Marx (1969), 5).
37 Compare Marx (1976).
38 Marx a. Engels (1969), 26.

ey's philosophy. This might seem surprising as Dilthey cannot be accused of a lack of engagement with the history of philosophy, much less an underestimation of history in general. Dilthey makes unmistakably clear that "what man is, his history tells him."[39] But it would be hasty to conclude from this that humanity and in particular their philosophies are historical, therefore obey an immanent determination, that they are subject to a progressive development that brings forth qualitatively new results in time. Dilthey takes a clear distance from this idea. Instead of this he introduces a typology of philosophies: all philosophies from antiquity up to the present, in his view, can be divided into "Naturalism", "Idealism of Freedom" and "Objective Idealism".[40] This typology—and this is the heart of the matter—does not correspond to a chronological order. Hence we find Pythagoras together with Bruno and Hegel in the category of objective idealists.[41]

Dilthey had apparently found a meta-historical schema that comprehends all philosophies from all times. A history of philosophy is thus impossible. In this respect Dilthey comes quite close to Grohmann's concept, which was discussed earlier. With Grohmann too philosophy ends with the establishment of a comprehensive typology of all philosophies. In that Dilthey also assigns each philosophy of each epoch to one of the three types, he states that it is always and forever a matter of a mere variation of three themes in philosophy, without development and without history.[42]

However Dilthey also differs significantly from Grohmann. In Grohmann the inner coherence of all possible philosophies was made visible through Kant's philosophy. Philosophy could thus be presented, despite its diversity, as a unity. According to Dilthey (and much to his dismay) philosophy strives in vain towards unity. The three types of philosophy exist for him side by side, unmediated and unmediatable.

This lack of unity establishes another difference between Dilthey and Grohmann. With Kantian philosophy in the background, Grohmann declares his systematic to be completed. In contrast Dilthey must gather his typology quasi-empirically from the history of philosophy. "There is no other aid to such an arrangement than historical comparison."[43] Thus there is no basis for declaring this typology to be completed. In fact Dilthey in no way holds his typology of philosophy as carved in granite for all time. "Thus, that I present in the following

---

39 Dilthey (1960), 226.
40 Dilthey (1960), 100–118.
41 Dilthey (1960), 221–223.
42 Compare Geldsetzer (1968), 189.
43 Dilthey (1960), 99.

has a wholly provisional character."[44] The presented typology is therefore no dogma. It is open for further development. With this, Dilthey's conception of history remains in contrast to the thinkers of development, namely Fries, Hegel and Engels. However at the very least historiography is a part of the "philosophy of philosophy", that is, philosophy's reflection on its own activity, and can look back to a history, can develop further and thus has not come to an end.[45] The discussion about the end of the history of philosophy can, in regard to Dilthey's typology, thus be rejected because this typology is itself historical.

However Dilthey's history of philosophy is pressured from another angle. As already in Engels, in Dilthey too philosophies are referred back to an instance that is itself no longer philosophy. For Engels this instance was represented by societal conditions understood as shaped by the economy and of which philosophies are the expression. For Dilthey each philosophy is ultimately based on a determinate world-view [*Weltanschauung*] and that world-view is in turn based on the concrete way of life of individuals. "The ultimate root of world-view is life."[46]

This emergence of philosophy from life, mediated by a world-view, concerns not only the genesis of philosophy but also concerns its validity. For as the different world-views cannot be reconciled conceptually, neither are the three types of philosophy reconcilable. Thus one sees that the conflict between metaphysical systems is ultimately *grounded in life itself*, in life experience, in attitudes towards the problem of life.[47] For this reason, the eternal conflict between different philosophical systems ultimately does not have its basis in philosophy itself. That is why it cannot be resolved on the level of philosophy.

But Dilthey goes still further: the conflict also cannot be resolved on the level of world-view. With this restriction it would be conceivable that a world-view could gain predominance discursively. Hence, the type of philosophy corresponding to this world-view would thus assume universal validity.[48] Dilthey makes clear, on the contrary, that

---

[44] Dilthey (1960), 99.
[45] Dilthey provides here a kind of gradation of levels of reflection: "1. Dogmatic systems. 2. The elevation of human activity, in particular philosophical methods of consciousness in the Socratic school. 2. Increasing this consciousness to the transcendental method (variation: scepticism). 4. Rules, laws and forms of insight into life should be found through historical self-reflection. Phenomenology of philosophical systematics." (Dilthey (1960), 37. Compare also 38.)
[46] Dilthey (1960), 78, compare X.
[47] Dilthey (1960), 98.
[48] There is no one, true world-view, just as there is no one, true philosophy. Truth shows itself to a finite being only partially: "The pure light of truth is only glimpsed by us in different refracted rays." (Dilthey (1960), 224).

no world-view can be raised to a universally valid science through metaphysics. And just as little can they be destroyed through any kind of critique. They have their roots in a relation that is neither accessible to proof nor refutation, they are eternal, only metaphysics is transitory.[49]

If philosophy is only the abstract expression of a world-view and if world-views are immune to the means of philosophy, then a change in philosophy only takes place as expressions of the change of world-views, which in turn is based in the change of life. Philosophy can in no way retroactively participate in this process. It is just a decoration. In Dilthey too there is no genuine, independent history of philosophy that follows its own laws. Here too philosophy has no history.

In Dilthey we find aspects of Grohmann's thought in that there is a typology or systematic of philosophy. But with Dilthey this is neither meta-historical nor closed. If one is so inclined, aspects of Fries and Grohmann's veneration of Kant can be found here too. For, instead of engaging with the internal arguments of the individual types of philosophy, Dilthey asks after the conditions for the genesis and validity of philosophy and he finds this in the respective world-view or way of life. The resulting pull towards relativism, vehemently denied by Dilthey, is reminiscent of Hegel, when he links the validity of certain philosophies to their times, embedding it in a comprehensive teleology—which teleology is of course absent in Dilthey. The leading back of philosophy, including its development, to an instance that is not philosophically accessible and that shows itself as immune to philosophy is something that Dilthey shares with Friedrich Engels.

VI Gottlob Frege

After Dilthey, as it were took up philosophically, the considerations presented above, there remains only for us to refer to the history of philosophy in Frege, who is taken somewhat arbitrarily as an example at this point. Frege's remarks on the history of philosophy are noticeable by their absence. With this he makes a significant contribution to reflection on the end of the history of philosophy in the 19th century. A history does not end—perhaps does not end especially and primarily—when it is declared to be at an end. The history of philosophy can bear witness to this. A history actually ends when it disappears from consciousness, when it is no longer narrated. It ends or it begins anew.

---

49 Dilthey (1960), 218.

Bibliography

Ast (1829): Friedrich Ast, *Hauptmomente der Geschichte der Philosophie*, München: Weber.
Bauer (1863): Wilhelm Bauer, *Geschichte der Philosophie für gebildete Leser, zugleich als Einleitung in das Studium der Philosophie*, Halle: Schwetschke.
Baumgartner (1995): Hans Michael Baumgartner, "Anspruch und Einlösbarkeit. Geschichtstheoretische Bemerkungen zur Idee einer adäquaten Philosophiegeschichte", in: Rolf W. Puster (Ed.), *Veritas filia temporis? Philosophiehistorie zwischen Wahrheit und Geschichte*, Berlin / New York: De Gruyter, 44–61.
Büchner (1869): Ludwig Büchner, *Die Stellung des Menschen in der Natur in Vergangenheit, Gegenwart und Zukunft*, Leipzig: T. Thomas.
Busse (1848): Wilhelm Busse, *J. G. Fichte und seine Beziehung zur Gegenwart des deutschen Volkes*, Erster Theil, *Fichte der Philosoph*, Halle: Heynemann.
Carnier (1836): Karl Carnier, *Kurze Geschichte der Staats- und Rechtsphilosophie*, Aschaffenburg: J. Hembt.
Dilthey (1960): Wilhelm Dilthey, *Weltanschauungslehre*, in: Wilhelm Dilthey, *Gesammelte Schriften*, vol. 8, Stuttgart: Teubner Verlagsgesellschaft, Göttingen: Vandenhoeck und Ruprecht.
Engels (1973): Friedrich Engels, *Ludwig Feuerbach und der Ausgang der Klassischen Deutschen Philosophie* [1888], in: Karl Marx a. Friedrich Engels, *Werke*, vol. 21, Berlin: Diez, 259–307.
Erdmann (1866): Johann Eduard Erdmann, *Grundriss der Geschichte der Philosophie*, vol. 2, *Philosophie der Neuzeit*, Berlin: Hertz.
Frantz (1844): Constantin Frantz, *Speculative Studien*, Berlin: Hermes.
Fries (1837): Jakob Friedrich Fries, *Die Geschichte der Philosophie dargestellt nach den Fortschritten ihrer wissenschaftlichen Entwicklung*, vol. 1, Halle: Verlag der Buchhandlung des Waisenhauses.
Fries (1840): Jakob Friedrich Fries, *Die Geschichte der Philosophie dargestellt nach den Fortschritten ihrer wissenschaftlichen Entwicklung*, vol. 2, Halle: Verlag der Buchhandlung des Waisenhauses.
Geldsetzer (1968): Lutz Geldsetzer, *Die Philosophie der Philosophiegeschichte im 19. Jahrhundert. Zur Wissenschaftstheorie der Philosophiegeschichtsschreibung und -betrachtung*, Meisenheim am Glahn: Verlag Anton Hein.
Gérando (1806): Joseph-Marie de Gérando, *Vergleichende Geschichte der Systeme der Philosophie mit Rücksicht auf die Grundsätze der menschlichen Erkenntnisse* (aus dem Französischen übersetzt mit Anmerkungen von Wilhelm Gottlieb Tennemann), vol. 2, Marburg: Neue academische Buchhandlung.
Grohmann (1797): Johann Christian August Grohmann, *Über den Begriff der Geschichte der Philosophie*, Wittenberg: Kühne.
Grohmann (1798): Johann Christian August Grohmann, "Was heißt: Geschichte der Philosophie", in: Johann Christian August Grohmann a. Karl Heinrich Ludwig Pölitz, *Neue Beyträge zur kritischen Philosophie und insbesondere zur Geschichte der Philosophie*, vol. 1, Berlin: Verlag der Königlich Preußischen Akademischen Kunst- und Buchhandlung, 1–78.

Hegel (1971): Georg Wilhelm Friedrich Hegel, *Vorlesungen über die Geschichte der Philosophie, Teil III*, in: Georg Wilhelm Friedrich Hegel, *Werke in zwanzig Bänden*, vol. 20, Frankfurt a. M.: Suhrkamp.

Hegel (1994): Georg Wilhelm Friedrich Hegel, *Vorlesungen über die Geschichte der Philosophie, Teil 1*, in: Georg Wilhelm Friedrich Hegel, *Vorlesungen*, vol. 6, ed. by Pierre Garniron a. Walter Jaeschke, Hamburg: Meiner.

Hegel (2009): Georg Wilhelm Friedrich Hegel, *Grundlinien der Philosophie des Rechts* (1821), in: Georg Wilhelm Friedrich Hegel, *Gesammelte Werke*, vol. 14,1, ed. by Klaus Grotzsch a. Elisabeth Weisser-Lohmann, Hamburg: Meiner.

Hermann (1861): Konrad Hermann, *Das Verhältniß der Philosophie zur Geschichte der Philosophie*, Leipzig: Breitkopf und Härtel.

Lichtenfels (1836): Johann Ritter von Lichtenfels, *Auszug des Wissenswürdigsten aus der Geschichte der Philosophie*, Wien: J.G. Heubner.

Marx (1969): Karl Marx, "Thesen über Feuerbach" (written 1845), in: Karl Marx a. Friedrich Engels, *Werke*, vol. 3, Berlin: Diez, 5–7.

Marx (1976): Karl Marx, "Zur Kritik der Hegelschen Rechtsphilosophie. Einleitung" (written 1843f.), in: Karl Marx a. Friedrich Engels, *Werke*, vol. 1, Berlin: Diez, 378–391.

Marx a. Engels (1969): Karl Marx a. Friedrich Engels, *Die deutsche Ideologie* (written 1845f.), in: Karl Marx a. Friedrich Engels, *Werke*, vol. 3, Berlin: Diez, 9–530.

Müglich (1849): Johann Karl Müglich, *Die Hegel-Weisheit und ihre Früchte. Oder: Arnold Ruge mit seinen Genossen in den hallischen Jahrbüchern und in der Paulskirche zu Frankfurt und anderswo: Briefe an den Pastor Fix*, Regensburg: Manz.

Reiff (1840): Jacob Friederich Reiff, *Der Anfang der Philosophie. Mit einer Grundlegung der Encyclopädie der philosophischen Wissenschaften*, Stuttgart: A. Liesching & Company.

Schneidawind (1825): Franz Josef Adolf Schneidawind, *Die Hauptmomente der Geschichte der Philosophie*, Bamberg: Schmidt.

Schubarth a. Carganico (1829): Karl Ernst Schubarth a. Karl Anton Carganico, *Ueber Philosophie überhaupt und Hegel's Encyclopädie der philosophischen Wissenschaften insbesondere. Ein Beitrag zur Beurtheilung der letztern*, Berlin: Enslin'sche Buchhandlung.

Vogt (1861): Carl Vogt, *Untersuchungen über die Absonderung des Harnstoffs und deren Verhältniss zum Stoffwechsel*, Giessen: Ferber.

Weiller (1813): Kajetan von Weiller, *Grundriß der Geschichte der Philosophie. Zunächst für seine Zuhörer*, München: Giel.

Helmut Heit
Hegel, Zeller and Nietzsche: Alternative Approaches to Philosophical Historiography

> ... the outcome of which may well be an artistically true and not a historically true painting. To think of history objectively in this fashion is the silent work of the dramatist; that is to say, to think of all things in relation to all others and to weave the isolated event into the whole: always with the presupposition that if a unity of plan does not already reside in things it must be implanted into them.[1]

When evaluating the historiography of philosophy in 19th century German thought, it might be useful to compare some different approaches to this issue. Georg Wilhelm Friedrich Hegel, Eduard Zeller and Friedrich Nietzsche mark the beginning, middle and end of philosophy-historical reflections during this century and they all devote significant parts of their work to methodological contemplations. Moreover, their views are not only connected to a broader intellectual framework, but the latter two also reflect on their relationship to Hegel and mutually acknowledge each other's work. However, the perspectives of each of these thinkers on *historiographical* methodologies differ significantly. While Hegel is generally seen as the last representative of metaphysical, philosophically oriented historical constructions, Nietzsche serves as turning point to the ultimate collapse of any such philosophical ambition to provide grand narratives. Both seem to pursue contradictory but essentially philosophical views on history, thus explaining Karl Löwith's metaphor of a bridge spanning between Hegel's speculative philosophical theology and Nietzsche's destructive anti-Christian philosophy.[2] Zeller, on the other hand, is typically regarded as one of the first proper historians, who wrote his history of Greek philosophy in a scientific spirit and whose historiographical work is still widely accepted. One might be inclined to take the speculative systematic, the sober historian, and

---
1 Nietzsche (1997), 91.
2 Löwith (1941), 193.

the philosophizing artist as paradigmatic incarnations of three different expressions of 19th century philosophy.

In the light of these different labels, their philosophy-historical works should display essential differences, which indeed they do. However, if we do not trust the methodological and philosophical expositions and self-expressions alone but analyze how they actually wrote the history of a certain period of Western philosophy, our image becomes more focused. A closer look at a case study will also reveal substantial overlap and agreement. Despite their very different perspectives and narratives, none of them escapes the necessity of philosophical preconceptions and all try to do justice to the source. I take as my case study early Greek philosophy because all three authors put special emphasis on the "first philosophers" and devote extensive work to them and because they all worked with more or less the same comparatively small corpus of ancient sources. For pragmatic reasons I will limit myself mainly to a single, though complex problem: how can we account for the beginning of philosophy in the 6th century BC?[3] This paper will particularly emphasize Nietzsche since his historiographic work on early Greek philosophers seems to be the least well known. Moreover, Nietzsche provides a different perspective and one which might prove relevant today. Before I turn to Hegel (section 1), Zeller (section 2), Nietzsche (section 3) and my conclusions (section 4), let me briefly introduce the topic of the Greek beginnings of philosophy and the main sources of this.

The earliest account of the historical and systematic beginnings of philosophy is found in Aristotle's *Metaphysics*. The widely accepted view that Thales of Miletus is the first philosopher derives from this source. For Aristotle Thales is the first philosopher because he supposedly introduced the idea of *archē:*

> That of which all things consist, from which they first come and into which on their destruction they are ultimately resolved, of which the essence persists although modified by its affections—this, they say, is an element and principle of existing things. [...] Thales, the founder of this school of philosophy, says the permanent entity is water.[4]

According to Aristotle, Thales initiated Greek philosophy because he allegedly recognized one of the four prime causes, which Aristotle distinguishes in his work. The historical reliability of Aristotle is questionable, his terminology is most surely anachronistic and his cautious phrasing indicates he had no direct

---

[3] I provide a more detailed analysis of this question, its implications and possible solutions in Heit (2007).
[4] Aristotle (*Met.*), 983b.

access to Thales teachings.⁵ Thales (or his Ionian compatriot Anaximander) is seen as the originator of philosophy because he implied a difference between essence and appearance, because he made a universal but non-religious statement about the nature of everything and because he founded a tradition of philosophical criticism. Aristotle also provided the standard genealogical explanation for the emergence of this new mode of thought. His *Metaphysics* opens with an anthropological assumption ("All men naturally desire knowledge"⁶) and continues with an argument that the most privileged and most desired form of wisdom consists in universal knowledge for its own sake. The driving force behind the origin of philosophy therefore is the human condition, which strives to fulfill itself by means of a certain kind of knowledge. The natural desire is particularly triggered by certain puzzles, problems and causes of concern. "It is through wonder that men now begin and originally began to philosophize" and "speculation of this kind began with a view to recreation and pastime, at a time when practically all the necessities of life were already supplied".⁷ The origin of philosophy therefore results from three elements: natural desire or striving, wonder or puzzlement, and a state of good conditions or leisure-time. It is explained in an almost deductive-nomological manner by a combination of a law-like natural drive for knowledge and applicable conditions (puzzles and leisure) which allow the human potentialities to become actualities. Within such a framework philosophy naturally emerges as soon as conditions apply.

However, in contrast to this founding of philosophy in human nature, Aristotle and most of his followers insist on philosophy's being an exclusively Greek achievement. Diogenes Laërtius, for example, dedicates the first passages of his collection of anecdotes and philosophical positions to defend its decisively Greek origins while refusing claims to philosophical or philosophy-like modes of thought in other, "barbaric" cultures. He takes it to be misleading to talk about Persian, Babylonian, Assyrian, Indian or Celtic philosophers. "These authors forget that the achievements which they attribute to the barbarians belong to the Greeks, with whom not merely philosophy but the human race itself began."⁸ Such strict demarcations between Greek and non-Greek cultures became prevalent among 19th century historians

---

5 It is most probable that Thales left no written texts, if he ever wrote any. On the reliability of Aristotle's account see Frede (2008).
6 Aristotle (*Met.*), 980a.
7 Aristotle (*Met.*), 982b.
8 Laërtius (*Bion*), I, 2.

from Hegel onwards and served—regardless of their validity—in the contexts of philo-Hellenistic identity-politics.[9]

I Georg Wilhelm Friedrich Hegel— the Speculative Historian?

Hegel's lectures were arguably the most influential history of philosophy in 19th century, held nine times between 1805/06 in Jena and his death 1831 in Berlin. Transcripts of these lectures were published in 1833–36 by Karl Ludwig Michelet and shortly thereafter became very influential.[10] Although it soon became habitual to reject Hegel's specific *logificatio post festum*, it is hardly an overstatement to claim these lectures were foundational for systematic historiography of philosophy.[11] Hegel was the first philosopher who provided a detailed theory of philosophical historiography and its necessary preconditions, and he tried to apply these standards in detail to the historical materials. He aspired to a scientific historiography, which would combine the Kantian analysis of Newtonian science with historicism. Hegel hoped to "reveal the laws governing the historical world just as Newton's physics had once discovered the laws of the natural world".[12] While the existence of historical laws is not formally disproven, confidence in deciphering them decreased significantly in the meantime. As Frederic Beiser rightly observed: "Hegel's history of philosophy breathes an optimism—a confidence in reason and progress—that is out of touch with our age."[13] However, few scholars are prepared to conclude that reconstructions of changes and developments in the history of philosophy are nothing but "nicely invented narratives" and that the supposed "unity of the history of philosophy is merely an

---

9 Ulrich Johannes Schneider (1990) showed in his archaeology of historiography of philosophy that 18th century treatises often began with non-Greek traditions while the process of the institutionalization and canonization of philosophy and history of philosophy through and after Hegel led to a generally accepted focus on solely Greek beginnings. On the development of the demarcation between Greeks and Barbarians from Laërtius, his predecessors and in later authors, see Heit (2005).
10 As regards Hegel's lectures (which are strictly speaking only a secondary source) I relied on the most recent critical edition by Garniron and Jaeschke. Translations are my own.
11 On the originality, reception and impact of Hegel's lectures cf. Düsing (1983), 7–16; or Lutz Geldsetzer, who reconstructs how Hegel's views became dominant despite widespread reservations regarding his general approach Geldsetzer (1968), 84.
12 Beiser (1995), XI.
13 Beiser (1995), XXIX.

'idea'."[14] We may have lost Hegel's speculative optimism for good reasons, but the commitment perceiving the history of philosophy as a coherent and somewhat rationally developing argumentative enterprise remains strong on a pragmatic level among many historians. Such a perspective relies on several assumptions. Without preconceptions about your topic, you cannot discriminate it and follow its course through history. Without judgments about the significance and relevance of sources, about their connection to others and about the validity and proper understanding of their content, historiography is impossible. In that regard Lutz Geldsetzer was justified in remarking that "it had already been known since Hegel at the latest that the true freedom of presuppositions consists in having the right presuppositions and therefore having presuppositions in any case."[15] If one denies the possibility of having the *right* presuppositions one may at least ask to be self-conscious and explicit about guiding principles and methodological paradigms as opposed to a pretention to objectivity. And Hegel is very explicit about his presuppositions.

Hegel emphasizes the plausible conviction that the first and basic requirement of any history of philosophy is a proper understanding of its topic, i.e. of philosophy. He therefore denies the possibility of a completely impartial and unprejudiced historiography. "Only an understanding of philosophy provides us with a point of departure of its history."[16] According to Hegel philosophy properly understood is the systematic development of our consciousness of freedom. In addition to the necessity of a preliminary understanding of philosophy as distinct from other human activities or forms of thought like religion or art, Hegel also assumes that philosophy, by virtue of being rational and argumentative, must historically develop in a rational way. "The whole must be perceived as a rational progress, as an organic proceeding. No coincidence. The history of philosophy must itself be something philosophical."[17] This perspective on the history of philosophy implies a distinction between its empirical appearance as a course of human weaknesses and opinions and its underlying rational essence. In consequence, Hegel denies the relevance of anecdotes, personalities and personal opinions because of their accidental status.[18] The rational essence, he also assumes, only becomes visible at a certain stage of development: the be-

---

14 Kolmer (1998), 51; 408.
15 Geldsetzer (1968), 122.
16 Hegel (1994a), 14.
17 Hegel (1994a), 14.
18 "There are no philosophical opinions; if and inasmuch they are opinions, they are nothing philosophical. It therefore indicates a lack of philosophical education to speak of philosophical opinions" Hegel (1994a), 18.

ginning and historical development of philosophy can only be recognized from its *result*. A historian therefore must conceive of his current point of view as a necessary result of a preceding development.[19] A further assumption is that the historical development coincides with the logical development and "that the succession of systems of philosophy in history is the same as the succession in the logical deduction of the definitions of the idea."[20]

After an extended argument to this effect Hegel demarcates early Greek philosophy from contemporary and earlier modes of thought in three respects. Philosophy proper is distinct from traditional Homeric myth and religion, from practical knowledge as present in the sayings of the seven sages, and from the cultural and cognitive achievements of the neighbouring civilisations. "The foregoing was only something preliminary. We restrain from talking about Mongolian, Persian, Syrian philosophy; it is merely erudition to speak about it"[21] Hegel did, however, entertain his students with extensive erudition about Oriental thought, but only to show its religious essence and to explain its inferior "relation to thought and to true philosophy."[22] Hegel, as much as the tradition introduced by Aristotle and Theophrastus, ascribes the honorific title of "first philosopher" to Thales of Miletus because of his claim that the *arche* is water, though for reasons different to this tradition. According to Hegel, Thales marks "the beginning of the completely abstract, unspecified general thought."[23] The source of Thales' assumption is neither perception nor tradition, its results are counter-intuitive and counter-empirical. According to Hegel, however, it captures the true essence of nature nonetheless and it displays the correct use of reason, according to his time. And since reason is the prime feature of human beings as distinguished from other animals, the rise of philosophy in ancient Greece is an essential step in the historical rise of mankind to its full capacities. Hegel sees a continuous development of philosophical principles following his concept of dialectical logic from Thales onwards.

In order to explain this extraordinary emergence, Hegel refers to certain historical features like trade, political and religious freedom, sufficient leisure and a crisis that encouraged philosophical reflection. Far from being merely speculative Hegel tries to flesh out his concept of "*Volksgeist.*" The rise of the Greek nation

---

19 A philosophical defence of this idea is laid out in Hegel's *Wissenschaft der Logik*; cf. Hegel (1999), 53–65.
20 Hegel (1994a), 27. On another occasion in the lectures he adds that there might be steps in history, which may "cease in development in history" Hegel (1989), 88.
21 Hegel (1989), 1.
22 Hegel (1994b), 365.
23 Hegel (1994a), 103f.

depended on conditions like economic leisure, freedom from religious indoctrination by a caste of priests, cultural contacts and other social features. But its underlying dynamic is more than the sum of these arbitrary conditions. It is the natural development of reason. Like Aristotle or Diogenes, Hegel sees the origin of philosophy not only as "a kind of luxury"[24] but also as the realization of the highest capacities of mankind and therefore as the proper beginning of humanity itself. And Hegel also reserves this achievement for the Greek and occidental tradition alone. The Greek thinkers did not invent philosophy out of the blue but transformed and improved everything they adopted from preceding and neighbouring cultures by means of an *interpretatio graeca*. Thales might have used Babylonian observational data to foretell a solar eclipse and Egyptian wisdom to calculate the heights of the pyramids but it remains his sole and unprecedented achievement to transform these isolated pieces of knowledge into philosophy. "The external was only material and impulse to them, they transformed and reshaped it; the spiritual breath is peculiar to them, the form of art and science, which is the pure form of thought."[25] Several scholars therefore diagnosed a certain Euro-centrism immanent to Hegel's perspective on history, in that he "lapsed into the very fallacy that historicism intended to expose: ethnocentrism, the belief that one's own age is the apotheosis of world history."[26] Nietzsche in particular opposed such apotheosis of the present and mocked Hegel in his polemic on the advantages and disadvantages of history.[27] However, the very claim as to the early Greek beginnings of Western philosophy relies on significant differences between this tradition and the alternatives. Some Euro-centrism therefore seems inevitable unless the idea of specifiable historical beginnings of some universally valid mode of thought is abandoned. We

---

24 Hegel (1994a), 59.
25 Hegel (1989), 2.
26 Beiser (1995), xxix. William Walsh has observed that Hegel's conception of world-history is "the success story of modern European man" Walsh (1971), 183; a story which is "distinctively, indeed aggressively, European, and appeals to European standards and ideals in judging the significance of historical conditions and happenings" Walsh (1971), 188f. However, Walsh also points out that Hegel's Euro-centrism is the immediate result of his ambition to reconcile reason and history: "It was not *simple* prejudice, as it may have been on the part of some of the travellers he quotes, since he does more than simply *appeal to* the European ideal in its Protestant form; he tries to justify it as *rational*" Walsh (1971), 193.
27 Nietzsche ridicules the idea that the godly world-spirit "became transparent and comprehensible to himself within the Hegelian craniums [...] so that for Hegel the climax and terminus of the world-process coincided with his own existence in Berlin" Nietzsche (1997), 104. A perspective which resulted in an "idolatry of the factual: [...] If every success is a rational necessity, if every event is a victory of the logical or the idea—then down on your knees quickly and do reverence to the whole stepladder of 'success'!" Nietzsche (1997), 105.

shall see that Zeller is not prepared to do so while Nietzsche makes some steps in that direction.

II Eduard Zeller—the Scientific Historian?

Soon after Hegel's death it became popular to reject his apotheosis of reason in history as an unconvincing deification of concepts which, indeed, it was. However, it is worth noting that Hegel's basic assumption of an autochthonous, continuous and progressive development of philosophy from its Ionian beginnings reappears in almost all alternative accounts nonetheless. Historians kept reconstructing early Greek philosophy as a process from earlier mythology via humble Ionian beginnings through the contrast between Heraclitean and Parmenidean doctrines, the refinements in Anaxagoras and the atomists up until its culmination in the classic works of Plato and Aristotle. Friedrich Ueberweg explicitly states that Hegel (only) "hyperbolized in an unacceptable manner the otherwise justified basic concept of a step-by-step development, which can be found in the course of events in general and particularly in the succession of philosophical systems."[28] His objection does not question the idea of retrospective and developmental reconstructions but rather Hegel's supposedly too hyperbolic version. A very similar attitude can be found in the works of Eduard Zeller, who is praised as the first systematic modern historian of Greek philosophy and as the "unavoidable starting point for any analysis or for any synthesis regarding ancient thought."[29] Zeller denies that there is a unity between Hegelian logic and history because historical appearance is more or less contingent and because philosophy does not coincide with logic and ontology.[30] Hegel's "project therefore is misled principally as well as practically", but he continues by saying that "the only thing justified about it is the general conviction regarding the inner lawfulness of historical evolution".[31] Scholars like Ueberweg or Zeller reject certain details as well as the broader philosophical background of Hegel's account and try to replace it with something supposedly more scientific and empirically minded, but they neither deny the inner lawfulness of historical evolution nor the idea that the first Greek philosophers made decisive progress in the history of human reason.

---

28 Ueberweg (1865), 10.
29 Reale (1987), 329. Zellers work, though obviously dated, still remains standard; cf. Long (1999), 366.
30 Zeller (1876), 10–13.
31 Zeller (1876), 11 f.

Only the Greeks achieved such freedom of thought, not to turn to religious tradition but to the things themselves to uncover the truth about the nature of things; only with them did strict scientific procedure and reasoning solely according to its own rules became possible. This formal character alone separates Greek philosophy completely from the systems and attempts of the Oriental [...] who stands un-free in nature and can therefore neither reach valid explanations of phenomena out of their natural causes nor the freedom of a civil society or a pure human education [*Bildung*], whereas the Greek is able to see a lawful order in nature and to aspire to a free and beautiful morality in human life.[32]

These lines repeat essential features of the Aristotelian-Hegelian model of continuous and general progress in early Greek thought. Considering our limited positive information about early Greek thought they are also highly speculative, to say the least. Its basic characteristics are not only naturalistic metaphysics and scientific explanations but the aspiration to a free and morally valid rational worldview. Greek philosophy appears as the historical origin of human reason proper, in strict distinction from *the* Oriental, who is, like *the* Greek, denoted by the German collective singular, pretty much in the spirit of Hegel's *Volksgeist*. And—like Hegel—Zeller also puts forward extensive introductory considerations wherein the originality and autonomy of Greek philosophy is defended. It is claimed that it neither emerged out of ancient near Eastern cultures nor was it continuous with archaic myth and religion or with empirical competence and practical wisdom. The character of Greek thought and Greek people separates their philosophy from preceding and neighbouring modes of thought; it solely "developed as an indigenous product out of Greek people's mind and educational conditions."[33] Concerning the roots of these specifically favourable Greek conditions, Zeller, much like many contemporary and later scholars, takes refuge to an idea dating back to Aristotle. Friedrich Ueberweg, for example, states in his *Grundriss der Geschichte der Philosophie*:

> The philosophy of the West, with which this compendium has to do primarily, could not emerge as a science among the Nordic peoples, which are distinguished by physical strength and courage though more or less uncultured, but only among the *Hellenes*, who harmoniously unite spiritual strength and susceptibility.[34]

---

32 Zeller (1876), 109
33 Zeller (1876), 21.
34 Ueberweg (1865), 8. Aristotle assumed that the Greeks unified the advantages of Northern and Oriental people and were particularly gifted to establish an ideal society in *Politics* 1327b19–38.

Since then, the idea of the Greeks as the "most talented of all nations" survived up until recent publications.[35] Such an idea is not only based on a post-metaphysically deflated conception of Hegel's spirit of the people (*Volksgeist*) and on some outdated 19th century philo-Hellenism. According to Jaap Mansfeld, "the contribution of genius is still an inescapable assumption" as long as one wants to defend the idea that a *miracle grec* occurred and that philosophy and scientific thought have a distinguished historical origin among ancient Greeks.[36] Zeller's reconstruction explicitly states these assumptions and therefore operates with a developmental perspective almost inevitably built into his reconstruction of Greek thought. His focus on significant contributions to the overall development of philosophy also explains why he shares Hegel's relative lack of interest in anecdotes about the lives and arbitrary opinions of his respective philosophers.

> The merely individual in a man is therefore also the ephemeral. The individual has a permanent and possibly large and continuous effect only if he puts himself with his personality into the service of the general and performs his special activity as part of the common work.[37]

Zeller belongs to the majority of European historians of philosophy who ascribe the world-historically original *Discovery of Reason* to early Greek philosophers.[38] This origin is explained by a combination of anthropology with a certain concept of rationality and certain favourable external conditions, especially the Greek genius. In consequence and despite several differences in detail, e. g. regarding the classification of chronological periods, *Die Philosophie der Griechen in ihrer geschichtlichen Entwicklung* can be "still and rightly regarded as a document of Hegelian historiography of philosophy."[39] His historiography is ultimately less impartial and objective than it pretends to be. Given the philosophical obstacles emphasized by Hegel this is hardly surprising. But if pure objectivity is unachiev-

---

35 Windelband (1892), 21. For further reference to 'the Greek genius' see Heit (2007), 50–54; 129–139.
36 Mansfeld (1990), 58.
37 Zeller (1876), 14.
38 Cf. Snell (1948).
39 Geldsetzer (1968), 95. Gadamer relates Hegel's eminent significance as a point of reference for 19th century historiography of philosophy to the impact of Zeller's "moderate Hegelianism" and goes on to suggest that the "interpretation of the philosophical tradition by the Hegelian scheme became a constant of our way of thinking, even if you cannot apply without restriction any perfect parallelism between the logical development of ideas and their progress in the history of philosophy" Gadamer (1996), 26.

able the question remains: what constraints and standards would distinguish philosophical historiography from merely subjective narratives?

III Friedrich Nietzsche—the Artistic Historian?

Nietzsche's engagement with early Greek philosophy is instructive not only to those with a genuine interest in Nietzsche but also because he approaches these so-called "first philosophers" somewhat differently to his predecessors. He mainly dealt with the early Greek philosophers during his active years as Professor for Classical Philology in Basel, where he composed his university-lectures on the "Pre-Platonic Philosophers" (PPP) between 1869 and 1876, and in an unfinished and unpublished essay written in 1873 on "Philosophy in the Tragic Age of Greece" (PTG). A third source from which Nietzsche's views on early Greek thought can be reconstructed is the treatise "Διαδοχαί of the Pre-Platonic Philosophers" from 1874, which is mainly a contribution to doxographic studies.[40] While his private notes for PPP, most probably written in 1872, cover detailed criticisms of the sources and scholarly debates, the essay PTG is written in a freer style and was meant for publication. The lecture-notes are the richest and most detailed source for Nietzsche's views and they are the closest to standard accounts of this period. To present-day readers the title of these lectures seems especially significant, but one should not overestimate its philosophical weight for Nietzsche. To speak of pre-Platonic instead of pre-Socratic philosophy is relevant in terms of historical classifications, but neither Nietzsche nor his contemporaries are consistent in that regard. The terminology was more flexible before Diels and Kranz published their seminal collection *Die Fragmente der Vorsokratiker* in 1903. Hegel has no general label for these thinkers, Zeller speaks of "pre-Socratic" philosophy, Ueberweg dubs them "pre-Sophist" (and in later editions "pre-Attic"). Other scholars wish to avoid the "not yet" implication of "pre-" and prefer the less charged notion of "early Greek philosophy". Nietzsche did not restrict himself to the usage of pre-Platonic and simultaneously used phrases

---

[40] It is important to keep in mind that we are dealing with the early Nietzsche, who had not yet fully developed his own philosophy. With the prominent exceptions of Empedocles and Heraclitus Nietzsche only seldom refers to pre-Platonic philosophers in later publications. It is also worth noting that his famous distinction between antiquarian, monumental and critical history in his second *Untimely Meditation* on the advantages and disadvantages of history for life (1874) did—as far as I can tell—not influence his own philosophical-historical studies. The only connections I see are his severe criticism of Hegel and the reservations against the ideal of historiography as an objective science.

like "tragic", "earlier, "archaic", or even "pre-Socratic".[41] In his first announcement of the lectures in autumn 1869 Nietzsche advertised a course on the "History of the older Greek philosophy".[42]

Nietzsche commanded profound knowledge of early Greek philosophy which he reconstructed from a multitude of sources. The lack of a standard edition such as that of Diels and Kranz was only partly ameliorated by earlier collections of fragments. A valuable source was Diogenes Laërtius, whom Nietzsche had studied repeatedly and in detail.[43] These studies were particularly decisive for his understanding of Greek philosophy from a doxo-biographic perspective.[44] In addition to Zeller, Ueberweg and—particularly with regard to Democritus—Friedrich Albert Lange's *Geschichte des Materialismus*, Nietzsche read other histories of philosophy such as Christoph Meiners' *Geschichte des Ursprungs, Fortgangs und Verfalls der Wissenschaften in Griechenland und Rom* (Lemgo 1781), Karl Prantl's *Übersicht der griechisch-römischen Philosophie* (Stuttgart 1854), and Jacob Bernays' studies on Heraclitus (Berlin 1869). But his main focus was on ancient sources. In an introductory course on classical philology he advises his students:

> The fragments must be studied in original: in Mullach fragm. philos. (poor esp. Democritus), the personal-notes in Laert. Diogenes. Numerous historical writings are lost. Valuable compendium with excerpts of sources Ritter a. Preller. Comprehensive account from Zeller, now 3 ed.[45]

Despite this philological focus *ad fontes*, Nietzsche is well aware of the limits of our sources. What we have and what we do not have results in almost every case from earlier prejudices and value-judgments of generations of scholars and scribes. Our sources illuminate and simultaneously obscure our view; the lack of reliable information about the early Greek philosophers is particularly unfortunate and misleading. "It is a true misfortune that we have so little left from

---

[41] Nietzsche (1962), 69.
[42] Nietzsche (1993a), 209. The majority of Nietzsche's *Nachlass* and lecture notes have not yet been translated. I refer to the standard German editions and provide my own translations.
[43] Actually about half of Nietzsche's published philologica deal with Diogenes Laertius; cf. Barnes (2014).
[44] Müller (2005), 103–117.
[45] Nietzsche (1993b), 407 – my translation. The two collections of fragments and testimonies he suggests are: Friedrich Wilhelm August Mullach (1860): *Fragmenta philosophorum graecorum. Collegit, recensuit, vertit annotationibus et prolegomenis illustravit indicibus* Paris (Didot); and: Heinrich Ritter and Ludwig Preller (1869): *Historia philosophiae graecae et romanae ex fontium locis contexta. Locos collegerunt, disposuerunt, notis auxerunt H. Ritter et L. Preller. Editio quarta.* Gotha (Perthes).

these original philosophers, and we involuntarily measure them too modestly, whereas from Plato onward voluminous literary legacies lie before us."[46] Nietzsche therefore argues that our image of Greek philosophy is involuntarily but severely determined by this long-lasting and value-laden process of tradition and neglect. The dominant and "classic" role of Plato and Aristotle derives to a significant degree from "the sheer accident that they never lacked connoisseurs and copyists,"[47] while the works of Heraclitus, Protagoras, Empedocles or Democritus are almost completely lost. If one keeps the poor taste and the mean and petty character of most people in mind, copyists included, it seems "very likely the most impressive part of Greek thought and its verbal expression is lost to us, a fate not to be wondered at."[48] But since every historian has to weave his tapestry with the available twines, Nietzsche too has to rely on the selected group of given sources.

It is therefore hardly surprising that his engagement with early Greek philosophy has some common ground with the standard views of 19th century scholarship. The selection of relevant figures is more or less traditional. In PTG Nietzsche reconstructs Thales (§ 3), Anaximander (§ 4), Heraclitus (§§ 5–8), Parmenides (§§ 9–13), and Anaxagoras (§§ 14–19). The fact that he does not deliver the announced treatment from Thales till Socrates is due to the fragmentary status of the text. PPP covers a broader spectrum including pre-Ionian and post-Anaxagorean thinkers like Democritus and Socrates. In a letter to his friend and colleague Erwin Rohde (June 11, 1872) Nietzsche proudly announced his having developed a "beautiful table of categories, main figure [*Hauptkerl*], precursor and follower."[49] However, this self-assessment is only partly justified as other historians made similar distinctions between central and less central figures within philosophical schools. It is almost common sense to treat Anaximander as the "main figure" of Ionian philosophy, preceded by Thales and followed by Anaximenes. But Nietzsche rejects the idea, prevalent in Hegel, that early Greek philosophy was an enterprise organized in schools. This, he argues, is an anachronistic prejudice introduced by Alexandrian *diadochai:* "Philosophical schools did not exist at that time."[50] Nietzsche also uses the established tools to determine biographical dates and chronological order. In questionable cases he usually opposes the Hegelian side. While Hegel and Zeller for example take Heraclitus' philosophy of becoming as a response to the Eleatic school of being,

---

46 Nietzsche (2006), 5.
47 Nietzsche (1962), 36.
48 Nietzsche (1962), 36.
49 Nietzsche (1986), 10.
50 Nietzsche (2006), 32; cf. Nietzsche (1995), 613.

Nietzsche sides with Ueberweg and assumes (like a majority of scholars since) that Parmenides responds to Heraclitus. His decision, against Zeller, to place the Pythagorean philosophy and mathematics a century after Pythagoras in Plato's time appears to have been confirmed by most modern scholars.[51]

Nietzsche also shares the widely acknowledged view that the Greeks were original. With respect to the "strange question" of Thales' supposed Phoenician descent, the solution he suggests coincides with the majority of his contemporaries: "He is a Phoenician only in the sense that his family may be traced back to Cadmus."[52] Nietzsche perceives this issue as a consequence of a "oriental tendency of later scholars", namely the Alexandrians: "Greek philosophy is said to have not originated in Greece."[53] Very similarly to Hegel or Zeller he argues that intercultural exchange must have been natural to the Ionian tradesmen and colonialists. They were not isolated, but embedded in various cultural interactions. However philosophy is a completely original Greek achievement nonetheless.

> Nothing would be sillier than to claim an autochthonous development for the Greeks. On the contrary, they invariably absorbed other living cultures. The very reason they got so far is that they knew how to pick up the spear and throw it onward from the point where others had left it.[54]

Therefore Nietzsche contends in accordance with most scholars in his time that the general context of Greek culture provides no support for the unjustified conclusion "that philosophy was thus merely imported into Greece rather than having grown and developed there in a soil natural and native to it."[55] He occasionally ridicules the idea of a parallelism between five early Greek philosophers or schools and five main non-Greek cultures without ever mentioning the originator of this idea, August Gladisch.[56] For Nietzsche, philosophy is an unparalleled and particularly Greek development and it is constitutive for the course of Western culture. However, despite his insistence on their foundational role, Nietzsche's interest in the pre-Platonic philosophers does not derive from a self-affirming search for humble beginnings of a glorious, distinguished and continuous prog-

---

51 Nietzsche (2006), 131; cf. Nietzsche (1986), 10 and Heit (2011), 54f.
52 Nietzsche (2006), 23.
53 Nietzsche (2006), 25.
54 Nietzsche (1962), 30.
55 Nietzsche (1962), 29.
56 See Nietzsche (2006), 3; Nietzsche (1962), 29; cf. Skowron (2004). In his criticism of Gladisch's oriental tendencies Nietzsche sides with Zeller (1876), 27–31. On the dispute between Gladisch and Zeller see Michael Forster's contribution to this volume.

ress. His view of early Greek philosophy and of Western culture respectively differs in significant ways from many 19th (and 20th) century thinkers.

The most obvious feature of Nietzsche's original perspective is his focus on *early* Greek culture. He reverses the standard order between archaic and classic Greek philosophy. Most scholars agree with Aristotle's dictum that the earlier philosophers "are like untrained soldiers in a battle, who rush about and often strike good blows, but without science" and that "the earliest philosophy speaks falteringly, as it were, on all subjects; being new and in its infancy".[57] In consequence, most appreciate Plato's and Aristotle's philosophy as the highest and "classic" culmination of earlier approaches. Nietzsche, on the other hand, tends to think of them as late, actually too late expressions of decline. While the Greek "knew precisely how to begin at the proper time [...] as a pursuit springing from the ardent joyousness of courageous and victorious maturity", they did not know when to stop; and by "the fact that they were unable to stop in time, they considerably diminished their merit."[58] The later Greek philosophers were lacking the creativity and unity of character that was present previously. "From Plato on there is something essentially amiss with philosophers when one compares them to that "republic of creative minds" ["*Genialen-Republik*"] from Thales to Socrates."[59] This judgment corresponds with his general enthusiasm for the early, the archaic, the tragic age of Greece. But is also expresses a different heuristics. Not only the subject but also his approach is original. As opposed to a search for predecessors, developments and continuities, Nietzsche is driven by the ambition to find alternative modes of living and thinking:

> Greek philosophy is generally considered by asking, How far, in comparison with more recent philosophers, did the Greeks recognize and advance philosophical problems? *We* desire to ask, What do we learn from the history of their philosophy *on behalf of the Greeks?* Not, What do we learn on behalf of philosophy.[60]

A prime requirement for such an illuminating experience of alterity is the development of an understanding of the different mindsets of these archaic people. "Whoever conceives of them as clear, sober, harmonious, practical people will be unable to explain how they arrived at philosophy."[61] The emergence and sustainability of philosophers among them is a remarkable fact itself because—un-

---

57 Aristotle (*Met.*), 985a; 993a.
58 Nietzsche (1962), 28.
59 Nietzsche (1962), 34.
60 Nietzsche (2006), 3
61 Nietzsche (2006), 3

like the Aristotelian tradition—for Nietzsche it seems to be far from natural to philosophize. Consequently, he focuses his attention on the conditions under which "the Greeks produced *archetypal philosophers*"[62] and on the characteristics of these "*typical philosopher-heads.*"[63] In order to draw up these personality-studies Nietzsche explicitly rehabilitates the long outmoded genre of anecdotes, because "the only thing of interest in a refuted system is the personal element. It alone is what is forever irrefutable. It is possible to present the image of a man in three anecdotes; I shall try to emphasize three anecdotes in each system and abandon the rest."[64] I have not been able to detect these three anecdotes in any of the following chapters, but the emphasis is clear. In direct contrast to Hegel, Nietzsche draws our attention to the individual person.[65]

> I am going to tell the story—simplified—of certain philosophers. I am going to emphasize only that point of each of their systems which constitutes a slice of personality and hence belongs to that incontrovertible, non-debatable evidence, which is the task of history to preserve.[66]

The focus on irrefutable and indisputable "great individual human beings"[67] experienced a mixed reception. Christof Rapp sees Nietzsche's account as characterized by an idiosyncratic obsession with biographical, i.e. with non-philosophical concerns, that should rather be ignored and—like Hegel—Rapp indeed explicitly ignores them.[68] Heinrich Niehues-Pröbsting, on the other hand, sympathizes with Nietzsche's focus on exemplarily personalities and on historically real, alternative ways of living and of looking at the human scene; he also shares Nietzsche's reservations about the "multi-volumed and thick-bodied handbooks on the history of philosophy, of which the 19th century produced so many."[69] However, Niehues-Pröbsting rightly complains that Nietzsche does not fully translate his program into action. He still concerns himself with the relation be-

---

62 Nietzsche (2006), 4.
63 Nietzsche (1962), 31.
64 Nietzsche (1962), 25.
65 In his introduction to the study of Platonic dialogues Nietzsche also takes Plato's philosophy as the main testimony for Plato as a man Nietzsche (1995), 148; and he later continuously applies a heuristics of reading philosophical systems as "a confession of faith on the part of its author, and a type of involuntary and unself-conscious memoir" Nietzsche (2002), 8.
66 Nietzsche (1962), 24.
67 Nietzsche (1962), 24.
68 Rapp (2007), 11.
69 Niehues-Pröbsting (2004), 148f.)

tween Heraclitus and Parmenides.[70] But his focus on unique personalities invites the very plausible assumption that early Greek thought does not represent a rational evolution of doctrines but rather a "multitude of largely conceptually unrelated voices."[71] This step towards a non-evolutionary and pluralistic historiography deserves further attention.

> It is meant to be a beginning, by means of a comparative approach, toward the recovery and re-creation of certain characters, so that the polyphony of Greek nature at long last may resound once more.[72]

One of those grand voices is Thales of Miletus. Nietzsche agrees with the tradition that we should take his remark about water as the origin of philosophy seriously and he gives three reasons: "First, because it tells us something about the primal origin of all things; second, because it does so in language devoid of image or fable, and finally, because contained in it, if only embryonically, is the thought, 'all things are one'."[73] While the first reason also applies to religious cosmogonies, Thales' naturalistic language indicates a completely different enterprise that lifts him to the status of science. Actually, Nietzsche relates the water-principle to later scientific developments and informs his audience that the theory of transformative water reappeared twice in the history of natural science, i.e. in Paracelsus and in Lavoisier. He also invites us to "recall the Kant-Laplace hypothesis concerning a gaseous precondition of the universe" as support for the Ionian idea that the universe emerged out of less solid aggregate conditions.[74] The profane naturalism, however, is something Thales has in common with his supposedly only practically and empirically minded contemporaries and preceding cultures, such as Babylonian science. But instead of merely proposing a mistaken cosmological hypothesis, "he went beyond scientific considerations."[75] Like Zeller et al., Nietzsche constructs an emergence of philosophy as a new mode of thought distinct from mythical poetry and practical knowledge. What separates the Ionian from the observational empiricism of Babylonian sci-

---

[70] Cf. Nietzsche (2006), 44, 75; Nietzsche (1962), 69. Gadamer, on the other hand, was convinced that the extensive debate about their historical and logical relation and "the whole problem 'Parmenides and Heraklitus' results from the overwhelming influence of Hegelian thought" Gadamer (1996), 46.
[71] Müller (2005), 4.
[72] Nietzsche (1962), 24.
[73] Nietzsche (1962), 39.
[74] Nietzsche (2006), 27. Such considerations, widespread in PPP but not in PTG, prove Nietzsche's early and continuous interest in natural sciences and contemporary scientific findings.
[75] Nietzsche (1962), 39.

ence is his speculative jump beyond contemporary religion, knowledge and common sense.

> The sparse and un-ordered observations of an empirical nature which he made regarding the occurrence and the transformations of water (more specifically, of moisture) would have allowed, much less made available, no such outrageous generalization. What drove him to it was a metaphysical conviction which had its origins in a mystic intuition. We meet it in every philosophy, together with the ever-renewed attempts at a more suitable expression, this proposition that "all things are one."[76]

Nietzsche thus agrees with the standard view that "Thales is the first philosopher",[77] but he gives a different meaning to this title. Thales is not the first representative of proper usage of human rationality who finally turned "to the things themselves to uncover the truth about the nature of things."[78] His water-hypothesis does not represent "the first really rational attempts to describe the nature of the world"[79] but expresses an outrageous generalization and a statement of faith that deals "high-handedly with all empiricism."[80] According to Nietzsche's interpretation, the tradition of metaphysical hypotheses inaugurated by the Ionian *physikoi* hardly appears like the work of "students of nature, who took nature as an independent realm to be understood in terms of its own capacities".[81] In contrast to such empiricist readings, Nietzsche sides with Hegel's insistence on the speculative elements in early Greek thought. But unlike Hegel he does not assume the truth of such speculations. They express, as he pointedly writes in a notepad, "the artistic impulse in the chrysalis of philosophy."[82] The impulse to clarify and unify the observational world of chaos and becoming by means of metaphysical speculation and logical purification served as a point of departure for Western philosophy. According to Nietzsche, Thales introduced a new perspective on the world, a perspective informed by other sources and directed by other needs and values than preceding ones, but a perspective nonetheless.

---

76 Nietzsche (1962), 39.
77 Nietzsche (2006), 8.
78 Zeller (1876), 109
79 Kirk, Raven a. Schofield (1983), 75.
80 Nietzsche (1962), 39.
81 Graham (2010), 1.
82 Nietzsche (1980a), 529.

IV Epilogue: Polyphonous Historiography

An evaluation of Hegel's, Zeller's and Nietzsche's reconstructions of early Greek philosophy seems to indicate that there is no such thing as a completely neutral and value-free historiography. It is always a current perspective that investigates the selective remains of earlier thinkers. Therefore the first methodological requirement is self-awareness and intellectual honesty. But despite the fact that the idea of a miraculous Greek "rise of civilization" has been challenged by several objections, enthusiasm for early Greek achievements remains widespread. For instance the most recent comprehensive English edition of early Greek philosophers states in its first sentences:

> The Presocratics introduced a new kind of wisdom to the world. They appeared suddenly in the sixth century BC as sages who wanted to explain, not just this or that fact or custom or institution, but everything at once. [...] They gave birth to two important disciplines that have characterized Western thought ever since: philosophy and science.[83]

The beginning of philosophy is still ascribed historically and geographically to ancient Greece at about 600 BC and taken to be unprecedented and spontaneous. In the light of these continuities, the lasting value of Nietzsche's engagement with early Greek philosophers derives from the fundamental change of perspective regarding the nature of their achievements. He invites us to perceive the pre-Platonic philosophers as creative thinkers, who introduce new images of the world and new modes of life, but who neither discover the objectively given essence of nature nor introduce the one and only proper way of thinking or living. They polyphonically and pluralistically represent opportunities of thinking and living, and they embody role models for philosophers. They did so by arguments, experimentation and an unreasonably optimistic trust in reason. It has been argued that Nietzsche is reading himself into the sparse ancient sources and that his concept of early Greek philosophy is only a human, all-too-human model and invention.[84] This is obviously the case and—as Nietzsche was particularly well aware—inevitably so. Our sparse sources are not only thick palimpsests of earlier value-judgments but the preserved texts also only speak to certain ears:

> When I carefully listened to the general sound of the older Greek philosophers, I meant to perceive tones which I was used to hear from Greek art, namely tragedy. How much this was

---

83 Graham (2010), 1.
84 Cf. Borsche (1985), 81; or Rehn (1992), 41.

due to the Greeks or how much only due to my ears (the ears of a very art-loving man)—this I cannot say with certainty even today.[85]

Nietzsche's account is construction, of course, but this fact alone does not separate him from any other historiography. It seems fair to speak of Hegel's antiquity, or Zeller's, or, for that matter, Aristotle's or Diogenes Laërtius'. Hegel provides an impressive systematic reconstruction with a particularly high degree of methodological reflection on the philosophical requirements of any history of philosophy. Zeller certainly delivers one of the most learned and elaborate history. However, unlike the traditional (and Euro-centric) euphoria about a world-historical break-through from myth to reason, Nietzsche invites a perception of the Greek miracle as a contribution to polyphony and as an essential variation in our human activities of world-making. This is a plausible narrative. Since our historiographical sources are always limited while it is obviously possible —even lege artis—to reconstruct them differently, we are perhaps best advised with tolerant pluralism.

Bibliography

Translations of German literature are—unless stated otherwise—my own.

Aristotle (Met.): Aristotle, "The Metaphysics. Books I-IX", in: Aristotle, *The Metaphysics Books I-IX*, vol. 1, ed. by Hugh Tredennick, Cambridge / London: Loeb Classical Library (1961), 1–473.

Barnes (2014): Jonathan Barnes, "Nietzsche and Diogenes Laertius", in: Anthony K. Jensen and Helmut Heit (Eds.), *Nietzsche as a Scholar of Antiquity*, London: Bloomsbury, 115–137.

Beiser (1995): Frederick C. Beiser, "Introduction", in: G.W.F. Hegel, *Lectures on the History of Philosophy. I. Greek Philosophy to Plato*, ed. by Frederick C. Beiser, Lincoln / London: University of Nebraska Press, XI-XL.

Borsche (1985): Tilman Borsche, "Nietzsches Erfindung der Vorsokratiker", in: Josef Simon (Ed.), *Nietzsche und die philosophische Tradition*, vol. 1, Würzburg: Königshausen & Neumann, 62–87.

Düsing (1983): Klaus Düsing, *Hegel und die Geschichte der Philosophie. Ontologie und Dialektik in Antike und Neuzeit*, Darmstadt: Wissenschaftliche Buchgesellschaft.

Frede (2008): Michael Frede, "Aristotle's Account of the Origin of Philosophy", in: Patricia Curd and Daniel W. Graham (Eds.), *The Oxford Handbook of Presocratic Philosophy*, Oxford: Oxford University Press, 501–529.

Gadamer (1996): Hans-Georg Gadamer, *Der Anfang der Philosophie*, Stuttgart: Reclam.

---

85 Nietzsche (1980b), 530.

Geldsetzer (1968): Lutz Geldsetzer, *Die Philosophie der Philosophiegeschichte im 19. Jahrhundert. Zur Wissenschaftstheorie der Philososphiegeschichtsschreibung und -betrachtung*, Meisenheim: Hain.

Graham (2010): Daniel W. Graham, *The Texts of Early Greek Philosophy. The Complete Fragments and Selected Testimonies of the Major Presocratics*, vol. 1, Cambridge: Cambridge University Press.

Hegel (1989): Georg Wilhelm Friedrich Hegel, *Vorlesungen. Ausgewählte Nachschriften und Manuskripte*, vol. 7, *Vorlesungen über die Geschichte der Philosophie. Teil 2: Griechische Philosophie I. Thales bis Kyniker*, ed. by Pierre Garniron and Walter Jaeschke, Hamburg: Meiner.

Hegel (1994a): Georg Wilhelm Friedrich Hegel, "Einleitung in die Geschichte der Philosophie" (1823), in: Georg Wilhelm Friedrich Hegel, *Vorlesungen. Ausgewählte Nachschriften und Manuskripte*, vol. 6, *Vorlesungen über die Geschichte der Philosophie. Teil 1: Einleitung in die Geschichte der Philosophie. Orientalische Philosophie*, ed. by Pierre Garniron and Walter Jaeschke, Hamburg: Meiner, 1–364.

Hegel (1994b): Georg Wilhelm Friedrich Hegel, "Orientalische Philosophie (Kollegmitschrift)" (1826), in: Georg Wilhelm Friedrich Hegel, *Vorlesungen. Ausgewählte Nachschriften und Manuskripte*, vol. 6, *Vorlesungen über die Geschichte der Philosophie. Teil 1: Einleitung in die Geschichte der Philosophie. Orientalische Philosophie*, ed. by Pierre Garniron and Walter Jaeschke, Hamburg: Meiner, 365–400.

Hegel (1999): Georg Wilhelm Friedrich Hegel, "Wissenschaft der Logik. Erster Band. Die objektive Logik. Erstes Buch. Die Lehre vom Sein" (1832), in: Georg Wilhelm Friedrich Hegel, *Gesammelte Werke*, vol. 21, ed. by Walter Jaeschke and Friedrich Hogemann, Hamburg: Meiner.

Heit (2005): Helmut Heit, "Western Identity, Barbarians, and the Inheritance of Greek Universalism", in: *The European Legacy* 10/7, 725–739.

Heit (2007): Helmut Heit, *Der Ursprungsmythos der Vernunft. Zur philosophiehistorischen Genealogie des griechischen Wunders*, Würzburg: Königshausen & Neumann.

Heit (2011): Helmut Heit, *Grundwissen Philosophie: Frühgriechische Philosophie*, Stuttgart: Reclam.

Kirk, Raven a. Schofield (1983): Geoffrey S. Kirk, John E. Raven and Malcolm Schofield, *The Presocratic Philosophers. A Critical History with a Selection of Texts*, 2nd rev. edition, Cambridge: Cambridge University Press.

Kolmer (1998): Petra Kolmer, *Philosophiegeschichte als philosophisches Problem. Kritische Überlegungen namentlich zu Kant und Hegel*, Freiburg: Alber.

Laërtius (*Bion*): Diogenes Laërtius, *Lives and Opinions of Eminent Philosophers*, ed. by R.D. Hicks, Cambridge / London: Loeb Classical Library (1966).

Long (1999): A. A. Long, "The Scope of Early Greek Philosophy", in: A. A. Long (Ed.), *The Cambridge Companion to Early Greek Philosophy*, Cambridge: Cambridge University Press, 1–28.

Löwith (1941): Karl Löwith, *Von Hegel zu Nietzsche. Der revolutionäre Bruch im Denken des neunzehnten Jahrhunderts*, Stuttgart: Kohlhammer.

Mansfeld (1990): Jaap Mansfeld, "Myth, Science, Philosophy. A Question of Origins" (1985), in: Jaap Mansfeld (Ed.), *Studies in the Historiography of Greek Philosophy*, Assen/Maastricht: Van Gorcum (1990), 1–21.

Müller (2005): Enrico Müller, *Die Griechen im Denken Nietzsches*, Berlin / NewYork: De Gruyter.

Niehues-Pröbsting (2004): Heinrich Niehues-Pröbsting, *Die antike Philosophie. Schrift, Schule, Lebensform*, Frankfurt a. M.: Fischer.
Nietzsche (1962): Friedrich Nietzsche, *Philosophy in the Tragic Age of Greeks* (1873), Translated, with an Introduction by Marianne Cowan, Washington: Regenery.
Nietzsche (1980a): Friedrich Nietzsche, *Sämtliche Werke. Kritische Studienausgabe in 15 Bänden*, vol. 7, *Nachgelassene Fragmente 1869–1874*, ed. by Giorgio Colli and Mazzino Montinari, Berlin / New York: De Gruyter.
Nietzsche (1980b): Friedrich Nietzsche, *Sämtliche Werke. Kritische Studienausgabe in 15 Bänden*, vol. 8, *Nachgelassene Fragmente 1875–1879*, ed. by Giorgio Colli and Mazzino Montinari, Berlin / New York: De Gruyter.
Nietzsche (1986): Friedrich Nietzsche, *Sämtliche Briefe. Kritische Studienausgabe in acht Bänden (KSB)*, vol. 4, ed. by Giorgio Colli and Mazino Montinari, München / Berlin / New York: dtv/De Gruyter.
Nietzsche (1993a): Friedrich Nietzsche, *Werke. Kritische Gesamtausgabe (KGW)*, II/2: *Vorlesungsaufzeichnungen (SS 1869 – WS 1869/70), Anhang: Nachschriften von Vorlesungen Nietzsches*, ed. by Fritz Bornemann, (begründet von Giorgio Colli und Mazzino Montinari, weitergeführt von Wolfgang Müller-Lauter und Karl Pestalozzi), Berlin / New York: De Gruyter.
Nietzsche (1993b): Friedrich Nietzsche, *Werke. Kritische Gesamtausgabe (KGW)*, II/3: *Vorlesungsaufzeichnungen (SS 1870 – SS 1871)*, ed. by Fritz Bornemann, (begründet von Giorgio Colli und Mazzino Montinari, weitergeführt von Wolfgang Müller-Lauter und Karl Pestalozzi), Berlin / New York: De Gruyter.
Nietzsche (1995): Friedrich Nietzsche, *Werke. Kritische Gesamtausgabe (KGW)*, II/4: *Vorlesungsaufzeichnungen (WS 1871/72 – WS 1874/75)*, ed. by Fritz Bornemann, (begründet von Giorgio Colli und Mazzino Montinari, weitergeführt von Wolfgang Müller-Lauter und Karl Pestalozzi), Berlin / New York: De Gruyter.
Nietzsche (1997): Friedrich Nietzsche, "On the Uses and Disadvantages of History for Live" (1874), in: Friedrich Nietzsche, *Untimely Meditations*, ed. by Daniel Breazeale, Cambridge: Cambridge University Press, 243–334.
Nietzsche (2002): Friedrich Nietzsche, *Beyond God and Evil. Prelude to a Philosophy of the Future* (1886), Edited by Rolf-Peter Horstmann and Judith Norman, Cambridge: Cambridge University Press.
Nietzsche (2006): Friedrich Nietzsche, *The Pre-Platonic Philosophers* (1872), Translated from the German and Edited with an Introduction and Commentary by Greg Whitlock, Urbana: University of Illinois Press.
Rapp (2007): Christof Rapp, *Vorsokratiker*, München: Beck.
Reale (1987): Giovanni Reale, *A History of Ancient Philosophy. I. From the Origins to Socrates*, New York: New York University Press.
Rehn (1992): Rudolf Rehn, "Nietzsches Modell der Vorsokratik", in: Rudolf Rehn and Daniel W. Conway (Eds.), *Nietzsche und die antike Philosophie*, Trier: wvt, 37–45.
Schneider (1990): Ulrich Johannes Schneider, *Die Vergangenheit des Geistes. Eine Archäologie der Philosophiegeschichte*, Frankfurt a. M.: Suhrkamp.
Skowron (2004): Michael Skowron, "Nachweis aus Gladisch, August: Herakleitos und Zoroaster", in: *Nietzsche Studien* 33, 373.
Snell (1948): Bruno Snell, *The Discovery of the Mind. The Greek Origins of European Thought*, NewYork: Harper.

Ueberweg (1865): Friedrich Ueberweg, *Grundriß der Geschichte der Philosophie – Erster Theil. Das Alterthum (die vorchristliche Zeit)*, 2nd revised edition, Berlin: Mittler.

Walsh (1971): William Henry Walsh, "Principle and prejudice in Hegel's philosophy of history", in: Z.A. Pelczynski, *Hegels Political Philosophy. Problems and Perspectives*, Cambridge: Cambridge University Press, 181–198.

Windelband (1892): Wilhelm Windelband, *Lehrbuch der Geschichte der Philosophie*, Tübingen: Mohr.

Zeller (1876): Eduard Zeller, *Die Philosophie der Griechen in ihrer geschichtlichen Entwicklung. 1. Teil, 1. Abteilung: Allgemeine Einleitung* (1844), 4th revised edition, Leipzig: Furs.

Michael Forster
Does Western Philosophy Have Non-Western Roots?

There is an interesting division among nineteenth-century historians of philosophy between those who believe that western philosophy has non-western, in particular eastern, roots and those who deny that it does.

The former group includes Friedrich Schlegel, Wilhelm von Humboldt, August Gladisch, and Eduard Röth, whose versions of the idea of eastern origins are quite various. Schlegel, following in the footsteps of the Englishmen Colebrooke and Jones, and to a lesser extent also certain German predecessors,[1] argued in his Cologne lectures of 1804–6 and then more elaborately in his seminal work on Sanskrit language and literature, *On the Language and Wisdom of the Indians* (1808), that very ancient Indian texts such as the *Bhagavad-Gita* contain genuine philosophy (especially in their doctrines concerning the soul and afterlife), that this is superior to western philosophy in certain respects, and moreover that it influenced the birth and development of western philosophy at crucial early periods (for example, the Pythagoreans and Plato).[2] Schlegel's pioneering work was subsequently followed and refined by other scholars in nineteenth-century Germany, especially Humboldt in two famous addresses on the *Bhagavad-Gita* that he delivered to the Berlin Academy in 1826. A very different and far more ambitious version of the thesis that western philosophy has eastern origins was developed by Gladisch in his book *Religion and Philosophy in their Worldhistorical Development and Relation to Each Other, According to the Documents* (1852).[3] Gladisch argued that each of the five main presocratic philosophies of ancient Greece had originated from one of the five main eastern nations: Pythagoras's philosophy from the Chinese, the Eleatic philosophy from the Indians, Heraclitus's philosophy from the Persians, Empedocles' philosophy from the Egyptians, and Anaxagoras's philosophy from the Jews. Yet another version of the idea of western philosophy's eastern origins was that of Röth in his *History*

---
[1] Concerning some of these eighteenth-century German forerunners, see Geldsetzer (1968), 184.
[2] Friedrich Schlegel, *Friedrich Schlegels philosophische Vorlesungen aus den Jahren 1804 bis 1806*, ed. by C.J.H. Windischmann, Bonn: Weber 1846. Friedrich Schlegel, *Über die Sprache und Weisheit der Indier*, in: Friedrich Schlegel, *Kritische Friedrich-Schlegel-Ausgabe*, vol. 8, Studien zur Philosophie und Theologie, ed. by Ernst Behler a. Ursula Struc-Oppenberg, Paderborn: F. Schöningh 1975, 105–433.
[3] August Gladisch, *Die Religion und die Philosophie in ihrer weltgeschichtlichen Entwicklung und Stellung zu einander nach den Urkunden*, Breslau: Hirt 1852.

of our Western Philosophy: Developmental History of our Speculative, Both Philosophical and Religious, Ideas from their First Beginnings up to the Present (1846/ 1858; second, revised edition 1862).[4] Röth argued that the origins of western philosophy lay in ancient Egypt (and also to some extent other areas and cultural traditions of the Near East, including Babylon and Zoroastrianism). In particular, he argued that presocratic philosophers such as Thales and Pythagoras had spent time in, and borrowed ideas from, Egypt. For example, according to Röth's account, ancient reports of Thales' travels to Egypt are historically credible, and Thales drew from there, among other things, his conception that everything is water and his knowledge of astronomy (exemplified in his famous prediction of an eclipse). Similarly, according to Röth, ancient reports of Pythagoras's long residence, and study with priests, in Egypt are historically credible, and such central features of Pythagoras's position as his strictly hierarchical, secretive, church-like school, his distinctive religious-philosophical views (including his conceptions of the soul as separable from the body, immortal, subject to judgment in an afterlife, and undergoing transmigration into animals), and his sophisticated mathematics all came from Egypt.

On the other side of the divide in the nineteenth century were people who in one way or another rejected the idea that western philosophy had significant non-western origins. Two of the century's early experts on Greek philosophy, Christian August Brandis and August Heinrich Ritter, were still relatively open-minded about the idea of eastern influences, but already tended towards skepticism about it. Brandis judiciously suspended judgment pending fuller information. Ritter in his *History of Philosophy* (1829–1853) showed great interest in the question of eastern, and in particular Indian, influences, devoting not just one but two extended discussions to it, but expressed great caution about the question due to his lack of relevant expertise and information, and was in the end inclined to deny that there had been significant eastern influences on the earlier phases of Greek philosophy.[5] With the Eurocentric Hegel and his follower Zeller this sort of skepticism hardened and came to dominate the field of writing history of philosophy. Thus, Hegel in his *Lectures on the History of Philosophy* (delivered 1805–31), while conceding that the ancient Chinese and Indians had had a rudimentary philosophy, was at pains to downplay its significance and value, saying for example that "the so-called Oriental [Philosophy] ... does not enter into the substance or range of our subject ... We only deal with it at all in

---

4 Eduard Maximilian Röth, *Geschichte unserer abendländischen Philosophie. Entwicklungsgeschichte unserer spekulativen, sowohl philosophischen als religiösen Ideen von ihren ersten Anfängen bis auf die Gegenwart*, 2 volumes, Mannheim: Bassermann 1846/1858.
5 August Heinrich Ritter, *Geschichte der Philosophie*, 12 volumes, Hamburg: Perthes 1829–1853.

order to account for not treating of it at greater length."[6] (Hegel accordingly mentions Schlegel's work on Indian philosophy condescendingly, and in a separate review of Humboldt's addresses likewise responds coolly to Humboldt's claims of Indian philosophy's importance.[7]) Then Hegel's follower Zeller made an even more uncompromising case for the virtual irrelevance of eastern thought to the history of western philosophy. Zeller in particular argued in *The Philosophy of the Greeks in its Historical Development* (1855–70; followed by several revised editions) against Gladisch and Röth that an Oriental influence on Greek philosophy was (1) unproven by them, (2) a completely superfluous hypothesis given that Greek philosophy began crude and its development could be explained *internally*, (3) unlikely given the difficulties of transmission, and (4) indeed impossible because whereas Greek philosophy was enabled by the fact that Greek society was free, Oriental society was not free.[8] Zeller's high reputation as a historian of Greek philosophy seems to have ensured that this position became widely accepted as the final word on the subject.

I would like in this article to re-consider this debate, and indeed to re-open it. For, although, as was just mentioned, the idea that western philosophy has non-western roots appears to have been virtually shut down by the end of the nineteenth century due to the influence of Hegel and Zeller, it seems to me very doubtful that their reasons for dismissing it were at all adequate. The recent publication of Edward Said's *Orientalism* and Martin Bernal's *Black Athena*, which have sensitized us to the large role that cultural prejudice played in such issues in the nineteenth century, perhaps makes this an especially appropriate time to re-examine and re-open the debate.[9]

However, in order to do so in a fruitful way, it seems to me very important to focus on the most plausible version of the thesis of eastern origins. While Schlegel's and Humboldt's insistence that early Indian philosophy is genuine philosophy and of considerable value still appears defensible, their idea that it *influenced* early western philosophy looks dubious. This is largely due to the absence of ancient Greek testimony that it did and to the absence of any plausible route of transmission at the period in question (as Zeller already convincingly

---

[6] Hegel (1974), 117.
[7] For Hegel's review of Humboldt, see Hegel (1986), 131–133.
[8] Eduard Zeller, *Die Philosophie der Griechen in ihrer geschichtlichen Entwicklung*, 5th edition, Leipzig: Reisland 1892.
[9] See esp. volume 1 (1987) and volume 2 (1991) of Martin Bernal's *Black Athena*, 3 volumes, New Brunswick/ New Jersey: Rutgers University Press.

argued).¹⁰ Gladisch's claim that the five main strands of Presocratic philosophy had their origins in as many eastern nations is even more fanciful and implausible (as Zeller again already convincingly argued).¹¹ However, Röth's version of the thesis seems to me another matter entirely, possessing a far higher level of scholarly seriousness and historical plausibility. So it is Röth's version of the thesis that I would like to consider more closely here.

Since Röth is almost unknown today, it may be worth beginning with a little biographical information about him. He was born in Hanau in 1807. He attended the Gymnasium in Wetzlar and then the University of Giessen. He subsequently studied Rabbinic literature with a Jewish scholar in Frankfurt, which led to his first publication, a work on Paul's Letter to the Hebrews, in 1835. In 1836 he moved to Paris, mainly in order to deepen his study of Oriental languages—notably including Egyptian hieroglyphics, which had just recently been deciphered by Jean-François Champollion and made accessible through his *Grammaire égyptienne* and *Dictionnaire égyptien* of 1832—with Sylvestre de Sacy, Eugène Burnouf, and Stanislas Julien, but also in order to study the natural sciences. These studies and his historical research led him to the conclusion that western philosophy was neither entirely autochthonous nor rooted in India or China, but instead rooted mainly in ancient Egypt (and to a certain extent also other Near Eastern regions and sources, including Babylon and Zoroastrianism). After Paris, he went to Heidelberg University, where he took his *Habilitation* in 1840, became associate professor in 1846, and then full professor for Philosophy and Sanskrit in 1850. He published his main work, *History of our Western Philosophy: Developmental History of our Speculative, Both Philosophical and Religious, Ideas from their First Beginnings up to the Present*, in 1846–58 (among the people to whom he dedicated it were the great classical philologist August Boeckh and the great natural scientist Alexander von Humboldt). During this period he also published a translation of, and commentary on, the first thirty-four chapters of the Egyptian *Book of the Dead*. Exhausted by his work on these projects, he died in 1858.¹²

In his *History of our Western Philosophy*, Röth is open-minded and respectful about ancient Indian and Chinese philosophy, but he rejects the idea that either of them had an actual influence on early periods of Greek philosophy.¹³ Instead,

---

10 For Zeller's criticisms of the idea that Greek philosophy had Indian origins, see Zeller (1892), 481–483.
11 Zeller (1892), 28–32. Interestingly enough, though, Nietzsche took Gladisch's work seriously in *Philosophy in the Tragic Age of the Greeks* (1872/3).
12 This biographical information is partly drawn from *Deutsche Biographie* (online).
13 Röth (1846), 24f.

he develops, with enormous erudition and force, a fascinating thesis—very much in the spirit of Martin Bernal's *Black Athena*, but about a century and a half earlier—to the effect that ancient Greek religion and philosophy, instead of being exclusively "Aryan" or autochthonous, as many eighteenth- and nineteenth-century classicists had claimed, largely arose from ancient Egyptian sources (and also to a lesser extent other Near Eastern sources, such as Babylonian science and Zoroastrianism), as the ancient Greeks had themselves commonly held. More specifically, he makes a case that there were three main phases of such influence: Concerning the first phase, he argues (very much as Bernal later would) that Egyptian religion was transported to Greece in the second millennium B.C. (in particular, by the "Pelasgians," whom—like Bernal—he identifies as Phoenicians coming out of Egypt), where it then formed the core of traditional Greek religion.[14] Concerning the second phase, he argues that beginning in the seventh century B.C., the earliest Greek philosophers, especially Thales and Pythagoras, traveled to Egypt (as well as to other parts of the Near East) and brought back from there Egyptian religious, philosophical, and scientific ideas to form the basis of their own philosophies, thereby establishing the foundations of the whole Greek (indeed, the whole western) philosophical and scientific tradition.[15] Finally (and much less controversially), he argues that there was a third phase of Eastern influence during the Hellenistic and early Christian periods, when new forms of religion and philosophy—especially, Neoplatonism, Christianity, and Christian philosophy—arose from yet another infusion of Eastern ideas.[16]

I would like here to set aside the first and third parts of this complex historical account in order to focus on the second part, the part concerning the origins of Greek philosophy. It may be helpful to begin with a brief summary of the core of Röth's argument in this part of his account.

As has already been mentioned, Röth's general thesis is that Greek philosophy first emerged through an appropriation of religious, philosophical, and scientific ideas from ancient Egypt (and to a lesser extent also other ancient Near Eastern sources).[17]

More specifically, he argues—in agreement with ancient Greek reports, but in sharp opposition to what he sees as predominantly and lamentably Eurocentric modern scholarship –[18] that five of the earliest and most important presocratic

---

14 Röth (1846), 82–326.
15 Röth (1846), 345–347.; Röth (1858) passim.
16 Röth (1846), 456–458. For a convenient summary of the whole three-part account, see Röth (1858), 78f.
17 Röth (1858), XV-XVL, 81–89.
18 Röth (1846), 330; Röth (1858), 80f., 363.

philosophers, all from the city of Miletus on the coast of Asia Minor (which had a colony in Egypt: Naucratis) or from the islands nearby, spent time in Egypt and drew their central doctrines from there, or at least learned from immediate predecessors who had done so: Thales, Anaximander, Anaximander's pupil Anaximenes, Pherecydes, and Pherecydes' pupil Pythagoras.[19]

Concerning *Thales*, Röth argues that ancient Greek accounts according to which he spent time in Egypt are historically credible;[20] that the knowledge of astronomy that enabled him to achieve his famous prediction of an eclipse and of the solstices came from there;[21] that his reported knowledge of a sun-based calendar (which contrasted strikingly with the Greeks' traditional moon-based calendar) came from there;[22] that his reported conception of the earth as a sphere (which contrasted strikingly with the Greeks' traditional conception of it as flat) likewise came from there;[23] that his reported mathematical, and in particular geometrical, knowledge, such as that which reportedly enabled him to measure the height of the pyramids, came from there as well;[24] that his famous thesis that everything is, or at least rests on, water likewise derived from a strikingly similar Egyptian conception;[25] and finally, that his reported doctrine that the soul is immortal was Egyptian in origin as well (as Herodotus implied).[26]

Concerning *Anaximander*, Röth argues that he too ultimately received his main ideas from Egypt, in this case largely through the influence of his countryman, friend, and teacher Thales, including his identification of water as a central aspect of the ultimate principle of things that he identifies, "the infinite [*to apeiron*]," and an implication that the world is a sphere.[27]

Concerning *Anaximenes*, Röth argues that, as Anaximander's pupil, he inherited the general Egyptian orientation of Anaximander's cosmology, but that

---

19 For a helpful overview, see Röth's detailed list of contents at Röth (1858), XV-XLIX. Röth's claim of an actual visit to Egypt extends only to Thales, Pherecydes, and Pythagoras; according to Röth, Anaximander's and Anaximenes' knowledge of Egypt and Egyptian ideas was indirect.
20 Röth (1858), 94 f.
21 Röth (1858), 96–98, 107, 115.
22 Röth (1858), 106–107. The source for this report is Diogenes Laertius, who more specifically ascribes to Thales a division of the year into 365 days and of each month into 30 days (just like the Egyptians, who had removed the mathematical discrepancy by inserting 5 intercalary days).
23 Röth (1858), 122. The sources for this report are Plutarch and Galen.
24 Röth (1858), 106–108.
25 Röth (1858), 116–119.
26 Röth (1858), 127–129. Cf. Röth (1846), 176–178.
27 Röth (1858), 129–160.

he also fused it with Xenophanes' monotheism and took the more original step of identifying air as the essence of both the divine mind and nature.[28]

Concerning *Pherecydes*, Röth argues that he traveled to Egypt,[29] and that accordingly his famous cosmogony is thoroughly Egyptian in character, [30] as is his reported belief in the immortality of the soul.[31]

Finally, concerning Pherecydes' pupil *Pythagoras*, who is the centerpiece of the whole account, Röth argues that reports by ancient authors according to which Pythagoras studied with priests in Egypt and drew his philosophical and religious conceptions from there are historically credible;[32] that his very un-Greek establishment of a school for young followers with an austere hierarchy, a sharp distinction between inner and outer circles, and strict rules of secrecy concerning certain doctrines was modeled on the practices of the Egyptian priesthood with whom he had himself studied;[33] that his very un-Greek insistence on numerous arbitrary-looking rules of diet, dress, and comportment (e.g. not eating beans, not wearing wool in religious contexts, and not stepping over a balance) and on their memorization was again largely Egyptian in inspiration (as Röth points out in passing, these rules are strikingly reminiscent in their general character of similarly numerous and arbitrary-looking rules in the Old Testament, which presumably likewise derived from the ancient Hebrews' residence in Egypt, namely during the period of their captivity there);[34] that his very un-Greek rules against animal sacrifice, and especially against the sacrifice of sacred animals, were also largely Egyptian-inspired;[35] that his religious-ethical conceptions, including his un-Greek (in particular, un-Homeric) beliefs in a soul (in the sense of a mind or self) that is separable from the body, immortal, subject to judgment in an afterlife, and undergoes transmigration or metempsychosis into animal forms, likewise came from Egypt (as Herodotus implied);[36] and finally, that his sophisticated knowledge of mathematics, including both number-theory and geometry, came from Egypt as well.[37]

---

28 Röth (1858), 243–254.
29 Röth (1858), 161–163.
30 Röth (1858), 165–167.
31 Röth (1858), 171.
32 Röth (1858), 264f., 312–314.
33 Röth (1858), 473f., 480–482, 595f., 602–608.
34 Röth (1858), 488–507.
35 Röth (1858), 497f.
36 Röth (1846), 176–178., 183, 233f.; cf. Röth (1858), 506f., 595–597. Röth concedes that versions of some of these ideas were already present in *certain strands* of Greek religion before Pythagoras, especially in the cults of Orpheus and Dionysus. But he sees those strands as themselves originally offshoots of the Egyptian cult of Osiris, which had become syncretized and distorted

As I mentioned, Zeller in *The Philosophy of the Greeks in its Historical Development* attempted to refute Röth's account, and in terms of public perception evidently won the day. But how convincing is his refutation really? It seems to me that it is not convincing at all. On the contrary, it seems to me that it largely consists of an unholy combination of inconsistencies, dubious judgments, and rhetorical foul-play, and that the main lines of Röth's account withstand it with flying colors.[38]

A large part of Zeller's attempted refutation lies in a set of very general claims that he makes which are supposed to tell against *any* account like Röth's: (1) Greek philosophy began crude and then developed in an immanent way.[39] (2) The emergence of Greek philosophy can be explained quite adequately in terms of earlier Greek culture, especially Homer, whose thought in particular already possessed the same sort of clarity, harmony, freedom, etc. that philosophy later would.[40] (3) Philosophy is secular, so how could it have come from Oriental priests?[41] (4) The Egyptians may have influenced the Greeks in *other* fields, such as science and religion—for example, as Herodotus implies, concerning astronomy, geometry, and the soul—but not in *philosophy*.[42] (5) There were insuperable obstacles standing in the way of a communication of ideas from the Egyptians to the Greeks, including the Greeks' notorious ignorance of foreign languages.[43] (6) The Egyptians and other Oriental peoples lacked the *freedom*, in particular the political-social freedom and the freedom in or from religion,

---

in Greece. His fuller position is that Pythagoras, on his return from Egypt, where he had become acquainted with the cult of Osiris in its pure form, recognized that those strands had such a source and consequently sought to link up with and purify them, thereby producing a transition from mere traditional Orphic cult to Orphism as a religious-philosophical movement, in particular by himself authoring the Orphic "Holy Story [*hieros logos*]." For this position, see Röth (1858), 356–387, 596, 600–602, 609–611, 715f.

37 Röth (1858), 515–591. Röth interprets Pythagoras as already extremely sophisticated in mathematics, and goes into this subject in great detail. There is a lot of speculation in this part of Röth's account, but its core thesis remains very plausible.

38 I do not, of course, mean here to endorse *every aspect* of Röth's account, which runs to many hundreds of pages and is certainly questionable on many points of detail (for example, in its attributions of extremely sophisticated mathematical achievements to Pythagoras and thence to the Egyptians).

39 Zeller (1892), 35f.
40 Zeller (1892), 41f.
41 Zeller (1892), 36.
42 Zeller (1892), 37–40; cf. 454–456.
43 Zeller (1892), 40.

that was a distinguishing trait of the Greeks and that made possible their philosophy.[44]

However, it seems to me that these general claims of Zeller's are virtually worthless as responses to an account like Röth's. Claim (1), the claim that Greek philosophy began crude and then developed immanently, is refuted by such features of its beginning as Thales' prediction of the eclipse and the solstices and Pythagoras's discovery of the theorem that bears his name—achievements that were anything but crude and which seem to have been quite without precedent in the Greek context.

Claim (2), the claim that the emergence of Greek philosophy can be explained quite adequately in terms of earlier Greek culture, especially Homer, whose thought already possessed the same sort of clarity, harmony, freedom, etc. that philosophy later would, succumbs to the same point (though of course there *are* important continuities between Homer and philosophy *as well*).

Claim (3), the claim that philosophy is secular, so that it could not have come from Oriental priests, is strangely obtuse. For one thing, the early Greek philosophers in question here, such as Thales and Pythagoras—and for that matter, also the majority of subsequent Greek philosophers, indeed the majority of philosophers *tout court*—were *not* secular thinkers; on the contrary, their thought included a large religious component (as Röth in particular rightly emphasizes). For another thing, even if they *had* been purely secular thinkers, a process in which they had extracted secular ideas from out of an originally religious context would have been perfectly intelligible. For yet another thing (to add a more ad hominem point), Zeller *himself* traces philosophy back to a religious source, namely to the religion of the Greeks.

Claim (4), the claim that the Egyptians may have influenced the Greeks in *other* fields, such as science and religion—for example, concerning astronomy, geometry, and the soul—but not in *philosophy*, is again obtuse. For one thing, there was no clear division between such intellectual activities in the early Greek context—or, for that matter, in most of the subsequent western intellectual tradition either. Indeed, to assume that there was is basically just to project back anachronistically in time a division of academic disciplines that really only emerged with the German university of the eighteenth and nineteenth centuries. For another thing, some of the most plausible parts of Röth's case are his theses that such rather paradigmatically "philosophical" doctrines in Thales and Pythagoras as that the soul (in the sense of the mind or self) is separable from

---

44 Zeller (1892), 47, 66, 122f.

the body, that it is immortal, and that everything is constituted by the single substance of water had Egyptian origins.

Claim (5), the claim that there were insuperable obstacles in the way of a communication of ideas from the Egyptians to the Greeks, including the Greeks' notorious ignorance of foreign languages, is extremely weak as well. For one thing, as we have just seen, Zeller himself concedes, very plausibly, that there was an early communication of *scientific and religious* ideas from the Egyptians to the Greeks. So he is (a) inconsistent here and (b) himself supplies good grounds for dismissing his own claim. For another thing, even Zeller concedes that his claim would be trumped if there were persuasive evidence for an early communication of philosophical ideas from Egypt to Greece, but Röth has arguably shown that especially in the cases of Thales and Pythagoras there precisely *is*. For yet another thing, the communication of ideas from Egypt to Greece was certainly at least perfectly possible within only a century or so after those thinkers, as can be clearly seen from the example of Herodotus, so why not a little earlier as well?

Finally, claim (6), the claim that the Egyptians lacked the freedom, in particular the socio-political freedom and the freedom in/from religion, that distinguished the Greeks and made possible their philosophy, is sufficiently refuted by recalling three obvious points: first, the earliest Greek philosophy *antedated* the establishment of Greek liberalism and democracy; second, it was itself religious in character; and third, the alleged lack of freedom among the Egyptians was clearly at least not so severe as to preclude major intellectual innovations among them, such as, for example, Akhenaten's introduction of monotheism.

This leaves as the remaining threads by which Zeller's case against Röth hangs his more detailed objections to Röth's specific claims of Egyptian influence on the presocratic philosophers. So let us now consider those objections, confining our attention to the two most important cases: Thales and Pythagoras.

In connection with Thales, Zeller pursues two completely inconsistent interpretive strategies, one in his Introduction, the other in his main text. Let us consider each of them in turn. Concerning his strategy in the Introduction, the first thing to note—and indeed to be thunderstruck by—is that he *concedes* Röth's claims that Thales went to Egypt and that his ideas had Egyptian origins.[45] His only qualification of this concession consists of an attempt to restrict the Egyptian influence in question to Thales' "religion" and "science" in contradistinction to his "philosophy." However, such a qualification is untenable, not only because (as I have already mentioned) the sort of distinction between disciplines

---

45 Zeller (1892), 26.

that it presupposes is quite anachronistic, but also because at least two historically credible examples of Egyptian influence on Thales, namely his doctrine that everything is constituted by the single substance of water and his doctrine of the immortality of the soul, are just about as "philosophical" in character as one could wish. Moreover, Zeller is clearly *right* to concede Röth's claims, because the evidence for them is extremely strong. Accordingly, they would still be essentially endorsed by many authorities on the presocratic philosophers today, such as Kirk, Raven, and Schofield for example.[46] Furthermore, while Zeller tries to pass over this concession that Röth is basically right about Thales in indecent haste, the concession is an enormous one. After all, Thales is generally and plausibly considered to be the very first Greek philosopher, and moreover the one who established, with his doctrine that everything is water, a whole tradition of cosmological speculation about the fundamental constitution of things that would drive Greek philosophy throughout its subsequent history and that indeed still drives it today.

Subsequently, in his more detailed treatment of Thales within the main text Zeller instead adopts a quite different and completely incompatible interpretive strategy, but one that is equally problematic in its own way. His new strategy is basically to endorse evidence that seems to point towards a Greek origin for

---

[46] See Kirk, Raven a. Schofield (1983), ch. 2. Like Röth, Kirk, Raven, and Schofield find the account in Aetius and Proclus that Thales visited Egypt plausible (79, 98); hold that he achieved such geometrical feats as measuring the height of the pyramids as a result of living in Egypt and learning the relevant geometrical techniques from the Egyptians (84–86); and argue that the opinion attributed to him by Aristotle that water is the first principle of everything, or that on which everything rests, came from Egypt, where the earth was commonly conceived as a dish resting on water (88–93, 98). Indeed, Kirk, Raven, and Schofield even add some further evidence for Thales' presence in Egypt and for an influence of Egyptian ideas on him that are omitted by Röth, for example arguing that he developed a theory of the cause of the flooding of the Nile that is first reported without attribution by Herodotus and then explicitly attributed to him by Aetius as a result of visiting Egypt (79 f.). On the other hand, Kirk, Raven, and Schofield also contradict or drop certain further arguments for an Egyptian influence on Thales' ideas that are adduced by Röth, but for reasons which seem to me quite questionable: First, unlike Röth, they attribute Thales' predictions of an eclipse and solstices to Babylonian influence instead of to Egyptian (82 f.). But their reason for doing so, namely that the Babylonians are known to have had such information but the Egyptians are not, seems dubious given (a) the possibility of transmission of the information from the Babylonians to the Egyptians and especially (b) the very striking fact that all of the predictions in question concern the *sun*, which was a central object of worship for the Egyptians at the relevant period. Second, unlike Röth, they fail to adduce the reports that Thales had a solar calendar and believed the earth to be a sphere as evidence of Egyptian influence on him. However, there seems little reason to doubt the veracity of those reports, and the argument from them to an Egyptian source for the ideas in question is a strong one.

Thales' ideas but to question evidence that seems to point towards an eastern origin. For example, he endorses the report that Thales held that everything is full of gods, since (as he says) this coheres with antecedent Greek religious conceptions.[47] And he endorses Aristotle's report that Thales identified water as the matter from which everything arises and by which everything is constituted (a position that would place Thales within, albeit at the start of, a Greek cosmological tradition).[48] But he expresses skepticism about Thales' reported astronomical and mathematical achievements,[49] his reported belief in the soul's immortality,[50] and his reported belief, again communicated by Aristotle, that the earth swims on water.[51] However, these judgments have little basis beyond the Eurocentric prejudice that evidently motivates them and are indeed largely perverse. For example, the reports of Thales' astronomical and mathematical achievements, such as his prediction of an eclipse and his measurement of the height of the pyramids, are among the most historically credible that we possess about him. Similarly, there is no really compelling reason to doubt the report in Diogenes Laertius, going back to Choerilus of Iasus in the third or second century B.C. and others, that Thales believed in the soul's immortality. And Zeller's preference for Aristotle's report that Thales identified water as the matter from which everything arises and by which everything is constituted over Aristotle's (at least prima facie) incompatible report that he held that the earth swims on water gets the balance of probability exactly the wrong way round. For the former report looks suspiciously like a typically Whiggish interpretation of Aristotle's resulting from his desire to represent the presocratic philosophers as already anticipating his own concern with first principles (*archai*), whereas his attribution to Thales of a belief that the earth swims on water is unlikely to be due to any such distortion.

Turning now to Pythagoras, Zeller's response to Röth is more self-consistent in this case, amounting to a flat denial of Röth's claims that Pythagoras was influenced by the Egyptians.[52] Zeller's argument against Röth mainly consists of four points: (1) He implies that Röth relies on very late and unreliable ancient sources: "The relationship between Egyptian and Persian doctrines and Greek myths and philosophical ideas that Röth assumes cannot be proved, even if one assumes his explanations, as soon as one denies credence to unreliable au-

---

47 Zeller (1892), 191.
48 Zeller (1892), 186 f., 195.
49 Zeller (1892), 193.
50 Zeller (1892), 193 f.
51 Zeller (1892), 194 f.
52 Zeller (1892), esp. 26, 32 f., 479 f.

thorities. [...] If Iamblichus and Hermes Trimegistos were classical witnesses concerning Egyptian antiquity, then we could delight in the primally ancient documents with which they make us acquainted and the Greek philosophical ideas that they claim to have found in the ancient Egyptian writings."[53] (2) Against Röth's thesis that there is a striking resemblance between the very un-Greek character of Pythagoras's school as an institution and Egyptian priestly institutions, Zeller's main objection is that Pythagoras had no Egyptian-style caste system.[54] (3) Against Röth's thesis that Pythagoras's conception of a soul (in the sense of a mind/self) that is separable from the body, survives death, is subject to judgment in the afterlife, and undergoes transmigration or metempsychosis into animals came from Egypt, Zeller objects (a) that earlier Greeks such as the Orphics and Pherecydes already had such conceptions,[55] and (b) that the ancient Egyptians did not even believe in the soul's metempsychosis into animals.[56] Finally, (4) against Röth's tracing of Pythagoras's knowledge of number-theory and geometry back to Egyptian influence, Zeller objects that the Egyptians had nothing like Pythagoras's number-theory in the sense of his theory that numbers are the fundamental constituents of all reality.[57]

However, this whole argument against Röth's account is again extremely weak. Let us consider each of Zeller's objections in turn. Concerning objection (1), the objection that Röth relies on late, unreliable sources such as Iamblichus and Hermes Trimegistos, Röth basically does no such thing. On the contrary, his account of Pythagoras mainly relies on two early sources that both deserve to be taken seriously as historical evidence: His main authority for the claim that Pythagoras lived in Egypt, learned from the priests there, and transmitted philosophical ideas from there to the Greeks is Isocrates' *Busiris* from the fourth century B.C.,[58] where Isocrates writes: "One might cite many admirable instances of the piety of the Egyptians, that piety which I am neither the first nor the only one to have observed; on the contrary, many contemporaries and predecessors have remarked it, of whom Pythagoras of Samos is one. On a visit to Egypt he became a student of the religion of the people, and was the first to bring to the Greeks all philosophy."[59] And Röth's main authority for his more specific claim that Pythagoras's doctrines concerning the soul came from Egypt is Herodotus from the

---

53 Zeller (1892), 32f.
54 Zeller (1892), 61f., 480.
55 Zeller (1892), 479f.; cf. 65, 117.
56 Zeller (1892), 479f.
57 Zeller (1892), 480.
58 Röth (1858), 264f.
59 Isocrates (1945), 119 (11.28).

fifth century B.C.,⁶⁰ who writes in one passage of certain religious and funerary practices that they are "Egyptian and Pythagorean," and in another passage which almost certainly likewise alludes to Pythagoras: "The Egyptians are the first to have maintained the doctrine that the soul of man is immortal, and that, when the body perishes, it enters another animal that is being born at the time, and when it has been the complete round of the creatures [...] it enters again into the body of a man at birth [...] There are some Greeks who have adopted this doctrine, some in former times, and some in later, as if it were their own invention; their names I know but refrain from writing down."⁶¹

In fairness to Zeller, he does eventually consider these early testimonies, but he dismisses the Isocrates passage on the grounds that it comes from a rhetorical exercise, and the Herodotus passages on the grounds that Herodotus does not assert Pythagoras's presence in Egypt and that his discussion of the doctrine of the soul does not mention Pythagoras but seems instead to be referring to earlier transmitters of the doctrine to the Greeks.⁶² However, these attempts to dismiss the evidence are not at all convincing. Concerning Isocrates, the appropriate reply is that even a competent rhetorical exercise does not just gratuitously lie about basic historical-biographical information that can easily be checked by the intended audience.⁶³ And concerning Herodotus, the mere fact that he fails to say explicitly that Pythagoras was in Egypt does not show that he does not believe it; on the contrary, the two passages just cited arguably imply it. And while he may indeed not be alluding to Pythagoras *exclusively* as a transmitter of Egyptian doctrines about the soul to the Greeks, it at least seems clear that Pythagoras is *among* the people to whom he is alluding. For in another passage he explicitly ascribes a doctrine of the soul's immortality to Pythagoras's supposed slave Zalmoxis, and that Pythagoras also believed in a transmigration of human souls into animals is already attested in a very early fragment by Xenophanes.

Concerning Zeller's objection (2), his objection to Röth's claims of a striking and detailed resemblance between the very un-Greek character of Pythagoras's school as an institution and Egyptian priestly institutions, that Pythagoras had

---

60 Röth (1858), 127.
61 Kirk, Raven a. Schofield (1983), 219–221.
62 Zeller (1892), 304–306.
63 It is perhaps also worth noting that Diogenes Laertius gives a very similar account of Pythagoras's residence in Egypt and learning from the priests there (*Lives of Eminent Philosophers*, VIII.i.2–3). Nor should this account be dismissed as quickly as some of Diogenes' other stories about philosophers can be, for he seems to have been unusually careful in his choice of sources for Pythagoras, for example drawing mainly on the relatively inaccessible and reliable writings of Alexander Polyhistor from the first century B.C. rather than on the large, fanciful, and unreliable neo-Pythagorean literature that had emerged subsequently.

no Egyptian-style caste system, merely to state this objection is almost enough to show how silly it is. For one thing, Röth's point concerned a *whole series* of ways in which Pythagoras's school strikingly departed from Greek precedent and instead resembled the Egyptian priesthood, including the very existence of a religious-philosophical school educating young followers at all, austere hierarchy within it, a sharp separation between an inner and outer circle, strict rules of secrecy, numerous arbitrary-looking rules of diet, dress, and comportment subject to memorization, and the proscription of animal sacrifice, especially the sacrifice of sacred animals.[64] For another thing, the idea of a caste-system played no role at all in Röth's elaborate and convincing case!

Concerning Zeller's objection (3), his twofold objection to Röth's thesis that Pythagoras's conception of a soul (in the sense of a mind/self) that is separable from the body, survives death, is subjected to judgment in the afterlife, and undergoes transmigration or metempsychosis into animals came from Egypt, that (a) earlier Greeks such as the Orphics and Pherecydes already had such conceptions and (b) the ancient Egyptians did not even believe in the soul's metempsychosis into animals, this objection is again very weak. Regarding point (a), Röth *himself* argues that such conceptions were already present in Orphic cult and in Pherecydes even before Pythagoras, but in both cases he traces their presence there back to Egyptian sources, as he does in the case of Pythagoras.[65] Nor does the existence of such indirect Egyptian influences on Pythagoras's conception through Greek predecessors either in Röth's view or in fact exclude the likelihood that he was also influenced by the Egyptians directly. And regarding point (b), two things should be noted: First and foremost, even if Zeller's claim that the Egyptians lacked a doctrine of metempsychosis into animals were correct, one would still need to ask, But what about all the *rest* of Pythagoras's strikingly un-Greek (in particular, un-Homeric) doctrines about the soul and Herodotus's testimony that they came from Egypt? In other words, even if one conceded Zeller's claim, the vast bulk of Röth's thesis would remain quite untouched. Second,

---

64 Zeller makes some competing attempts to explain the character of the Pythagorean school from Greek precedents, such as political clubs. Compare Zeller (1892), 326. But these attempts are quite unconvincing.

65 Röth's fuller position is that certain ancient strands of Greek religion such as Orphic cult and the cult of Dionysus already contained similar conceptions of the soul due to the very early forming influence of Egyptian religion on Greek religion, and that Pythagoras when he returned from Egypt recognized their presence in those strands of traditional religion and therefore attempted to purify them in order to restore them to a purer, Egyptian form (in the process effecting a transformation of mere Orphic cult into Orphism as a religious-philosophical movement). Similarly, Röth implies that Pythagoras became acquainted with such conceptions not only through the Egyptians but also through his teacher Pherecydes.

while Zeller's denial that the doctrine of metempsychosis into animals was a part of the ancient Egyptians' religion may be correct, and is still widely accepted today, due to the lack of independent confirmation that they held it,[66] the denial is not beyond dispute. After all, Herodotus, who was actually there, states unequivocally that the Egyptians held the doctrine and that they were the first to do so.[67] Röth in the light of this testimony hypothesizes that the doctrine was a relatively late innovation in Egyptian religion (though still early enough to have preceded and influenced Greek versions of it).[68] And I would suggest that such traditional Egyptian practices as respecting and embalming sacred animals, depicting certain gods as having partly human and partly animal form (for example, the falcon god Horus and the Sphinx), and representing the departing soul of the dead as a bird make such a late innovation fairly likely. Moreover, even if these practices did *not* lead the Egyptians to any such innovation, they would at least make it easy to explain how Greek thinkers such as Pythagoras and Herodotus *reasonably supposed* that the Egyptians believed in metempsychosis into animals—which would still support the view that Pythagoras's general position on the soul came from Egypt (albeit with this modest element of distortion) and that Herodotus is largely reliable (even if not completely infallible) in his testimony that it did so.

Finally, concerning objection (4), Zeller's objection to Röth's derivation of Pythagoras's knowledge of number-theory and geometry from Egypt, that the Egyptians had no trace of his number-theory in the sense of his theory that numbers are fundamental constituents of the rest of reality, this objection is again obtuse (and indeed in a way very similar to that in which his previous objections were obtuse, namely by disregarding what is essential in Röth's case and instead criticizing what is at best inessential or at worst no part of it at all). First and most importantly, Röth's *fundamental* point here is of course just that Pythagoras's (for his time) strikingly un-Greek strong interest in and knowledge of number-theory and geometry can be plausibly traced back to Egypt, where such interest and knowledge are known to have already been cultivated, not that he borrowed such specific metaphysical doctrines about numbers as the doctrine that they constitute all reality from Egypt. Second, Röth indeed (and moreover with some historical plausibility) *contradicts* the ascription to Pythagoras himself of a doctrine that numbers constitute all reality, instead interpreting his position as one that merely treated numbers as *symbols* of the fundamental constit-

---

66 See Kirk, Raven a. Schofield (1983), 220.
67 See Kirk, Raven a. Schofield (1983), 219f.
68 Röth (1846), 218–220.

uents of reality, and attributing the more ambitious doctrine in question only to later Pythagoreans such as Telauges and Philolaus.[69]

In sum, it seems to me that Zeller completely fails to undermine the credibility of Röth's account that Pythagoras resided in Egypt, studied with the priests there, and drew the main lines of his philosophy from there, and that the account remains extremely plausible.

My general conclusion, therefore, is that when one considers Röth's overall case and Zeller's reply to it carefully, it is hard to resist the assessment that, just as Röth argued, at least two of the earliest and most fundamental pillars of western philosophy, Thales and Pythagoras, lived and learned in Egypt, drawing central features of their philosophies from there, and that Zeller entirely fails to undermine the plausibility of this account. At least to judge the historical question on the strength of this debate, it seems that western philosophy really did have non-western roots.

Let me, though, end this article by qualifying that dramatic assessment just a little. One qualification required here is that since my primary concern in this article has been to explore and adjudicate a certain nineteenth-century debate over the question of the origins of western philosophy rather than to address that question itself, such an assessment must be tentative. Nor do I mean to deny that western philosophy *also* had autochthonous Greek roots, for example roots in Homer. Nor do I mean to deny that the non-western roots involved underwent any changes as they grew into Greek philosophy. For example, one especially important change that occurred resulted from the Greeks' contribution to philosophy of a strong strand of *skepticism* (and also anti-skepticism), a strand that was in certain ways already anticipated by Homer and that was subsequently developed in a wide variety of forms by such thinkers as Xenophanes, Parmenides, Zeno, Protagoras, Gorgias, Socrates, the Pyrrhonists, and the Academic skeptics.

If one would like a vivid illustration of the sort of process that occurred here (and indeed also some significant additional evidence that it did), one might usefully think of the birth of Greek temple architecture and sculpture during the same historical period: It seems quite clear that Pharaonic Egyptian temple architecture and sculpture were the main source of Greek temple architecture and sculpture (this is obvious even to the comparing eye: just compare the religious function, the spatial layout, the materials, the columns, etc. of Pharaonic Egyptian temples with those of the earliest Greek temples; just compare the genre, the general appearance of the body, the rigid frontal stance, the character-

---

[69] Röth (1858), 880–882.

istic one-foot-slightly-before-the-other posture, etc. of Pharaonic Egyptian portrait sculptures with those of the earliest Greek *kouroi* sculptures). But it also clear that between the time of the earliest Greek temples and sculptures from the seventh century B.C. and those from the classical period just two or three centuries later (for example, the Parthenon and its sculptures) a change occurred that turned them into something much more distinctively Greek. Roughly the same thing happened with philosophy.

Bibliography

Geldsetzer (1968): Lutz Geldsetzer, *Die Philosophie der Philosophiegeschichte im 19. Jahrhundert. Zur Wissenschaftstheorie der Philosophiegeschichtsschreibung und -betrachtung*, Meisenheim am Glan: Hein.
Hegel (1986): G.W.F. Hegel, *Berliner Schriften 1818–1831*, in: G.W.F. Hegel, *Werke in zwanzig Bänden*, vol. 11, ed. by E. Moldenhauer and K.M. Michel, Frankfurt a. M.: Suhrkamp.
Hegel (1974): G.W.F. Hegel, *Lectures on the History of Philosophy*, vol. 1, tr. by E.S. Haldane and F.H. Simson, Reprint New York: The Humanities Press.
Isocrates (1945): Isocrates, Busiris, in: Isocrates, vol. 3, with an English translation by Larue van Hook, London: William Heinemann LTD, 100–131.
Kirk, Raven a. Schofield (1983): G.S. Kirk, J.E. Raven and M. Schofield, *The Presocratic Philosophers*, 2nd edition, Cambridge: Cambridge University Press.
Röth (1846): Eduard Maximilian Röth, *Geschichte unserer abendländischen Philosophie. Entwicklungsgeschichte unserer spekulativen, sowohl philosophischen als religiösen Ideen von ihren ersten Anfängen bis auf die Gegenwart*, vol. 1, *Die ältesten Quellen unserer spekulativen Ideen*, Mannheim: Bassermann.
Röth (1858): Eduard Maximilian Röth, *Geschichte unserer abendländischen Philosophie. Entwicklungsgeschichte unserer spekulativen, sowohl philosophischen als religiösen Ideen von ihren ersten Anfängen bis auf die Gegenwart*, vol. 2, *Griechische Philosophie. Die ältesten Jonischen Denker und Pythagoras*, Mannheim: Bassermann.
Zeller (1892): Eduard Zeller, *Die Philosophie der Griechen in ihrer geschichtlichen Entwicklung*, vol. 1,1, *Allgemeine Einleitung. Vorsokratische Philosophie. Erste Hälfte*, 5th edition, Leipzig: Reisland.

Andreas Urs Sommer
The History of Philosophy as Counter-History: Strategies of Philosophico-Historiographical Dissidence[1]

Our image of the philosophical historiography of the 19th century is dominated by multi-volume, monumental works penned by philosophy professors—monumental works which consider philosophy as a region of fully independent reflection, decoupled from both the history of the sciences as well as from general history. To put it in a somewhat exaggerated way, in these works philosophy appears to be a fully sovereign sphere of the highest reflectivity, concerned exclusively with its own fully independent problems, whose solutions then retroactively impact the course of scientific and general history inasmuch as these solutions are formative of a world-picture ("Weltanschauung"). In the face of these monumental works one easily loses sight of not only the detailed and highly specialized research exploring countless philosophical-historical themes in the the 19th century, research that has set the standard in many fields up to today. At times we lose also sight of those examinations of the history of philosophy that are neither prepared to consider philosophy as detached from all other forms of history nor to see it as treating absolutely autonomous problems in a space of the most sacred seclusion. When I speak in the following of philosophico-historiographical dissidence, I have the latter forms of philosophical historiography in mind. The dissidence or the refusal concerns the isolationism of the dominant form of philosophical historiography, an isolationism which comprises both the understanding of philosophy itself as well as of its history. The discussion below gives three examples of such a dissidence, examples that offer different views of what constitutes philosophy and what constitutes the history of philosophy. Such dissidence often refers itself to the philosophical model of interpretation according to which the history of philosophy is typically constructed as *a history*—and especially to the interpretative model of continuity, development, progress. Dissident philosophical historiography can also be practiced where the respective writer does not understand himself primarily (or at all) as a historian of philosophy or a philosopher. In the following I will thus seek dissident philosophical historiography particularly where it does not explicitly

---

[1] I want to thank Mr Daniel Unger and Ms Julia Maas for the critical review of the German version of this manuscript.

present itself as philosophical history. Dissidence means then not only the refusal to agree with the prevailing models but also a saying otherwise. Dissidence means to emphasize something that is hidden in what currently prevails. Dissident philosophical historiography brings to light alternatives for thinking. This is true especially when this philosophical historiography is pursued quasi-left-handedly, by non-philosophers who do not aspire to be historians of philosophy in the first place.

I Discontinuity and the "purely historical view"

On the 7th of June 1870 Franz Overbeck (1837–1905) held his inaugural lecture at Basel University as the newly appointed Professor for the New Testament and Early Church History. On the 23rd of May Overbeck had let his friend the historian Heinrich von Treitschke know that:

> As much as I would have wished to avoid this work [i.e. the inaugural lecture], still it is of great concern to me, since I would like it to serve me in making my position in the local theological and ecclesiastical entanglements clear. My specialized colleagues have all welcomed me very courteously, there is a will to happy consensus almost everywhere, and only a few of them have such a radically different standpoint that no real understanding is to be expected. Another not so pleasant yet unavoidable duty of my local position is to support the local reform association, although for the moment my unfamiliarity with local circumstances will enable to keep it from too much intrusiveness.[2]

Overbeck probably already succeeded in warding off such "intrusiveness" with his inaugural lecture. He embraced a "purely historical view of New Testament writings" in his lecture, without of course—as conciliation had to be made—granting to this approach the *sole* right to exist in theology. And although three years later in his polemic *Concerning the Christianity of Our Current Theology* (1873) Overbeck is inclined to call the disposition to theology into question in principle and to see the contrast between faith and reason as irrevocable, in his inaugural lecture a compromise appeared to be still possible—but not a compromise, of course, that would hamper or diminish purely scientific historical analysis.

The radicalization to which the *Christianity of our Current Theology* testifies is also essentially owed to discussions with a colleague seven years younger with whom Overbeck was to come into contact only after his inaugural lecture and subsequently developed and fostered a lifelong friendship with him. This collea-

---

2 Overbeck (2008), 44.

gue was Professor for Classical Philology in Basel since 1869 and was called Friedrich Nietzsche.

The inaugural lecture *Concerning the Origination and Right of a Pure Historical View of New Testament Writings in Theology* runs through the history of theology from the 2nd century up to the 19th century with the question of if, when, why and how a genuine historical interest in the New Testament had arisen. The findings remain largely negative with the exception of the most recent past. The first sentence explains what Overbeck understands by a "purely historical view": one "resting on no other presupposition than that of general historical-scientific investigation".[3] This first sentence makes it unmistakeably clear that for Overbeck the method of profane historiography is self-evident without restriction and that no dogmatic or religious regard is to be applied to the subjects of church history. For Overbeck the "purely historical view" is not to be made coincide with a specific theological view which asserts the autonomy and inherent lawfulness of ecclesiastical history and which thinks, for example, that it can read the influence of God on the constituent facts of church history.

This brings me at last to the question of why I take the reflective work of a church historian on his profession to be a substantial contribution to a dissident philosophical historiography. The implicit repudiation of all philosophical-historical speculation is even more striking than the implicit delimitation of the modern heritage as against the ancient *historia sacra*. This is worth noting because later in the lecture Ferdinand Christian Baur is not only strongly indicated as being the real founder of a "purely historical" approach, but also because in other places Overbeck looks back at his first academic steps as "a stout, even arrogant Tübinger"[4], therewith characterizing himself as one of Baur's followers, despite his neither having studied in Tübingen nor having personally met Baur. Baur stands not only for a programme of "characterizing Christianity purely historically, as it actually was",[5] but also for understanding this history philosophically or, more accurately, understanding it with the help of the Hegelian philosophy of history as a dialectical occurrence, as the historically unfolding mediation of contraries and thus as a continually developing unity. This historical-philosophical perspective remained "[t]otally alien" to Overbeck, as he later admitted.[6] The opening of his inaugural lecture confirms this retrospective self-evaluation for his proposed procedure is "purely historical" not only in its religious-dogmatic abstinence but also in its philosophical-metaphysical absti-

---

3 Overbeck (1871), 3.
4 Overbeck (1903), 3.
5 Overbeck (1903), 4.
6 Overbeck (1903), 3.

nence. "Purely historically" means essentially free from historical-philosophical prejudices and free from endeavouring to see overarching, universal laws running through the course of history. Without referring directly to Baur, Overbeck takes the demand for a purely historical view seriously and sees the history of Christianity in the light of this in that he discards the philosophical-speculative model of history as the inheritance of the ancient providential *historia sacra* and allows nothing beyond the merely factual knowledge which goes beyond the function of providing orientation.

Overbeck wants to show "[w]ith a brief historical overview" (which actually constitutes the main part of the lecture) that the "task" of a "purely historical view" of theology was "not pushed forward through the accidental scepticism of the few" but "rather [it], so to speak, unfolded through the centuries", such that "theology cannot be taken otherwise".[7] In other words Overbeck postulates a kind of developmental-historical necessity which acts with Baur's adaption of the speculative-universalistic philosophy of history to ecclesiastical historiography in the background as a kind of residual Hegelianism. At any rate, on this model history is totally dissimilar to that which Overbeck's secret philosophical informant, Arthur Schopenhauer, was inclined towards, namely, a succession of circumstances in which there was no higher order to be seen, such that no science of history is possible.[8] In this lecture Overbeck seems not to have abandoned the thought of development and seems to be inclined to see, in the flow of historical appearances, a constant lawfulness, without of course this lawfulness being specified beyond the postulated *Factum* that theology arrived at a "purely historical" manner of consideration through an inner necessity. Whether the suggestion of such a necessity actually accords with Overbeck's own persuasions or whether he stated it with the strategic purpose in mind of making his interest in a "purely historical view" palatable to the public, remains an open question. However, the history that he narrates in the passages that follow testify to the exact opposite of historical inevitability, such that theologians have for a long time successfully avoided a "purely historical view".

During the introduction into the historical narrative Overbeck reminds us that the lament about lost origins and the original innocence in Christianity was always prevalent and that one can recognize the core of a historical consciousness therein. The consciousness "that our knowledge of Christendom appeals to tradition [and that] this tradition is itself subject to changes in time" was never wholly lost. However, "this consciousness [has] only existed in the greatest

---

7 Overbeck (1871), 4.
8 See § 38 "Ueber Geschichte" in Schopenhauer (1977), 516–525.

obscurity up until the present".⁹ And bringing these considerations together, the following conclusion suggests itself: it is not only the tradition that is subject to historical processes of transformation but origins themselves can only to be understood as products of a very specific time. The "purely historical examination" of the "historical essence of Christendom" will later lead Overbeck to the insight that this essence is an antiquated relic that cannot in any way be normative for the present. For us the transfer of Overbeck's view to the theory and praxis of philosophical historiography follows easily. For in what is considered classical or ancient philosophy we are, perhaps, not so much dealing with normative origins as with historically contingent formations of thinking whose binding power for the philosophy of the present is, if anything, loose?

Overbeck's historical narrative in the inaugural lecture begins at the end of the second century when the understanding of the original Christian world is already extinct: "One [then] lives in a world that is thought wholly differently and one places the concepts of an entirely different formative sphere into that of early Christianity."¹⁰ Clemens of Alexandria in particular here becomes determinative for Christian theology. With him the writings of Plato won a meaning equivalent to the Biblical texts in the search for true knowledge. Accordingly it is incredible to him "that the Apostle Paul despised the philosophy of the Greeks. That he had even warned against it is something Clemens is unable to acknowledge. If the Apostle did this nonetheless, [then for Clemens] he can only mean a certain philosophy, [or] certain reprehensible systems, such as that of the Epicureans."¹¹ It is instructive that Overbeck sees the total deficiency of historical consciousness in Clemens (which is then propagated by Origenes) as rooted in the amalgamation of Christianity with Platonism. For it is precisely the Alexandrian synthesis of religion and philosophy that he regards as incapable of legitimation in terms of the "historical essence of Christendom". This fundamental distinction between the (original) Christian and the Platonic-philosophical shows Overbeck's implicit hostility towards the philosophical-theological attempts at reconciliation, such as those of German idealism, which had been cultivated by Hegel and Baur and which still essentially defined reflective theology right up to Overbeck's time. Baur's famous book *Die Christliche Gnosis* [The Christian Gnosis] not only deals in detail with Clemens but also pays tribute to his religious-philosophical synthesis¹² which, as little as Clemens and his anti-gnostic comrades were able to "consider the relevant question of relationship of heathenism, Judaism

---

9 Overbeck (1871), 5.
10 Overbeck (1871), 8 f.
11 Overbeck (1871), 9.
12 Baur (1835), 488–543.

and Christendom [...] in its true speculative meaning".[13] According to Baur this true speculative meaning had been first granted with modern philosophy of religion, whose summit was reached with Hegel.[14] Thus, for Overbeck's self-chosen teacher Baur, the problem of the history of Christendom lay principally in the as yet insufficient dialectical mediation of Judaism and heathenism, a mediation which could only be accomplished in the present thus allowing this history of Christendom to be interpreted as a positive developmental process, as a progress. In Overbeck's inaugural lecture, however, the pre-dominant thought is that of a straying from the spirit of the beginning. Dialectical mediations and positive historical syntheses do not occur in Overbeck's narrative and the adaption to the situations and needs of the current environment and the current situation steps into its place. Thus, because Clemens' public thought in a Greek-philosophical manner, one had to make Christendom popular by using a Platonic garb and because this public held the capacity to act in high esteem one had to make Paul's rejection of free will disappear in the exegesis of the Biblical texts. Overbeck thus maintains the basic difference between Platonism and original Christendom, a difference that speculative philosophy and the historiography of theology in the 19th century tended to sublate. Overbeck refuses to play these dialectic games. In his inaugural lecture he conceals Baur's endeavours in this direction. And later, when looking back at the dialectic, Overbeck mimics incomprehension. He shows *en passant* the incompatibility of philosophy and Christendom—which is not to say that he directly maintains this incompatibility but rather he represents all attempts at synthesizing the heterogeneously existing traditions from the second century on as unable to do justice to the "historical essence of Christendom".

We will now turn from the wider errors and confusions of the history of Christendom and speak instead of the problem of Biblical accounts of miracles which the inaugural lecture deals with towards the end. After Overbeck, this problem was to win a catalytic function for the development of the historical interest in theology, because miracles, as a first irritating element, drew attention to the other peculiarities of Biblical writings, enabling the knowledge that

> the historical facts of evangelical and apostolic history are not, in any individual book of the New Testament, printed in plain immediacy, but in each case the facts are already placed within a definite perspective by the author of each individual book.[15]

---

13 Baur (1835), 542.
14 Baur (1835), 668–735.
15 Overbeck (1871), 25.

Overbeck thus in no way takes the New Testament writings to be mere decolomania of original Christian realities but as already interpretations, such that the modern discussion of them turns above all on "the *degree* to which one wants to concede that the medium of the narrative has a modifying influence on the facts of the matter."[16] To today's readers of Overbeck, this attention to the literary workmanship of the text in question seems to provide an important pointer towards another kind of philosophical historiography. In this the history of philosophy has to do with texts first of all and only secondly with thoughts— and as such its primary, if not its exclusive, attention is to be applied to the specificity of these texts. The notion that we can directly grasp the underlying thoughts is a naïve idea that the pre-critical church historiography shares with long dominant forms of philosophical historiography.

In contrast to Baur's dialectical model, in Overbeck history proves itself to be a *discontinuous process* in which, although many moments reoccur, there is much that simply cannot be sublated. When, as Overbeck writes, the origins of Christendom have "become our past",[17] it is only a small step to the subsequent conclusion that these origins are no longer of concern to the present and, as purely historical, have forfeited every normative power. The "purely historical view" can thus become a strategy for a radical apathetization.

In 1871 Overbeck does not follow this course through to the end but still grants theology a mediating role between faith and knowledge. This task of mediation is itself "highly changeable"[18] and determined by the contingencies of the respective situation. Considered purely historically, theology too is a wholly historical essence, without a supernal binding power or an inalienable core. Theology is always only a momentary and a situational balance of the antagonistic tendencies of faith and knowledge. Theology is contingent. And when transferred to philosophy, the verdict of contingency is close also at hand. When Overbeck speaks of "Biblical critique as in part sublating [*aufhebenden*] the influence [*Geltung*] of the past",[19] one would question which "influence" this critique can allow to survive. Which aspect is not sublated? And who determines influence and sublation? Sublation has lost its Hegelian multi-dimensionality here: it only indicates losses and discontinuities. Overbeck's "purely historical view" is a school of sobriety, even of an anti-speculative and anti-dogmatic sobering up. And Overbeck's objections to the previous historical approaches to Christian origins can be transferred alarmingly easily to a philosophical historiography

---

16 Overbeck (1871), 26.
17 Overbeck (1871), 30.
18 Overbeck (1871), 32.
19 Overbeck (1871), 34.

which tends to dogmatism, an obsession with origins and a speculative-dialectical retouching of discontinuities. A dissident historiography of philosophy, according to Overbeck's scientific model, would have to be purely scientific—not, of course, that Overbeck ever wanted to dictate a model to philosophy or its historiography.

Generally speaking, Biblical exegesis is hardly in suspicion of being a leading discipline of science as, because of its dogmatic biases, we are not accustomed to expect any methodological-historical innovations on its part. However when its dogmatic biases are dispensed with, as in Franz Overbeck's work, intellectual powers are released and their findings can spread to other regions. Overbeck's handling of the discontinuities of history, his refusal to submit its course to a historical-philosophical schema, his attention to the necessary textuality of intellectual traditions and his critical distancing from allegedly normative origins (in which he is far superior to his friend Nietzsche who in his inaugural lecture on Homer as well as in *Geburt der Tragödie* [The Birth of Tragedy] 1872 pays tribute to a cult of normative origins) can also inspire other areas of historiography, particularly philosophical historiography. The normative orientation of the dominant German philosophical historiography in the 19th century seems, grossly oversimplified, to have been acquainted with two directions for inquiry: either one directed oneself towards the normative origins of philosophical thinking, to figures who were considered unsurpassed such as Socrates, Plato and Aristotle (or Thomas Aquinas in the neo-Scholastic variation) or one directed oneself towards thinking's development, which development is conceptualized as continuous or as dialectically fractured. In his discipline, Overbeck renounces both of these possibilities. Above all he challenges the philosophical model (that is the Hegelian model in particular in its various stages of atrophy) which had spread widely to the different fields of historiography. Accordingly, the Hegelianized method of philosophical history ceased to be normative for the scientific historiography. Philosophical history lost its interpretative power regarding other areas of history, if it ever had it. When one transfers this Overbeckian renunciation from the area of ecclesiastical historiography to philosophical historiography, this latter is strongly advised to give up its philosophical fixation upon normative origins or upon historical development and to sober itself up.

II Philosophy as communicative event

In 1880 a volume was published with the title *Menschen des XVIII. Jahrhunderts nach den Causeries du Lundi* by a publisher almost exclusively concerned with Antisemitica, Ernst Schmeitzner in Chemnitz. The author was named (although without mentioning his first name) as Charles-Augustin Sainte-Beuve (1804–1869); information about the editor and translator was missing from the title page as well as from the text and nor was there an introduction, a preface, or any explanation of the translations or the choice of the texts. It is worth noting that this was the first ever German translation of a selection from Sainte-Beuve's chief work of literary criticism, a book that appeared a decade after his death. It consisted of writings which had regularly appeared since 1849 on Mondays in the daily Paris press as the *Causeries du lundi* and which sought to bring into view of the newspaper reading public the richness of world literature, and French literature in particular, in an enjoyable and at the same time discerning way. The enormous resonance of the *Causeries*, soon to be available in book form, made Sainte-Beuve the most influential literary critic of his century, one whose judgments claimed a canonical status while at the same time not failing to be regarded with suspicion. The volume *Menschen des XVIII. Jahrhunderts* assembles a series of such literary critical portraits from the *siècle des lumières*.[20] The unnamed translator is Ida Overbeck, nee Rothpletz (1848–1933), Franz Overbeck's wife. The translation had been suggested by a friend of the couple, Friedrich Nietzsche. He had also directly influenced the choice of texts: "in the end was it not best to leave out M. Chamfort? The article in question was probably not a masterpiece; perhaps you are considering whether Fontenelle fits in with your 'Persons of the 18th century'?", Nietzsche asked Ida Overbeck in his letter of the 5th November 1879.[21] Nietzsche also initiated contact with the publisher who was, at that time, also his own: "I let slip a few words to Schmeitzner concerning the St. Beuve translation and he took them up with great joy."[22] And on the 18th November 1879 Nietzsche wrote to the publisher saying:

> Dearest Sir, the Sainte-Beuve translation is finished: do you want to contact Mr.Prof. Overbeck on account of it? (Mrs. Prof. Overbeck desperately wants to remain out of play, so please, act as if you knew nothing of her participation.) As the title perhaps: '*Sainte Beuve. Personalities of the 18th century.* The first German translation.' There are 8 personalities; it is a nice *little* volume to get your teeth into).[23]

And when the volume became available, Nietzsche wrote enthusiastically to Ida Overbeck:

---

20 Compare Sainte-Beuve (1880) and Sainte-Beuve (2014).
21 Nietzsche (2003a), 461, Nietzsche to Ida Overbeck, 5.11.1879.
22 Nietzsche (2003a), 456, Nietzsche to Franz Overbeck, 22.10.1879.
23 Nietzsche (2003a), 465, Nietzsche to Ernst Schmeitzner, 18.11.1879.

> One hour ago, dear Frau Professor, I received the 'Personalities of the 18th Century', I browsed therein and saw this and that good word and behind every good word so *much, much more!* It captivated me and at the same time I was captured by the feeling of a deep inexpressible *privation*. I feel I have wept, and it would be strange if this excellent little book did not arouse in many others such a sensation.[24]

The hope for bookselling success would not be fulfilled. Schmeitzner was not the right man to position it on the market and to secure the necessary attention. To this day the original print is only available in a few libraries; a new edition was just recently published together with the first edition of Ida Overbeck's diaries (Sainte-Beuve 2014).

What has all this to do with the historiography of philosophy, even in its dissident variety? Certainly, Sainte-Beuve's studies of the prominent personalities and constellations of personalities in the *siècle des lumières* give a deep insight into the world of the Enlightenment in its "customs", in its "pleasures",[25] but also in its virtues, to speak with that vehement opponent of Sainte-Beuve, Marcel Proust. Certainly, Sainte-Beuve succeeds at the same time in summarizing the forms of life, thinking and writing of an intellectual elite and in making the personages vividly clear in their respective individual peculiarities: Fontenelle, Montesquieu, Mme de Grafigny and Voltaire, Mme du Châtelet, Mme Latour-Franqueville and Rousseau, Diderot, Vauvenargues, Mlle de Lespinasse and Beaumarchais, to whom Ida Overbeck's selection is devoted, are depicted as very different characters. At the same time these profiles show how the bourgeois Parisian literary business had fitted a by-gone epoch into their own order of values and adjusted it to their own needs—a process that would later drive Nietzsche in his *Götzen-Dämmerung* [Twilight of the Idols] (1888)[26] as well Marcel Proust alike into a rage because they both sought to distance themselves from this order of values. However, what does all this yield for the understanding of the history of philosophy? Is the interest in Sainte-Beuve, be it as a reader, as a translator or as editor, more than a bourgeois amusement, analogous to house music and a visit to the pub?

There is nothing wrong with house music and visits to the pub, but I am not primarily interested in the entertainment factor of Sainte-Beuves *Causeries*

---

24 Nietzsche (2003b), 35, Nietzsche to Ida Overbeck, 18. 8.1880.
25 Proust thinks that Sainte-Beuve's "method consists in not separating the person from the work", thus completely by-passing the reality of artistic creation: "this method fails to recognize what a little deeper dealing with ourselves teaches: that a book is created a different I to the one which is allowed to come to light in our habits, in society and in our vices". Proust (1962), 14.
26 For details see Sommer (2012a), 407–412.

which, as opposed to, for example, Friedrich Ueberwegs *Grundriß der Geschichte der Philosophie*, was certainly borne *ab ovo* by the powers conferred onto literary criticism by Horace's *prodesse et delectare:* Monday's literary reflections should be useful as well as entertaining. The selection, probably made in joint discussions between the Overbecks and Nietzsche, is much more than entertaining and opening not only on to a temporal but also on to a thematic horizon: it focuses far more strongly on the thought rather than the literary compositions of the French Enlightenment. It is clearly concerned with bringing the German public closer to this thinking in all its diversity through its most outstanding representatives and it does this not through a conventional philosophical-historical doxography but practically through personal records. This publication was paralleled by the printing, also by Schmeitzner, of *Menschliches, Allzumenschliches* [Human, all too Human] in 1878—a work to whose title page Nietzsche had affixed the highly visible dedication: "In memory of Voltaire / dedicated to the remembrance of his death / 23rd May 1778".[27] Nietzsche's next two works too, both *Vermischte Meinungen und Sprüche* [Miscellaneous Opinions and Maxims] (1879) as well as *Der Wanderer und sein Schatten* [The Wanderer and his Shadow] (1880), conceived of as supplements and appendages to *Menschliches, Allzumenschliches*, further develop the Enlightenment idea of a free spirit.

Ever since Marcel Proust (see note 24) the accusation has haunted those who have not read Sainte-Beuve that he reduces literary works to the biography of their author. But if one looks at his *Menschen des XVIII. Jahrhunderts* such a remonstrance could hardly be more drastically amiss. It rejects literary-historical biographism as consistently as it does philosophical-historical biographism. The underlying historiographical model is rather a form of history of communications. Sainte-Beuve is interested in the practicalities of exchange and in how literary-philosophical works may have originated out of these practicalities— and in how the new and the unheard emerged. In contrast to overarching philosophical interpretative schemata and particularly in contrast to the speculative-universalistic philosophy of history developed in the Enlightenment, Sainte-Beuve maintains a noble abstinence and does not push the many individual histories of the century of the Enlightenment into a developmental and progressive framework but largely leaves the sources in their own right. True, he is concerned with the life of his protagonists, but still only insofar as this shows something individual and at the same time exemplary—something that pushes towards a specific work. One can say that Sainte-Beuve is interested in the philosophical form of life of the proponents of the Enlightenment—and this is according to

---

27 Nietzsche (1878). The later editions remove this prominent dedication from the title page.

him also something exemplary for the present. Particularly striking are the passages where he deals with Salon culture, to which he accords central significance in the emergence of the new Enlightenment.

With the *Causeries* Sainte-Beuve devised a new medium on the one hand for the presentation of thinking and on the other for its formation. The texts selected for the *Menschen des XVIII. Jahrhunderts* convey this thinking itself as the eminent formative power which progressively managed to revolutionize society from its roots up. Enlightenment thinking in Sainte-Beuve's portraits thereby found wholly different forms and fields of activity—and it itself becomes different through these forms and fields of activity. Sainte-Beuve shows how philosophy—taken in the widest sense of the 18th century—won an interpretative sovereignty over the understanding of life and world among the upper bourgeoisie and the nobility and he showed that philosophy knew how to employ different media. Two examples: the salons and with them the *Salonnières*, as depicted by Sainte-Beuve, are revealed to be an crucial aspect of philosophical culture. The salons acted as a melting pot for utterly different thoughts, and *Salonnières* such as for example Julie de Lespinasse managed, at times masterfully, to amalgamate different intellectual temperaments and ideas. Significant literary-philosophical works from the *siècle des lumières* owe their origination and their character to the salons, whose inspirations they worked through.

The second example of the new philosophical virtuosity with media is the experimentation with the form of the aphorism, which is rendered vividly in Ida Overbeck's translation, especially in the penetrating portrait of the Marquis de Vauvenargues. Under the conditions of censorship, Vauvenargues practiced a radically insinuating, brief writing that is on the one hand based on formal requirements of a La Rouchefoucauld, but on the other overcomes his radical pessimism.

Sainte-Beuves *Causeries* are themselves a means—a means of shaping the world in thought. The newspaper article on literature takes the place of the salons as a still unknown medium for intellectuals—it inspires thinking by pleading for agreement, by defying antagonism or by provoking further reflective work. In their regular appearance on Mondays the *Causeries* contribute to an unexpectedly revolutionary course. For the emergence of the newspaper industry in the 19th century addressed a wholly new strata of readers. Sainte-Beuve had seized upon the press so as to attain his purpose, namely the dissemination and democratization of literary-philosophical high culture.[28] And in this high culture was at the

---

28 Sainte-Beuve did not abstain, however, from recasting his ephemeral newspaper articles in

same time transformed—the salon is open to anyone who wanted to participate in it. One can understand this as a Socratism transposed to modernity: after high culture and philosophy had been enclosed for two and a half thousand years in a kind of refuge in the academy[29] and had thus fostered their own elite status, Sainte-Beuve made higher education accessible for all. And what philosophy is and can be changes with this; and that is why the history of philosophy too should not be confined to the mere reproduction of systems of thought and theories. The history of philosophy must also change as philosophy changes. Philosophy does not seek other media simply as a means of expression, so as to be able to cope with a more diverse world. Rather philosophy itself changes through its means of expression, it changes its form and with this its circle of addressees and producers. The philosophy that crystallized in the salons as a competitive performance and as an *agon* of spirits is something fundamentally different to the philosophy of a *persona*, of an individual mask in a solitary study, as exemplified in Descartes' setting in the *Meditationes*. Descartes could still imagine away the world of others and the world in general. Sainte-Beuve on the other hand is driven by the salon genesis of the spirit because it is there that the interaction, the non-isolation and the inability to be isolated of persons, of thinking individuals is located. The *Causeries* want to salvage the communicative situation of the salons for the world of the 19th century.

One result of Sainte-Beuve's efforts in the history of thought, considered as a dissident philosophical historiographical achievement, is that it shows philosophy to its advantage in all its diversity. Philosophy is the Proteus of thought; it is the master of transformation *par excellence*, it can serve a variety of mediums and is itself the medium of various different discourses. The formative power of philosophy is won only by those who let themselves play in different fields —who grant to her an abundance of resources for expression and thinking. If one takes Sainte-Beuve's *Causeries* of the 18th century as the product of a man who was in no way a 'professional philosopher' (actually Sainte-Beuve was a physician by formation!) and as testimony to a dissident philosophical historiography, one thus turns from a limited and limiting understanding of philosophy. Dissident philosophical historiography can try to be seen otherwise than as philosophy's street-scavenging sister. This was also done in the philosopher of whose portrait in the *Causeries* Wolf Lepenies remarked Sainte-Beuve really "talks in full flow about himself".[30] It is Denis Diderot to whom Sainte-Beuve feels clos-

---

the form of a book and from allowing his *Causeries* to appear in that classical genre oriented towards bourgeois edification.
29 On this question generally see Mirelli (2013).
30 Lepenies (2006), 142.

est, the philosopher who refuses all determination. His portrait stands right at the centre of Ida Overbeck's *Menschen des XVIII. Jahrhunderts* and forms the heart of the translation.

It is characteristic that Nietzsche, at the time when he dedicated a book to Voltaire, in no way wished Ida Overbeck to translate Sainte-Beuve's countless *Causeries* of contemporary writers or even those from the 19th century generally, or those of the putatively elegant 17th century which was taken just as classical by Sainte-Beuve as by the Nietzsche of the 1880s. The French Enlightenment should be the sole subject of the book, according to the judgment of the initiators of the German edition, because the German public patently lacked knowledge of the French Enlightenment, not least as a consequence of the disparaging handling of this topic in the monumental works of 19th century German historiography. It is not absurd to assume that Nietzsche, with appearance of the Sainte-Beuve volume in his own publishing house, wanted to prepare the reader hitherto prejudiced against the French Enlightenment for his own radical free thinking. Over and above that, the edition of a book from the pen of one of the most important French intellectuals concerning the zenith of French culture is an unmistakeable cultural-political message. The thinking of the Enlightenment and the thinking of a traditional foe is of all things recommended as a serious alternative to the Prussian dominated *Reichskultur*. A transcultural perspective is inescapable and it is particularly directed against the Germanocentricism of 19th century German academic philosophical historiography, which gives the impression that the Germans were the only worthy successors to the Greeks and which also regards the French philosophy of the Enlightenment with suspicion. One's own Germanocentric view was consciously first alienated and then honed through the contrasting French view of the French Enlightenment. Here too a philosophico-historiographical dissidence is intended—but in this case not by the author but by the initiators of a translation.

III Agonal philosophical history

Nietzsche made his antipathy to traditional historians of philosophy clear in his eulogy to Arthur Schopenhauer:

> for the genius, which pure and with love, like the poet, looks at things and cannot go sufficiently deeply into them, the rummaging in countless strange and preposterous opinions

is as the most adverse and inopportune business [...]. The scholarly history of the past was never the business of a true philosopher.[31]

The products of these professorial historians of philosophy do not even fulfil the most elementary requirements of a "philologist", because

> they are poorly made, without scientific rigor and for the most part written with a hateful boredom. Who saves, for example, the history of the Greek philosophers from the soporific vapours which the learned though all-too-unscientific and unfortunately altogether boring works of Ritter, Brandis and Zeller have spread about it?[32]

The real argument against the history of philosophy is one that is well-known:

> What is the history of philosophy to our youth? Should they be discouraged from having opinions by the entangled confusion of opinions? Should they be taught to join in the jubilation about how we have progressed so wonderfully far? Should they even learn to hate or despise philosophy? [...] The only criticism of a philosophy that is possible and that also proves something, namely, to try to see whether one can live by it, has never been taught in universities, which is instead the constant criticism of words about words.[33]

With this last point in his assault on the popular history of philosophy he names the criterion or, better, the point of reference towards which he gravitates in his otherwise just sporadic reflections on the history of philosophy: life. To render what was just said into a philosophical historiographical concept, one would have to imagine the philosophical historian as a researcher doing field work, administering more or less concentrated doses of different philosophies to more or less unsuspecting subjects so as to check their suitability for or their lethality to life.

The keyword "life", by which every philosophy is to be measured and which is also supposed to preface philosophical historiography, represents the counterpart to Sainte-Beuve's attempt in *Menschen des XVIII. Jahrhunderts* to depict the power of philosophy to shape the world and itself. This power was only depicted by Sainte-Beuve, modestly posing as a historian and not as a philosopher, in its being carried and he himself did not preach it. In his choice of means Sainte-Beuve is a virtuoso or thoroughly modern in that he cleverly uses the contemporary press, defamed by Nietzsche in the aftermath of Schopenhauer, instrumentally for his own purposes. On the other hand the professor from Basel himself indulged in very awkward polemics against journalists as "servants of the mo-

---

31 Nietzsche (1999b), 416.
32 Nietzsche (1999b), 417.
33 Nietzsche (1999b), 417.

ment" who had replaced "the greatest genius, the leader for all time, the redeemer of the moment".[34] In a supposedly untimely manner Nietzsche—with the exception of two open letters on behalf of Wagner and on his own behalf—uses exclusively the medium of books, thus regressing in terms of medial development, which initially seemed to condemn him to remain without an echo because his books were so little received by his contemporaries.[35] However these books are not books in the traditional style.[36] Inscribed therein are medial developments of the 18th and 19th century—the aphorism of the 18th century, the brief observation so common in periodical literature of the 19th century. With this Nietzsche very consciously, not always successfully, sought to influence his own public perception in his favour.

In Nietzsche's explicit reflections on the history of philosophy the demand for orientation towards life surfaces again and again. However despite the keyword remaining the same, there are remarkable underlying shifts. He wrote to Lou von Salomé, probably on the 16th of September 1882:

> My dearest Lou, your thought of a reduction of philosophical systems to the personal records of their originators is really a thought from the 'sibling-brain': in Basel I myself have narrated the history of ancient philosophy in *this* sense and liked to say to my listeners: 'this system is refuted and dead—but the *person* behind it is irrefutable, the person cannot die—Plato, for example.[37]

Nietzsche then took up this idea in 1886 in the sixth section of *Jenseits von Gut und Böse* [Beyond Good and Evil], where he ignores the critical point against systematic thinking and instead puts the determination of every philosophy by drive at the centre:

> Little by little it has become clear to me what every great philosophy hitherto has been: namely the confession of its originator and a kind of unwanted and surreptious *mémoires*; just as the moralistic (or immoralistic) intentions in every philosophy each time constitute the real seed of life from out of which the whole plant grew. I thus do not believe that a 'drive to knowledge' is the father of philosophy, but rather that another drive, here and elsewhere, has utilised knowledge [*Erkenntniss*] (and pseudo-knowledge [*Verkenntniss*]) merely as a tool.[38]

---

34 Nietzsche (1999a), 671.
35 Nevertheless there were a surprising large number of contemporary discussions although they do not seem to have been of benefit to the sales of Nietzsche's books. Compare Reich (2013).
36 Compare Sommer (2009).
37 Nietzsche (2003b), 259.
38 Nietzsche (1999c), 19 f.

While in his 'Schopenhauer as Educator' from *Unzeitgemässen Betrachtung* [Untimely Meditations] of 1874, Nietzsche, in a manner reminiscent of traditional antiquity, recollects the relevance of philosophy in determining life and wants to measure all philosophy by whether it is good for life, twelve years later he opts for the contrary perspective. Life—condensed into the concept of drive, which remains nebulous throughout section six of *Jenseits von Gut und Böse*—takes shape in particular philosophies according to the type of life the respective philosopher leads. At this point, it is no longer about philosophy determining life but rather about philosophy's being determined by life. If one renders this proposition into a philosophico-historiographical concept, the philosophical historian would be busy identifying the dominant drive behind every philosophy (for there seem to be different possibilities) and so showing which drives bring about which philosophies. How such a programme of dissident philosophical historiography can be transferred to concrete research praxis remains an open question—as does the question as to whether such a research praxis could even be realized in the first place. For how does one pin down 'drives' if research only has their alleged products (philosophies and philosophical personalities) as the objects of its research? Must not such a philosophical historiography necessarily remain hypothetical as it does not itself disclose underlying drives but can only ever posit them?

We stand on firmer ground when, instead of accompanying Nietzsche and his hypothesis of formation by drives, we speak with Lou von Salomé and, by way of conclusion, throw a glance at Nietzsche's own 'personal-records' as 'originator' of a philosophy. In doing so we are only interested in how he dealt with philosophico-historical materials and philosophico-historical findings. The answer is simple: the way philosopher dealt with the thought of the past and academic researchers concerned with thought of the past was predatory through and through. We need only remember, for example, *Schopenhauer als Erzieher* where he pours caustic sarcasm on Eduard Zeller and other heavyweights in the historiography of ancient philosophy. Nevertheless Nietzsche helped himself, unscrupulously and without any references to these sources so as to provide historical nourishment for his philosophical ideas (today this would cost any Minister his office on account of 'plagiarism'). Another example is Nietzsche's so highly praised Spinoza. Whole generations of researchers were convinced, on the basis of notes in the *Nachlass*, that Nietzsche had an intimate first-hand knowledge not only of the *Ethics* but also of many smaller pieces by Spinoza. The fact is, however, that Nietzsche had probably never read Spinoza's works:

in 1875 he sent an edition of the *Ethics* offered to him back to the bookseller.[39] The notes in the *Nachlass* as well as the references to Spinoza and Nietzsche's specific conception of the architecture and intention of Spinoza's work too are owed instead (but never openly acknowledged as being owed) to one of the monumental works of classical academic German philosophical historiography, namely Kuno Fischer's *Geschichte der neuern Philosophie* [History of Recent Philosophy].[40]

If the personal records prove Nietzsche to be a poacher in the field of the history of philosophy, this bandit temperament is by no means an end in itself. It serves his re-instrumentalization the history of philosophy which seeks to make the past subservient to the philosophizing individual Friedrich Nietzsche's interest in the present and future. Philosophical historiography no longer dictates the interpretive frame concerning what philosophy is or should be but instead the history of philosophy is subjected to the present philosophical will to interpretation. Nietzsche shows no specific interest in the philosophical past as such, neither normatively nor developmental-historically but seeks histories and constellations that he can integrate and situate in his own philosophizing (especially notable here: Heraclitus). Authors of philosophical-historical dissidence can certainly make use of the "normal science" of the "history of philosophy". Nietzsche does so but only insofar as the past seems useful to the present and the future. He maintains a purely instrumental relationship to the history of philosophy. If one wanted to be sarcastic, one could see Nietzsche as the paradigmatic embodiment of the violent handling of the history of philosophy as it is today practiced by countless university philosophers and touted as the history of philosophy: Making history radically serviceable to one's own interests and at the same time giving the impression that you are only reproducing the findings of the ancients!

Nietzsche's dealings with the established historiography of philosophy can be described as a struggle, a struggle for interpretative sovereignty. Perhaps Nietzsche has remained philosophically indispensible because he sets the agonality of philosophy before our eyes in an exemplary way, because he practices this agonality in an exemplary way, because he embodies the agonality of philosophy in an exemplary way. Incidentally we see in this an affinity to Sainte-Beuve who, in the *Causeries*, shows how philosophy is an unstable event, a situated product of discussion, a relationship that occurs as dispute and controversy.

---

39 See Campioni et al. (2003), 719.
40 For details on this see Sommer (2012b) as well as Scandella (2012).

IV The refusal of constraints

Refusal is characteristic of the alternative approaches to the history of philosophy we have examined here. Overbeck refused the Hegelian reading of the history of Christianity and thus provided the measure of a purely historical examination of the history of philosophy. Sainte-Beuve refused the focus on conceptual history and instead proposed philosophy to be considered as a polymorphous and unstable communicative event. Nietzsche finally made an attitude of refusal of philosophical conventionalism and tradition into a basic principle of his thinking in that he vehemently denied the normativity of past philosophy for the present and for the future. Philosophico-historical dissidence thus means the conscious deviation from certain philosophico-historical models of interpretation and from dominant philosophical concepts. The condition for such dissidence is the existence of a normal type of philosophical historiography. This was the case in the 19th century: it was doxographical first of all, then developmental-historical and German university Professors of philosophy studied it, the queen of the philosophical disciplines. The consequence of the above discussed texts was stripping this normal type of philosophical historiography of its royal prerogative and the revealing of alternatives.[41]

Today this philosophical-historical 'normal type' has been disposed for some time. Scarcely anyone today takes the history of philosophy to be the queen of all the philosophical disciplines. Perhaps dissidence *in philosophicis* today would consist in helping philosophical historiography to have an audible voice once again.

Bibliography

Baur (1835): Ferdinand Christian Baur, *Die christliche Gnosis oder die christliche Religions-Philosophie in ihrer geschichtlichen Entwicklung*, Tübingen: Osiander.
Campioni et al. (2003): Giuliano Campioni, Paolo D'Iorio, Maria Cristina Fornari, Francesco Fronterotta a. Andrea Orsucci (Eds.), unter Mitarbeit von Renate Müller-Buck, *Nietzsches persönliche Bibliothek*, Berlin / New York: De Gruyter.
Lepenies (2006): Wolf Lepenies, *Sainte-Beuve. Auf der Schwelle zur Moderne*, München: dtv.

---

[41] An author such as Sainte-Beuve, of a wholly different intellectual environment, obviously never had the intention of dethroning German historiography. Through the transplantation of his *Causeries* to the German context his text could have—had they actually been received in Germany—yielded such a critical effect.

Mirelli (2013): Raffaele Mirelli, *Der Daimon und die Figur des Sokrates. Entstehung einer gegenwärtigen, akademischen Subjektivität am Leitfaden von Platon und Nietzsche*, Würzburg: Königshausen & Neumann.

Nietzsche (1878): *Menschliches, Allzumenschliches. Ein Buch für freie Geister. Dem Andenken Voltaire's geweiht zur Gedächtniss-Feier seines Todestages, des 30. Mai 1778*, Chemnitz: Verlag von Ernst Schmeitzner.

Nietzsche (1999a): Friedrich Nietzsche, *Ueber die Zukunft unserer Bildungsanstalten. Sechs öffentliche Vorträge* (1872), in: Friedrich Nietzsche, *Sämtliche Werke. Kritische Studienausgabe in 15 Einzelbänden*, vol. 1, ed. by Giorgio Colli and Mazzino Montinari, 3rd edition, München / Berlin / New York: De Gruyter, 641–752.

Nietzsche (1999b): Friedrich Nietzsche, *Unzeitgemässe Betrachtungen. Drittes Stück: Schopenhauer als Erzieher* (1874), in: Friedrich Nietzsche, *Sämtliche Werke, Kritische Studienausgabe in 15 Einzelbänden*, vol. 1, ed. by Giorgio Colli and Mazzino Montinari, 3rd edition, München / Berlin / New York: De Gruyter, 335–427.

Nietzsche (1999c): Friedrich Nietzsche, *Jenseits von Gut und Böse. Vorspiel einer Philosophie der Zukunft* (1886), in: Friedrich Nietzsche, *Sämtliche Werke. Kritische Studienausgabe in 15 Einzelbänden*, vol. 5, ed. by Giorgio Colli and Mazzino Montinari, 3rd edition, München / Berlin / New York: De Gruyter, 9–243.

Nietzsche (2003a): Friedrich Nietzsche, *Sämtliche Briefe. Kritische Studienausgabe in 8 Bänden*, vol. 5, ed. by Giorgio Colli and Mazzino Montinari, 2nd edition, München / Berlin / New York: De Gruyter.

Nietzsche (2003b): Friedrich Nietzsche, *Sämtliche Briefe. Kritische Studienausgabe in 8 Bänden*, volume 6, ed. by Giorgio Colli and Mazzino Montinari, 2nd edition, München / Berlin / New York: De Gruyter.

Overbeck (1871): Franz Overbeck, *Ueber Entstehung und Recht einer rein historischen Betrachtung der Neutestamentlichen Schriften in der Theologie. Antritts-Vorlesung, gehalten in der Aula zu Basel am 7. Juni 1870*, Basel: Schwabe.

Overbeck (1903): Franz Overbeck, *Ueber die Christlichkeit unserer heutigen Theologie* [1873], 2nd um eine Einleitung und ein Nachwort vermehrte edition, Leipzig: Naumann.

Overbeck (2008): Franz Overbeck, *Werke und Nachlass*, vol. 8, *Briefe*, unter Mitarbeit von Andreas Urs Sommer ausgewählt, ed. and commented by Niklaus Peter and Frank Bestebreurtje, Stuttgart / Weimar: Metzler.

Proust (1962): Marcel Proust, *Gegen Sainte-Beuve*, translated by Helmut Scheffel, Frankfurt a. M.: Suhrkamp.

Reich (2013): Hauke Reich, *Rezensionen und Reaktionen zu Nietzsches Werken 1872–1889*, Berlin / Boston: De Gruyter.

Sainte-Beuve (1880): Charles-Augustin Sainte-Beuve, *Menschen des XVIII. Jahrhunderts nach den Causeries du Lundi*, translated by Ida Overbeck, Chemnitz: Schmeitzner.

Saint-Beuve (2014): Charles-Augustin Sainte-Beuve, *Menschen des XVIII. Jahrhunderts*, translated by Ida Overbeck (initiiert by Friedrich Nietzsche. Mit frisch entdeckten Aufzeichnungen von Ida Overbeck neu ediert von Andreas Urs Sommer), Berlin: Die andere Bibliothek.

Scandella (2012): Maurizio Scandella, "Did Nietzsche Read Spinoza? Some Preliminary Notes on the Nietzsche-Spinoza-Problem, Kuno Fischer and Other Sources", in: *Nietzsche-Studien* 41, 308–332.

Schopenhauer (1977): Arthur Schopenhauer, *Die Welt als Wille und als Vorstellung. Zweiter Band. Zweiter Teilband. Ergänzungen zum 3. Buch*, in: Arthur Schopenhauer, *Werke in 10 Bänden*, vol. 4, Zürcher Ausgabe, Zürich: Diogenes.
Sommer (2009): Andreas Urs Sommer, "Ein philosophisch-historischer Kommentar zu Nietzsches Götzen-Dämmerung. Probleme und Perspektiven", in: *Perspektiven der Philosophie. Neues Jahrbuch* 35, 45–66.
Sommer (2012a): Andreas Urs Sommer, *Kommentar zu Nietzsches "Der Fall Wagner". "Götzen-Dämmerung"* (= Heidelberger Akademie der Wissenschaften (Ed.), *Historischer und kritischer Kommentar zu Friedrich Nietzsches Werken*, vol. 6/1), Berlin / Boston: De Gruyter.
Sommer (2012b): Andreas Urs Sommer, "Nietzsche's Readings on Spinoza. A Contextualist Study, Particularly on the Reception of Kuno Fischer", in: *Journal of Nietzsche Studies* 43/2, 156–184.

Sebastian Luft
Philosophical Historiography in Marburg Neo-Kantianism: The Example of Cassirer's *Erkenntnisproblem*

I Introduction: Philosophical Historiography as Problem-History. Windelband as Paradigm

We can think that "problem-history"[1] is exclusively a name for one way of philosophical historiography among others. As such it is a method that recounts the history of philosophy in terms of its problems, and not in terms of philosophical personalities or cultural epochs. In this understanding, problem-history proceeds with the naïve assumption that problems exist "in themselves", that they are merely repeated and manifested differently in different epochs. Plainly stated, this sounds both trivial and problematic. And if this reading is true then it is no wonder that problem-history is accorded little interest today, despite the fact that the classical authors of problem-history writing are still readily consulted. Apart from the fact that such writers are still being constantly exploited for research purposes in the present, their works are granted no independent philosophical value. This applies equally to the authors of these works: they are not considered as independent philosophers but "only" as historians. Generally speaking, whosoever dedicates one's philosophical existence to philosophical history, turned backwards and naïvely engaged in the history of problems, actually just carries on a desperate retreating battle because a sense of the actual business of philosophy has become lost. On this view, only someone who has forgotten what the authentic domain of philosophy is concerns himself with the history of philosophy. As a much-appreciated colleague once disparagingly put it: "Someone who has no new ideas will retreat into the history of philosophy."

---

[1] "Problem-history" here translates the standard term *Problemgeschichte*, which is sometimes translated as "history of problems", presumably in analogy to other coinages, such as *Wirkungsgeschichte* ("history of effects", but also "effective history"). In English, there is the fairly recent coinage "intellectual history" (introduced and popularized by Isaiah Berlin), which may be an apt translation for *Problemgeschichte*. Nonetheless, the term has been translated here as "problem-history" to acknowledge the proximity to "intellectual history", while also retaining the peculiar character of the German term and its history.

Such a judgment could be expected from a "classical" analytical philosopher. That such a judgment is, for its part, naïve in manifold respects is hopefully clear to all true historians of philosophy, even if it was an unquestioned dogma for a long time in analytic philosophy. But by now philosophical history has become a problem for analytic philosophy too, albeit one characterized by a real perplexity or helplessness concerning how best to proceed. Even when it explicitly concerns itself with the history of philosophy, analytic philosophy finds itself faced with the dilemma that Rorty so strikingly formulated: "Either we anachronistically impose enough of our problems and vocabulary on the dead to make them conversational partners, or we confine our interpretive activity to making their falsehoods look less silly by placing them in the context of the benighted times in which they were written"[2]. In the following it should become clear, through the consideration of neo-Kantian philosophical historiography as an exemplar, why precisely this dilemma need not exist in the first place. The dilemma is, on its part, the result of a naivety in the face of the history of philosophy, which is considered—if one is to follow Rorty here—merely as a quarry for one's own ideas or as a self-serving doxographical finger exercise without any independent systematic value.

But in fact anyone who, like the neo-Kantians, has a good look at the history of philosophy with systematic intent will find this dilemma absurd. Nevertheless, philosophical historians feel obliged to defend themselves in the face of such attitudes towards their work. When one looks at the great philosophical-historical works of the so-called age of historicism in the 19th century, one quickly discovers that the motive for this devotion to the history of the discipline was altogether different to that of the historical-antiquarian approach and also was not an unquestioned end-in-itself. Rather they turn to it as the source from which originate the highest and most compelling systematic questions, and ultimately the central question of what in actual fact philosophy *itself* is. The dimension of history, a dimension that since Hegel has become essential to philosophy, becomes recognised as a systematic problem and ranked among the traditional "central problems" of philosophy. In this case, it takes the shape of the central question regarding the historicity of philosophy itself. It may well be that such a question is already a symptom of a crisis as well as an indication of the dissolution of traditional conceptions. In the second half of the 19th century this was undoubtedly the case. But, as is well-known, crises always do philosophy good, and more good and in a wholly differently way than could be said about the sciences. And the question has a renewed significance today in the

---

2 Rorty (1984), 49.

light of the fact that the separation of ahistorical analytic philosophy and historically-orientated Continental philosophy has itself been superseded. With regard to the overcoming of this stalemate, the question of the historicity of philosophy and accordingly of the history of philosophy itself can be posed anew. As such, the question of the method of writing the history of philosophy is once again highly relevant.

The question of the way one should approach the study of the history of philosophy is intimately bound up with the question of what philosophy itself is. We owe this insight to the neo-Kantians, themselves under the influence of Hegel. An inquiry into this debate is particularly relevant for our contemporary situation, in that the role of philosophy in the framework of culture in general, and particularly inside university curricula is no longer self-evident. Philosophy finds itself, as consequence, either drawn back into an ivory tower of highly abstract questions or it dissolves itself in empirical research or—a third new possibility recently considered by Hösle—it lapses into a feuilleton-style popular philosophy.[3] None of these alternatives were feasible for either school of neo-Kantianism. On the contrary, they maintained, philosophy must remain in existence but it must itself always work out anew its "what" and "how". Philosophy is not a sublime body of thought that can naively insist on being continued in its "ancient form". It is, on the contrary, a task to be accomplished within the framework of cultural work. However, as is obvious, this self-positioning becomes possible only through reflection upon the history of the discipline.

Thus, the neo-Kantian treatment of philosophical history as problem-history is, in principle and transcending the differences between its schools, fundamentally the attempt to appropriate history with a forward regard, not in order to drive forward a steady progress (in this it differs from Hegel's teleology), but out of the insight into the historicity of philosophy itself. Anyone who desires to "scientifically assess and evaluate our contemporary world and human life" will have to understand the development of these principles "in the course of historical movement".[4] Accordingly, only someone who studies the history of philosophy can philosophize properly. This is the considered view of Windelband, and with this intention in mind, the history of philosophy is to be regarded as *"the history of problems and concepts"*.[5] The great philosophical historical works of neo-Kantianism adhere to this paradigm. One can legitimately characterize them as "problem-histories".

---

3 See Hösle (2013), 308.
4 Windelband (1957), VII, italics added.
5 Windelband (1957), VII.

Hence, Cassirer's work *Das Erkenntnisproblem in der Philosophie und Wissenschaft der neueren Zeit* was—rightly—regarded as a monumental work of problem-history orientated philosophical historiography. If it is true that Cassirer's philosophical historical work should be classified as problem-history, then it is first of all important to develop an understanding of philosophical problem-history. This will occur in the first part of this essay, in which I discuss Windelband's theory of problem-orientated philosophical historiography. At this very juncture, I will show that Gadamer's critique (among others) that problem-history is a "bastard of historicism" (Gadamer's famous phrase) does not apply to Windelband and *a fortiori* neither does it apply to Cassirer. In truth this method of philosophical historiography is a highly reflective and subtle procedure which thematizes systematically the history of the discipline in connection with the development of the sciences. The programme of problem-history should be distinguished from Gadamer's caricature.

If Cassirer takes over the paradigm of problem-history from Windelband, however, he does not do so without reflection. For Cassirer combines the problem-historical paradigm with the method of the Marburg School, the transcendental method. The application of the method that actually is supposed to serve the critique of knowledge is on first sight highly surprising but on second sight quite original. In this respect, Cassirer also pursues his own interests, which in the end remain critical towards Windelband and point ahead towards his own systematic ambitions. Similarly to critiquing Windelband's distinction between nomothetic and idiographic sciences, philosophical historiography, as a discipline for the humanities, is to Cassirer, properly speaking, not an idiographic science, diagnosing particulars, but instead strives towards universal knowledge. But how should the universal be ascertainable if it is subject to historical change? That philosophical problems can be reduced to the epoch of their occurrence, is the problem of relativism, which here appears in the form of historicism. Cassirer has clearly seen this problem. His procedure in his philosophical historiography, as can be seen in the *Erkenntnisproblem*, is, although orientated towards problem-history, a response to the danger of historicism. The answer is seen in the conception of the *a priori* as *historical*. In this he shows, as against Windelband, a heightened sensitivity for the historical dimension of philosophy, a dimension that in spite of its historicity must come forth as *transcendental*. A presentation of problem-history, as carried out in the Marburg School, specifically in Cassirer's work in which it finds its apex, thus simultaneously throws a light on the philosophical standpoint of this entire school. Hence, Cassirer's achievement can only adequately be appreciated as a narrowing of the distance between historical and systematic research. When this achievement is overlooked, one judges neither the historical nor the systematic purpose of his work correctly. Thus, in conclusion, from the example of problem-history a view of Cassirer's whole system becomes possible. Problem-historical philosophical historiography in the Marburg School illuminates the profile of this school in general and on Cassirer in particular.

II Windelband's Definition of Problem-History and the Three Factors of Philosophical Historiography

Windelband's works in philosophical historiography are, as was already stated, not ends in themselves, but are instead directed by a systematic problem, namely the question of what philosophy itself is. Just a glance at the history of Western philosophy, to which Windelband consciously restricts himself, shows that this tradition does not allow for a unified definition of philosophy (and how much more precarious the problem would be if non-Western traditions were to be included). The respective conceptions and definitions of philosophy are too divergent and the attitudes of humanity towards it change over the course of history. Windelband rejects a unified formula, because in the face of this heterogeneity, this "many-coloured diversity"[6] it is simply impossible to put one together. A generally valid conception of philosophy cannot be given either in terms of content or in terms of method and as such it is "not advisable to venture to obtain a general concept of philosophy through historical comparison".[7]

Windelband, though, is not satisfied with a scepticism or agnosticism towards the decisive question of how to define philosophy. And the only way to progress with this matter is a look at the *history* of philosophy itself, at that which has actually been thought and which one has characterized as philosophy.[8] Consequently, it

---

6 Windelband (1957), 7.
7 Windelband (1957), 3.
8 To be best of my knowledge, Windelband has not reflected on the problem that many thinkers have become regarded by us today as philosophers who were not so regarded in their own time, or inversely, that they were once seen as philosophers but are no longer seen as such according to our contemporary judgment. On the other hand his minimalistic concept of philosophy makes possible, in this regard, a relatively *laissez-faire* attitude regarding this issue because his historical considerations are in the end orientated towards the present, and that is why our judgment on previous thinkers is presumably more interesting for him than anything else. One must also add that this relaxed attitude that is appropriate when approaching philosophical history does not apply to his own opinion on what philosophy is. As he makes clear in several texts from the *Präludien* (for instance "Kritische und genetische Methode" and "Was ist Philosophie?"), for

must be borne in mind in advance that an interest in the history of the discipline, which is no more than tangentially relevant in other disciplines, originates out of the dilemma that a definition of philosophy is impossible in the face of its different historical forms. The study of the history of discipline is as it were a makeshift solution, in order to escape the fact that every definition of philosophy can be revised in later times. Accordingly, what is searched for cannot be a substantial definition that is timelessly valid. The insight into the historicity of philosophy is at the same time the refusal of the question of what philosophy is "in itself" is, *because there is no supratemporal "in itself"*.

Windelband's procedure for determining what philosophy is can be characterized as pragmatic, insofar he rejects, or at least does not consider, nobler or more majestic concepts of what philosophy is, such as "love of wisdom". Such definition was never universally valid for the Greeks. To the latter, philosophy was already present in terms of an unbridgeable dualism between the search for generally valid knowledge as science and the search for the right direction in life, between what we today characterize as theoretical and practical philosophy. The only thing that the depictions of philosophy in the course of Western history have in common is the name, and this too is a contingent construction. Windelband also rejects—as against for instance Hegel—the idea of progress or "a gradual approach" to a cognitive ideal, something which is absolutely the case in other sciences which from their "rhapsodical beginnings have won methodological security".[9]

Thus, the only thing that the different efforts on the part of philosophers have in common is equally modestly expressed in their "*common achievement which was brought about in spite of all differences of content and purpose in their occupation*".[10] To formulate it in a wholly prosaic way, this is what has been brought forth by those who have characterized themselves as philosophers as against scientists and other cultural creators: written works. But this is not meant trivially, rather it has an accurately defined meaning. No matter how philosophy understood itself and positioned itself vis-à-vis other cultural activities,

> whether it took as its point of departure the project of a general world knowledge which it wanted to obtain either as a total science or as a general synopsis of the results of the particular sciences or whether it sought for an insight into life, giving a conclusive expression to the high-

---

Windelband *a priori* philosophy is alone genuine philosophy, all others result in empiricism and finally in scepticism. This discrepancy in Windelband's concept of philosophy is therefore paradoxical on first glance but becomes understandable in this way: Windelband obviously separates his work on the history philosophy from his own understanding of philosophy "proper".
9 Windelband (1957), 8.
10 Windelband (1957), 8.

est values of willing and feeling or whether it sought reason's self-knowledge with clear restriction as its goal—it always succeeded in working towards a conscious expression of the necessary forms and content of the human activity of reason and freeing them from their original frames of ideology, emotions, and drives, transforming them into the frame of concepts. *The history of philosophy is the process through which European humanity has set down its conception of the world and its assessment of life in scientific terms.*[11]

The work of philosophy is therefore to find concepts for that which worries and moves humanity. It is, in good Hegelian fashion, work with concepts, *Arbeit am Begriff*. Its problem is that which afflicts humanity. This is brought to concepts in philosophy which act as a "formal indication" of the problems, of the problematic matter itself. Hence, the concrete work of problem-history is work on concepts and their history: it is a concept-history (*Begriffsgeschichte*). Concepts are *signs* or *indications* of problems. As such they do not refer to problems that philosophers simply make up but are expressions of the soul and the value judgments of humanity in different epochs, insofar as these have been subjected to rationality and transformed into concepts. However, this determination must also be applied to philosophy itself insofar as something like "reason" cannot be allowed to be anything other than a concept that indicates a problem. Otherwise put, it was the achievement of philosophers in the course of history to bring lifeworldly affairs to abstract conceptuality. To put it phenomenologically, philosophy reflects the lifeworld and is never independent of it. This proposition should certainly also be understood normatively.

Problems arise in these lifeworldly relations. What are the problems that problem-history dedicates itself to? In the course of describing the method of philosophical history, Windelband now distinguishes three "factors", as he calls them, only one of which—this has to be mentioned right away—is problem-history. The three factors are irreducible to one another which is, as the following will show, particularly relevant with regard to the later critiques of problem-history. The two others shall be mentioned first (problem-history is the second factor in Windelband's order, and in this presentation I deviate from his). *One* factor is *cultural history*, because "philosophy receives its problems as well as the material for its resolution from the ideas of the general consciousness of its time and from the requirements of society".[12] In some circumstances "a philosophical system [can] be like the self-knowledge of a determinate age", although the opposite is also possible, that is to say, philosophy can position itself against its age; and this need not necessarily be a Hegelian scenario, that is,

---

11 Windelband (1957), 8.
12 Windelband (1957), 11.

in any profound sense of dialectics. But in any case philosophy is never independent of its time.

The *third* factor, which in Windelband's discussion is the first mentioned, is the individual. The philosophical-historical process is only "carried out in the thinking of individual personalities".[13] And insofar as it is a creation of individuals a philosophical system thus shows a similarity with artistic works. This factor too is neither reducible nor trivial. It is therefore no accident that one finds the knowledge of respective authors and their peculiarities, of their personal motivations and their place in life, of philosophical interest. As against an abstract conception of philosophy, according to which neither its history nor its actors are relevant, this conception of philosophical-historical processes should be remembered. Of course, it can be grasped in a Hegelian fashion as the progress of the spirit. But at the same time it insists that the spirit consists of flesh and blood, must be fed and possesses passions, values and ideological leanings. No passionless spirit philosophizes. One must not be ashamed of an interest in the human-all-too-human side of philosophy. Who knows, perhaps such propositions as "Aristotle lived, worked, died" apply more to the speaker of these words and are even said on his own behalf? If you like, this is the recognition of the existentialist moment in all representations of philosophy.

Now, the third irreducible factor, which Windelband characterized as the "pragmatic factor" is actual problem-history insofar as it is to be "understood through the inner necessity of thought and through the "logic of the matters" [*durch die "Logik der Dinge"*]".[14] Again, insofar as it starts out from the manner of givenness of the matters, this sounds quite phenomenological inasmuch as Windelband characterizes as a problem that which the "logic of the matters" present to us of themselves, that is, what gives itself as a problem on its own accord, disregarding our access to it. But what are these problems? Here, Windelband applies formulations which can lead, and in fact have led, to misunderstandings. Let us look at exactly what he writes:

> The problems of philosophy, then, are in essence given, and thus it becomes clear that in the historical course of thinking they continuously recur as the "ancient enigmas of existence"[15] and always imperiously demand the solution which is never completely achieved. They emerge, as it is, from the insufficiency and contradictory imbalance of the content of

---

13 Windelband (1957), 12.
14 Windelband (1957), 10.
15 According to Beiser's indication this formulation, and also the anti-historical attitude itself, stems from Schopenhauer. The quotation marks could therefore also signify a reference to the well-known quotation of the pessimist. It could not be ascertained where this formulation is to be found in Schopenhauer.

imagination underlying philosophical contemplation. Hence, the problems of philosophy [are] inescapable tasks for the human spirit.[16]

These formulations have led people to interpret Windelband's idea of problem-history as a process in which certain timeless problems are always refashioned in new robes over the course of philosophical history. We will have to return to this criticism.[17] However, this superficial reading is rendered implausible by two things. In explicating these we will gain a complete picture of problem-history. First of all it should be pointed out that Windelband himself puts the formulation "ancient enigmas of existence" in quotation marks, thus ironizing it. The idea that these "ancient enigmas", which "continuously return", are supratemporal, is already refuted by their temporal definition as "ancient or primordial". And because of this it is not at all implied that the same thing is asked again and again. Problems pose themselves always anew, but as what and how is left open.

This reading is reinforced by a highly interesting suggestion in a footnote at this point in the discussion, where Windelband suggests "historically and systematically extending" Kant's antinomy of pure reason.[18] I understand these comments to imply that, as little as there are "ancient enigmas of existence" *in themselves*, there is no antinomy of reason correlative to it, which always again gets entangled in *the same* contradictions (as Kant claims) and thus never exceeds its antinomical status. That the antinomy of reason is to be historically and systematically extended can only mean, that what *gives* itself as antinomy of reason is historically alterable and can systematically take different forms, *generating* wholly new *kinds* of antinomies, not just the ones Kant identifies as static.

The problems are therefore that which gives itself from the matters in their intricate logic, which we initially do not understand, and which therefore appear to us as a problem which demands a solution, but appears as such always differently and in a historically changeable manner. Whether all that poses itself to us as a problem thus originates out of the "womb" of such ancient enigmas is in any case empty speculation. Therefore, problems are that which appears to humanity as tasks in a historically contingent and systematically changeable manner. Phi-

---

16 Windelband (1957), 10.
17 Compare Gadamer (1924) and (1990). Windelband was also defended against Gadamer's critique in Hofer's depiction in a manner similar to the above, although without relating itself to phenomenology (cf. Hofer (1997)).
18 Windelband, (1957), 10, note 46: "The result of Kant's investigations into the "antinomy of pure reason" (*Critique of Pure Reason*, Transcendental Dialectics, second Main Part) would need to be, in this manner, expanded historically as well as systematically."

losophy is obliged to grasp these problems conceptually and therewith to make them amenable to rational treatment. Accordingly, the business of philosophical historiography is both "philological-historical" inasmuch as these problems must be both (1.) *ascertained* and (2.) *genetically* elucidated, and it is also "critical-philosophical", inasmuch as (3.) these problems must be *assessed*. Genetic considerations are, naturally, focused on the question of how to make "understandable the partial dependence of every philosopher's theories on those of their predecessors",[19] hence, in this regard a certain continuity of different problems and constellations can be ascertained. But this consideration is, in the sense of the three irreducible factors, only one element among others, such as the dependence on the "general ideas of time" (the cultural-historical factor) as well as the "own nature and course of education"[20] of the individual philosophers (the individual factor).

Problem-history is therefore only one of three factors in the treatment of philosophical history. Further problems are not supratemporal ideas but are that which gives itself to us from out of the logic of the matters, each time differently and in different constellations. We, as humans, respond to these problems with the means at our disposal. Philosophy provides or works out the conceptual instruments for this response, instruments which the person on the street would not be immediately familiar with. Thus philosophy is not only the handmaiden of the sciences but of the whole of cultural activity. Hence, there is no general human nature which gets repeatedly caught up in the same general antinomies or seeks to answer each time anew ancient enigmas of humanity. Rather, what philosophy *is*, gives itself from out of the problems that the current cultural epoch and its representatives have to face. The work of philosophy exists in the effort "to bring to conceptualization" ("*auf den Begriff bringen*") these problems.

But this work is not purely arbitrary. For the mark of "good" philosophical work is, then, to provide the problematic *du jour* of the lifeworld with the right conceptuality, insofar as "many philosophers have battled with questions that have lacked natural justification, so that all of the effort of their thought was in vain, and on the other hand also with the solution of real problems unhappy attempts at conceptual construction have occurred, which have formed obstacles rather than furthering the resolution of the matter".[21] The errors that might occur thus go in both directions, that of the concretion of the lifeworld and the abstraction of philosophical concepts.

---

[19] Windelband (1957), 13.
[20] Windelband (1957), 13.
[21] Windelband (1957), 13.

The bottom line is that the "history of philosophy [is] the noblest organon of philosophy itself and belongs as an integral part of its system. For in its totality it constitutes the most extensive and most conclusive development of the problems of philosophy itself".[22] However, I would like to emphasise that the concept "system" here is not to be understood substantially, either. The system of philosophy is nothing other than the historical development of problems that philosophy adopts. That is why the history of philosophy exists in the service of philosophy itself and that is why philosophy is only graspable in terms of its historical development. A philosophy without history is just as absurd as a philosophical reduction of problems to their epoch (the absurdity of historicism). The honest philosophical historian is able to see the *genuine* problem, and so to see the facts of the matter from the point of view of the person for whom it is a problem instead of seeing it from the position of an absolute spirit examining it from above, for whom nothing is a real problem because all is resolved in absolute spirit. The absolute spirit, like a divine mind, is no longer bothered by any problems. The philosophical historian, who recognizes problems as problems, is accordingly the authentic philosopher. Whoever, from the history of Western thought, can show a problem as a problem, has already successfully accomplished the hermeneutic leap into the present.

As such, access to the history of philosophy as problem-history is a recollection of the problems, insofar as they were problems. It is a repositioning of the present self into the situation of those *for whom* these problems posed themselves. And these actors are not in the first place vocational philosophers but were those who, including scientists, were involved in the cultural formation of their time. The procedure is hermeneutic in that a leap of understanding has to be performed to enter another cultural horizon (in Windelband's terms, another cultural epoch or another philosopher). But for Windelband such an act is never antiquarian and backward-looking but instead always has a systematic interest. It tells us of the discussion of a problem from a different era of philosophy itself and this discussion is essentially contemporary with us. To anticipate Cassirer, the identification of a problem as common to an epoch already throws a light on this epoch. This is a view which only a philosopher can open up. And naturally the view that we presently take on an epoch says something about us. The identification of such a problem is already an interpretation that is only possible *ex post* and which understands an author better than he himself was capable of doing.

---

22 Windelband (1957), 13.

For these reasons, Gadamer's critique of problem-history should be conclusively rejected. As we recall, Gadamer had accused problem-history of accepting the "identity of problems" over time, problems which were merely answered differently in different epochs, whereas such an identity is an "empty abstraction".[23] As Gadamer puts it "[t]here is no standpoint outside history from which the identity of the problem over and above the changes in the historical attempts at its solution could be thought." If problem-history could be so understood, it could in fact be described as the "bastard of historicism" and it would be necessary to "destroy the illusion that problems are given like the stars in the heavens."[24] However, after what has been said it must be clear that this depiction and subsequent critique of Windelband's conception of problems and of history is not accurate. On the contrary his concept of problems is so unassuming that his standpoint, as I said, could best be described as pragmatic. What a problem is, is nothing other than what is unclearly given to us at a certain point in time from out of the logic of the matter at hand, the *Sache*. The identification of something *as* a problem is the authentic philosophical-historical achievement, an achievement in which the philosophical historian can never hope to free himself of his own time and leave it behind him either for an absolute or for a different historical standpoint, at least not by a leap that would separate him from the present. The preoccupation with the history of problems is consequently always motivated by problems of the present.

With this basic characterisation of problem-history in mind, we will now turn to Cassirer's conception thereof.

III Cassirer's Problem-History as an Application of the Transcendental Method. The Historicized *A Priori*

Cassirer does not directly examine Windelband's conception of problem-history. He rather implicitly classifies himself in this tradition when he calls his multi-volume philosophical-historical work *Das Erkenntnisproblem*, which, superficially at least, presents a history of the problem of knowledge. Cassirer never opposed the popular conception of this work as problem-historical. However, Cas-

---

[23] Gadamer (1990), 381.
[24] Gadamer (1990), 382. Note that Gadamer himself is adopting an ahistoricist position when stating this.

sirer was critical of Windelband and Rickert, and specifically of their classification of sciences into idiographic and nomothetic, respectively. In Windelband it is not clear if, on its part, problem-history is a discipline of the humanities and therefore idiographic. According to the above criteria, it is certainly so, at least in part. But it is in fact questionable whether problems such as cultural-historical factors can be ascribed a law-like character and if the individual factor is expressly unlawful and rather radically individual.

It is true that Cassirer recognizes the idiographic dimension of historiography that appears in Windelband's second factor as individuality. But he sees this as having a subordinate role: "The psychology of the individual 'subject' is first elucidated through the manner in which we relate it to the overall development of genre".[25] In this Cassirer follows Cohen's line of rejecting all psychological explanations. Cassirer's other statements about Windelband go in a similar direction, so it is predictable that Cassirer will grasp the concept of problem-history differently as it is bound with his own systematic interests. Cassirer's theory makes a universal claim, but one that is defined more encompassingly than Windelband's narrower conception of the nomothetic. Fundamentally, although some aspects of Windelband's concept of problem-history are applicable to Cassirer's conception of it, the latter's problem history is, in the end, decisively "Marburgian." In the first part of this section we will see how from Cassirer's theory of problem-history the general philosophical position of the Marburg school can be illustrated. In the second, following from this, I will develop Cassirer's position showing that while it remains fundamentally committed to the approach of the Marburg School he develops it into his own project. Thus, the project of problem-history will receive its proper systematic embedding. In a short conclusion I will sketch how one arrives at Cassirer's system of symbolic forms from problem-history.

To get right to the core of the problem, it should be emphasized, as regards the history of this work, that *Das Erkenntnisproblem* (first volume of four in 1906) appeared in the wake of Cohen's philosophical system, the first volume of which, the *Logik der reinen Erkenntnis*, was published in 1902. Cassirer also cites Cohen's work at strategic places in the *Erkenntnisproblem*, referring to its thesis of the historical *a priori*, a thesis which makes possible Cassirer's own problem-history. This notion was itself developed by Cohen, though more abstractly than in Cassirer's interpretation. Also, according to Cassirer's self-understanding its concrete application is seen with regard to historical detail rather than Cohen's broad pronouncements. Furthermore, the publication of the first two volumes

---

25 Cassirer (1994), 7.

(1906 and 1907) and of the third volume (1919) of the *Erkenntnisproblem* was interrupted by Cassirer's first systematic work, which according to his own assessment constituted his breakthrough to independent philosophizing, the 1910 *Substanzbegriff und Funktionsbegriff* [*Substance and Function*]. However, a little over a decade will have passed before the complete formulation of his system in the shape of his *Philosophy of Symbolic Forms*. Accordingly *Substanzbegriff und Funktionsbegriff* formulates and systematically justifies the double tasks of historical and systematic consideration, tasks that for Cassirer are "closely associated".[26] This close association is characteristic for Cassirer's work as a whole. In *Substanzbegriff und Funktionsbegriff* the "systematization of disciplines of knowledge is placed as a complement to the development of the history of the problem of knowledge".[27] This bringing together of historical and systematic tasks is the signature of the Marburg School. The proper classification of philosophical work was first explicated by the Marburg School's systematic position, which in turn leads the presentation of problem-history. For this reason, some basic paradigms of the Marburg School, which put problem-history in the appropriate light, need to be set out first.

First, the Marburg understanding of philosophy itself has to be explained, an understanding which is closely related to Windelband's. For the Marburg School too philosophy actually has no domain of its own but it works with pre-given material, that for the Marburg philosophers is chiefly given from the sciences. This was Cohen's original programme: The *factum* from which philosophy departs, is the *factum* of the sciences, each of which deal with different parts of culture. To put it simply, the task of philosophy is to legitimate these *facta*. Above all the natural sciences are paradigmatic here and it is with regard to these that the Marburg School has exerted the greatest influence. Ideally philosophy should approach all areas of culture through the *factum* of the respective sciences; accordingly it should also approach the regions of ethics and aesthetics in this manner. However, in this the other Marburg philosophers did not exactly follow the master. Therefore, the popular characterization of the Marburg School as being orientated towards a theory of scientific cognition, specifically that of the exact sciences, is quite legitimate. Yet Cassirer's ambition was to present a philosophical theory of *all* cultural regions that was not to be led by the natural-scientific paradigm. This is the mark of his proximity to as well as his distance from the Marburg School.

---

26 Cassirer (1994), IX.
27 Kreis (2010), 59.

To take as a starting point the *factum* of science means to reconstruct this *factum* in its genesis, that is to say, to elucidate the cognitive conditions of its emergence. However, these conditions are not the psychological processes of thinking, but "pure thought" ("*das reine Denken*", following Cohen) or the pure conceptual-logical element in knowledge formation, that is to say, concepts (categories) and functions of thinking. Here it is important to see that what stands before us as finished fact of knowing is not simply a "process, in which we bring a reproduction of an existing, ordered and structured reality to consciousness"[28], but is the result of conceptual work which, in turn, first of all constructs the object of knowledge. The true object of experience, for Cohen, is the knowledge worked out in science. The true object is thus not so much "the stars in the heavens" but rather the laws to which they are subject and according to which they function.[29] Only then can one speak meaningfully of the experience of reality. This reconstruction of what is always already constructed in the sciences is the Marburg "transcendental method." Philosophy distinguishes itself from Kantian *epistemology* as transcendental exploration of the condition of the possibility of experience and knowledge, to become the critique of knowledge that already exists, whereby experience and knowledge are taken as essentially synonymous. Accordingly, critique of knowledge [*Erkenntniskritik*] is the name for the Marburgian variation of theory of knowledge or epistemology [*Erkenntnistheorie*]. It is a critique of what is already experienced, that is, cognized, in the sciences.

This conception of epistemology as critique of knowledge has two closely related consequences. First: the insight that the objects of experience are formations of thought constructed by the human mind is counter-intuitive to the naïve conception of our ever progressive eliciting of immanent secrets from things in the world. Rather the objects of modern science, as Kant says in his famous image, are in the witness stand and subject to our questions as to their being, questions which we ourselves formulate according to our epistemological interests. And according to Kant, we only recognize of things that which we lay into them based on rational capacities. This theory was conceived by Vico with respect to history.[30] It is applied by Kant to the natural sciences. The *being* of things in the world is constructed by our conceptual work on them. The naïve conception, which even scientists tend to subscribe to, hence fails to recognize that these things are nothing other than the "free positings of the understand-

---

28 Cassirer (1994), 1.
29 Cf. Cohen (1977), esp. the systematic introduction.
30 Verene has emphasized the significance of Vico on this issue, cf. Verene (1969).

ing". The reality that we perceive as existing in itself is in truth created by us, insofar as we penetrate it using exact scientific methods. We see the human spirit in nature: it, so to speak, finds itself mirrored in nature. This is the continuously emancipating progress of modern sciences, which signifies a reversal of the mirror metaphor which Rorty assigned to modern philosophy. In truth nature is the mirror of the human soul.[31]

In the course of its becoming self-aware scientific progress recognizes that scientific knowledge is not superimposed onto reality as a second reality, but rather that *only through it* do we *have* reality in the first place. What something *is* depends on the conceptual and theoretical framework in which it is seen. "Science gradually eliminates the illusion which makes us attach our subjective sensations to the objects themselves".[32] The *factum*, which we take as our starting point in the naïve view of the world, is in truth a *fieri:* a being-made though conceptual construction. This is an insight that follows from the application of the transcendental method. This insight itself receives its meaning from the Copernican turn, which is here reinterpreted from being a mere standpoint into a concrete research programme. The interpretation of the *factum* as *factum* of science whose meaning is the always provisional, self-modifying result of a *fieri*, can be identified as the first important pillar of the Marburg School.

Secondly, this interpretation has a decisive consequence for the interpretation of scientific progress. If it is the case that science has gradually undermined the naïve conception of knowledge, such that knowledge is not a discovery of the secrets of things or of "what holds the world together in its innermost being" ("*Was die Welt im Innersten zusammenhält,*" Goethe), but is instead a conceptual-logical construction on the part of the scientific subject, then it follows from this that modern science has essentially and without realizing it *already carried out the Copernican turn and is gradually carrying it further.* This insight is first brought about through the philosopher reflecting on this scientific progress in Modernity. Accordingly, the Marburg interpretation of Kant's Copernican turn maintains that with the turn to the knowing subject no new district of metaphysics, as for instance of philosophy *itself,* becomes opened up. Rather Kant's transcendental philosophy is the philosophical *articulation* of the transcendental turn already happening in the *sciences*. The exact sciences are already transcendental, without an explicit knowledge of this, insofar as their achievement *is* the condition for the possibility of experience, according to Cohen's concept of expe-

---

[31] With regard to Rorty's influential thesis, if Cassirer's hypothesis is correct his *Erkenntnisproblem* would be a general refutation of Rorty's idea that modern philosophy is afflicted by the problem of representationalism, that it could be even adequately grasped by that label.
[32] Cassirer (1994), VI.

rience. The philosopher merely reconstructs how knowledge in the sciences is carried out and how it becomes further produced. Thus, the Kantian position of transcendental idealism takes on a concrete research programme, one that henceforth is characterized as "critical idealism" inasmuch as modern natural science has taken the strategic path to idealism that is never—not even in the distant future—going to be possession acquired once and for all. It is rather gradually worked out and continually modified. Idealism is thus the methodological projection of science itself. The objection that philosophy is thus the handmaiden of the sciences is consequently correct. But for the Marburg School this is not a reproach. For on the one hand with the intimate connection to science all metaphysical speculation is prohibited for all future; it is thus metaphysically-critically restrictive. On the other hand, if an experience of that which transcends normal experience cannot exist then there cannot be a domain belonging *inherently* to philosophy *alone*. To demand this is a philosophical dogma, which is finally eliminated.[33] Philosophy has to dwell in the "rich bathos" of experience, which gradually becomes recognized by the sciences.

Against this background it is therefore clear why the problem-historical depiction of philosophical and scientific history and the transcendental method of reconstructing the logical knowledge conditions of scientific work fit like *lock and key*. Because if the appropriate work of the transcendental method is the justification of the sciences' on-going epistemological work and if science necessarily runs its course historically, then epistemological criticism cannot but progressively work in close relation to this very historical processes. Nor is the choice of the theme of "knowledge as a problem" accidental. The identification of knowledge as the *problem* of the "modern age" is not a thesis forced on from above. Rather it is given by itself through a philosophical meditation on the modern scientific process itself, on precisely how the process of progressive knowledge *problematizes* what knowledge *itself* is and should be. Qualitatively new kinds of knowledge, beyond that yielded by the sciences, do not exist. Identifying something as a problem can thus be understood as the problematization of that which ought to be a problem. It is not a once-established and henceforth definite statement. Knowledge *becomes a problem*. The *factum* is thus again resolved into the *fieri* for the philosopher. Or to say it with another Marburg formulation, that which is a fixed given [*Gabe*] for the scientist becomes the task [*Aufgabe*] of philosophical reconstruction for the philosopher. Cognition and knowledge that, for Kant, were obtained once and remained immutable, in

---

[33] One can see Husserl's insistence on phenomenology occupying its ownmost region, as true philosophy, as a protest against this hypothesis.

truth develop historically. Thus the reconstruction of the problem of knowledge by way of the historical path is *necessary*.

> [T]he illusion of the "Absolute" disappears here ... of itself. By considering the presuppositions of the sciences as having *become*, we recognize that they are *creations* of thought. In that we see clearly their historical *relativity* and conditionality we open for ourselves a perspective into their inexorable progress and their always renewed productivity. Both directions of the consideration here are integrated with each other effortlessly and spontaneously [*zwanglos und ungesucht*]. The systematic structure of basic cognitions and the relations of their inner dependence confronts us once again clearly and comprehensibly in the image of their historical emergence.[34]

Against this systematic background—that "effortlessly and spontaneously" demands the historical viewpoint and wherein they both reciprocally support each other—we can now move on to the method of problem-history. That the systematic standpoint of the Marburg School also grasps the history of philosophy itself as a method is not surprising:

> by virtue of being a science the history of philosophy cannot be a miscellany through which we encounter facts in a colourful sequence; it wants to be a *method*, through which we learn to understand them.[35]

However, as we shall see, considerable difficulties arise at this point that must be cleared out of the way. The resolution of these difficulties opens the way to for Cassirer's mature system of symbolic forms.

What are these difficulties and how does Cassirer deal with them, then? As a philosophical reconstruction of the problem of knowledge, this reconstruction is guided by the thesis that modern scientific progress is the conceptual-theoretical mastery of reality—here that of nature (thus, it is pro-Vico and anti-Rorty). In doing this the sciences themselves are not conscious of their actual achievement. They themselves cling to the naïve belief in the being-in-itself of nature and the gradual discovery of its timeless being. However, increasingly the domination of nature is no longer interested in the individual thing in isolation. Guided by the logic of scientific progress, this change was carried out in modern science analogous to the way in which Cassirer observes a paradigm change from the concept of substance to the concept of function in modern concept formation, a shift which emphasises the functional nexus over individual substances:

---

34 Cassirer (1994), VIf.
35 Cassirer (1994), VIII.

[It is] no longer simply the individual thing, but the demand of internal coherence and internal freedom from contradictions which this thought poses that constitutes hencewith the ultimate archetype by which we measure the truth of our ideas[36],

an archetype through which the "primal elements of being itself" henceforth

> become understood and reinterpreted as *creations of thought*. The concepts of science appear now no longer as imitations of thingly beings, but as symbols for the orders and functional nexuses within reality.[37]

With this process the relativity of sensible appearance is to be overcome, but at this very point the scientific process is confronted with a new problem, namely a second-order relativity, so to speak, on the level of science itself. Because those theories and concepts once attained are no Platonic ideas but are themselves in the process of becoming, so that every "given" ["*Gabe*"] becomes a "task" ["*Aufgabe*"], every fixed standpoint is dissolved in the course of its development and is swept away by progress. However, this is no defect, because if we cognize only what we put into nature, this cycle of standing still and further advancing is *constitutive* for science.

> Thus the very essence of those logical foundational concepts which science has developed demands that we view these concepts not as separate and detached from one another but instead grasp them in their *historical* sequence and dependency. However, thereby any firm systematic foothold threatens to slip away.[38]

But why is that a problem? Is the progress of science not self-evident? Yes, but it puts a fundamental assumption of Kant's in question, namely that of the *a priori*. Kant had presumed that the categories identified by him as the constitutive core concepts of the understanding were both fixed and complete. As *a priori*, therefore independent of all experience, they were according to his classical understanding *necessary* and *universally valid*. Newton's scientific paradigm, which operated with these categories, was unsurpassable for Kant. However, this paradigm was, after Kant, overturned and falsified in various ways, thus making way for new paradigms. As Cassirer in particular shows, the Newtonian paradigm itself is the result of a conflict of paradigms, which suggests that Kant himself would have had to grasp his conception of the *a priori* differently. This change of paradigms is in fact the biggest stumbling block in the reception of the Kantian system, but progress in modern

---

36 Cassirer (1994), 2.
37 Cassirer (1994), 3.
38 Cassirer (1994), 4.

logic has "established full clarity on this point"[39], namely that the *a priori* has to be conceived as in a way that moves beyond Kant's understanding of it. The problem goes as follows: if modern science is supposed to be the confirmation of Kant's Copernican turn, how then can Kant's conception of the *a priori*, which is a necessary component of his system (and which Cassirer wants to preserve, as well) be retained? Is it not simpler to go the way of positivism and naturalism and to wholly give up all pretension to the *a priori?*

The Marburg conception of the *a priori* comes to bear on this point. The reason why the *a priori* cannot be dispensed with is that doing so would open the floodgates to relativism. For the sequence of changing scientific paradigms is not relativist in the sense of arbitrariness and does not amount to the denial of truth if one emphasizes that the respective concepts and theories of a scientific epoch —for example that which after Kuhn could be called *"normal science"*—are not arbitrary but were *necessary* for their time and with regard to their means and methods. They are the necessary ways in which at any one time the *"problem of the reciprocal relation between being and thinking* [is] *formulated anew"*.[40] What is *"a priori"* would here simply be the fundamental relation between being and thinking—but as a *problem*, insofar as this fundamental relation reveals itself differently in different epochs. Consequently to the problem-historically orientated philosopher the prevailing relations of being and thinking, of world and humanity respectively, are not given but he is tasked with them as a problem, they are to be reconstructed in their "relative absoluteness" inasmuch as *for the point in time of its validity* each standpoint claims and must claim absolute truth. However, in doing so one has precisely not succumbed to a succession of arbitrary paradigms:

> that we in [science] always find only a *relative* basis, that consequently we must maintain the *categories,* with which we consider historical processes, themselves changeable and transformable is of course true, but this kind of relativism characterizes not so much the boundary but rather the authentic life of knowledge.[41]

These bases are therefore provisional milestones, but nevertheless necessary points, at which clear and determinate categories exist, which, however, first can appear *as necessary at this point in time* through the problem-historical view. So the absolute is manifested as a relative absolute within history.

---

39 Cassirer (1994), 18.
40 Cassirer (1994), 9.
41 Cassirer (1994), 16.

But if the categories can change to correspond to the current state of science, then what remains as unchanging and therefore *a priori* in the more rigorous sense of the concept?

This is the continuity of the scientific processes itself, the *factum* of science: "the concept of the *history of science* already contains in itself the thought of a *preservation of* a *general logical structure* throughout the succession of particular conceptual systems".[42] That is the first "insight into the genuine "*a priori*" of history".[43] Strictly speaking one must divide the *a priori* again, distinguishing between a rigorous and a less rigorous notion of it. The continuity of scientific progress is unchanging and certain basic convictions inside science are unchanging such as

> the idea of the "unity of nature", that is to say, "the lawfulness of experience in general", ... but how this idea currently specifies particular principles and presuppositions: for me this, too, only reveals itself in the progress of scientific experience.[44]

Moreover, the fact that nature can only become known through the categories of pure thinking is unchanging, but as Cohen says *"new problems will bring new categories."*[45] But whatever evolves, they will be *categories*, having originated from pure thinking.

In good Marburg manner scientific progress is not a given [*Gabe*], but a task [*Aufgabe*]; it is a "postulate"[46] for seeing the unity of the history of science *in* its apparently haphazard succession. One must not, subversively, celebrate chaos and brilliant creativity, but rather one is called, precisely in the face of chaos, to detect from out of this the logical structure of the historical sequence. Accordingly, the problem-history of modern science itself has a systematic intent and without this systematic positioning of problems each problem-historical consideration would be futile. Historical consideration itself is a necessary contribution to reconstruction of what which knowledge in modern western thinking in general *is*.

Only with this conception of the historical *a priori* one can begin to practice problem-history in the true sense, insofar as one can explain only now the logic of the succession of scientific *a prioris* (in the plural).[47] This explanation is now

---

42 Cassirer (1994), 16.
43 Cassirer (1994), 17.
44 Cassirer (2009), 51: Letter to Schlick of October 10th, 1920.
45 Cohen (1977), 398.
46 Cassirer (1994), 18.
47 As already indicated, Cohen believed an *a priori* like that of the exact natural sciences could be demonstrable for all cultural givens. Cassirer does not subscribe to this conception: all symbolic forms in their *respective* meanings are the condition for the possibility of world experience.

expressis verbis construction as re-construction of the prevailing logics and their sequence. Construction cannot occur in a deductive-speculative manner. It is nevertheless a dialectic but not one that is a "steady growth" to an absolute, unsurpassable standpoint, rather "in the truly critical epochs of knowledge the manifold basic basic postions oppose each other in the sharpest dialectic contradiction".[48] "Dialectic" is in this case not a high-minded concept for the Hegelian threefold development of the spirit (of thesis, antithesis and synthesis), but the problematization of what was taken as self-evident in the old paradigm (of the dominant *a priori*) through the new paradigm, which thereby formulates its new *a priori* (and so on). Accordingly, it is the critical gaze of the problem-historical philosophers which ascertains what the "actual critical epochs" are. Finally, regarding knowledge in the present, it also can never be the last word, but the constant and unchangeable can only be the law of eternal becoming; that, so long as human beings "live and strive" (as says Goethe's *Faust*), their search for knowledge will not be complete, even if this search is only a part and a very specific development of cultural life as a whole. Although scientific knowledge surpasses other cultural achievements in its precision and its methodological rigour, it is, with regard to cultural life as a whole, a cultural form next to others which stand in productive competition, in shaping and experiencing reality.

IV Conclusion and Further Considerations: From Problem-History to Symbolic Forms

It now remains to briefly indicate how one can reconstruct Cassirer's entire system from this point, as it becomes executed in the philosophy of symbolic forms, even though here, too, the problem-historical insight must be applied to this philosophy itself such that any systematic programme of philosophy cannot in principle be brought to a finish, insofar as it is carried out by humans conceived as cultural beings and not as purely rational creatures. The problem-historical approach is in fact never given up by Cassirer. One can see the latter in his reoccurring tendency to approach a problem in question through the history of science with respect to it. Present-day philosophy has little patience for such extravagant panorama paintings, but what has been said makes clear that this method of approaching systematic problems historically is itself guided by systematic insight. Accordingly one does not do justice to Cassirer's philosophy itself, either, if one strips of it of its historical robes.

---

48 Cassirer (1994), 5.

The simple thought, which frees Cassirer from Cohen's rigorous logicism, is that the *factum* of science is only *one* manifestation of the human spirit. Cohen's idea that one must take one's point of departure from the fact of the respective science in every form of culture and not just in science is too restrictive for Cassirer. Cassirer understands every cultural form including myth, speech and religion, according to the replacement of the substance paradigm with the function paradigm, as functional contexts of meaning. In this respect, it is the work of philosophy in the context of the study of the respective culture to describe the functional structures that determine a cultural form. Of these, the purely logical reconstruction of the sciences reveals only one structure of meaning among others. Every cultural form is a way of constructing reality: each is, in Cassirer's words, symbolic. Transcendental idealism thus becomes symbolic idealism, insofar as we never have direct access to the world, but this access is always mediated through the constructions and the perspective of the spirit, which at any one time constitutes different structural forms. Accordingly, Cassirer furthermore even understands the *a priori* as plural, as a valid functional series for a respective context of meaning. Cassirer calls such a functional series or context a symbolic form.

Like science every cultural form is subject to historical change. As such the task of the philosophy of symbolic forms is not merely to statically describe the prevailing symbolic forms but also to reconstruct their origin and development. These two can only go hand in hand. History itself is no symbolic form but is the element in which symbolic forms and we as *animalia symbolica* live. If thus the history of science is considered according to its problem, that of knowledge, then other symbolic forms are to be considered in terms of the history of their constitutive elements, which cannot be adequately determined as knowledge, as for example religion, insofar as its problem cannot demand a solution through knowledge. "Knowledge" is perhaps not an adequate category for religion or it perhaps has, as a category, another meaning than exact knowledge. Applied to the totality of symbolic forms, problem-history becomes symbolic history insofar as the prevailing symbolic form cannot be understood without understanding the history of its development.

If then symbolic forms as a whole are subject to historical change, then it is also valid to say of these that a prevailing *a priori* can only be understood historically. As a result of this, many of the criticisms levelled at Cassirer's work become untenable. For instance Cassirer's enumeration of the symbolic forms just listed has been accused of being rhapsodic and unsystematic. But a look at the history of a symbol may well show that it once appeared as necessary, just as for example the Christian religion in the Middle Ages was constitutive for the human and world understanding of humanity in that period, but that it necessarily lost its standing in most parts of Western society in an age of secularization. Whereas another symbolic form is probably always going to be constitutive for what it is to be a human: language. It is likewise subjected to a change of its function as becomes apparent in the age of new (virtual) social interactions, but it will in all likeliness not disappear as a symbolic function for world-disclosure. And so one can finally explain the emergence of new forms from out of the changing relations between humanity and the world, if one wants to thus describe Cassirer's *a priori* as correlational.

Thus, it becomes clear that problem-history, as Cassirer exemplifies in the reconstruction of modern science, is a narrower form of historiography, which should be written for *all* symbolic forms. Every symbolic form has its *own* history and therewith its own historicity, and the respective historiography focuses, accordingly, on different kinds of problems and categories. Thus, problem-history and the Marburg School theory of science have been demonstrated as being particular forms of a wider historicity and a construction of the human spirit in its symbolic universality. In this manner, the contours of Cassirer's distinctive system of symbolic idealism, as a philosophical reconstruction and justification of all cultural forms, has been indicated. To put it formulaically, the critique of reason thus becomes a critique of culture. However, this critique of culture also and necessarily includes in its reflections the dimension of history while maintaining—as against Windelband and Dilthey's empiricist undersellings—its status as a transcendental theory.[49]

Bibliography

Bast (2000): Rainer A. Bast, *Problem, Geschichte, Form. Das Verhältnis von Philosophie und Geschichte bei Ernst Cassirer im historischen Kontext*, Berlin: Duncker & Humblot.

Cassirer (1994): Ernst Cassirer, *Das Erkenntnisproblem in der Philosophie und Wissenschaft der neueren Zeit*, vol. 1, reprint of the original edition, Darmstadt: Wissenschaftliche Buchgesellschaft.

Cassirer (2009): Ernst Cassirer, *Briefe. Ausgewählter wissenschaftlicher Briefwechsel*, in: Ernst Cassirer, *Nachgelassene Manuskripte und Texte*, ed. by John Michael Krois, Hamburg: Meiner.

Cohen (1977): Hermann Cohen, *Logik des reinen Denkens*, Hildesheim: Olms.

Gadamer (1924): Hans-Georg Gadamer, "Zur Systemidee in der Philosophie", in: Ernst Cassirer (Ed.), *Festschrift für Paul Natorp zum 70. Geburtstage*, Berlin/Leipzig: De Gruyter, 55–75.

---

[49] I would like to thank Rochus Sowa and Frederick Beiser for their critical but helpful comments on an earlier version of this essay.

Gadamer (1990): Hans-Georg Gadamer, *Wahrheit und Methode. Grundzüge einer philosophischen Hermeneutik*, Tübingen: Mohr/Siebeck.
Hofer (1997): Roger Hofer, *Gegenstand und Methode. Untersuchungen zur frühen Wissenschaftslehre Emil Lasks*, Würzburg: K&N.
Hösle (2013): Vittorio Hösle, *Eine kurze Geschichte der deutschen Philosophie*, München: Beck.
Kreis (2010): Guido Kreis, *Cassirer und die Formen des Geistes*, Frankfurt a. M.: Suhrkamp.
Krüger (1984): Lorenz Krüger, "Why Do We Study the History of Philosophy?", in: R. Rorty, J. B. Schneewind and Q. Skinner (Eds.), *Philosophy in History. Essays on the Historiography of Philosophy*, Cambridge: Cambridge University Press, 77–101.
Rorty (1984): Richard Rorty, "The Historiography of Philosophy: Four Genres", in: R. Rorty, J. B. Schneewind and Q. Skinner (Eds.), *Philosophy in History. Essays on the historiography of philosophy*, Cambridge: Cambridge University Press, 49–75.
Verene (1969): Donald P. Verene, "Kant, Hegel, and Cassirer: The Origins of the Philosophy of Symbolic Forms", in: *Journal of the History of Ideas* 30, 33–46.
Windelband (1924): Wilhelm Windelband, *Präludien. Studien und Aufsätze zur Philosophie*, 5th edition, Tübingen: Mohr.
Windelband (1957): Wilhelm Windelband, *Lehrbuch der Geschichte der Philosophie*, 15th edition, Neuauflage mit einem Zusatz ed. by Heinz Heimsoeth, Tübingen: Mohr.

Paul Ziche
Indecisionism and Anti-Relativism: Wilhelm Windelband as a Philosophical Historiographer of Philosophy

I Windelband's Problem: Integrating History's Empiricism and Philosophy's Truth-Claims

Wilhelm Windelband (1848–1915) was undeniably one of the most prominent and ambitious historians of philosophy of the period around 1900. As a historiographer, he authored a number of highly acclaimed textbooks in the history of philosophy[1] and championed the study of philosophy's history as a history of "problems". As a philosophical analyst of history as a scientific discipline, he presented the hugely influential analysis of the difference between the natural sciences and the humanities in terms of "nomothetic" general laws vs. "idiographic" individual descriptions.[2] As a systematic philosopher, he was the leading figure of the Baden school of neo-Kantianism that made "values" the core concept of philosophy. Although he never published a comprehensive systematic presentation of his philosophy, Windelband's early biographers praise him in virtual unison for having combined the history of philosophy with a systematic approach to philosophy.[3] In his

---

[1] All his handbooks appeared in various editions and were frequently reworked. He covered the entire history of philosophy in his handbooks, the most important of which is his *Lehrbuch der Geschichte der Philosophie* [in earlier editions: *Geschichte der Philosophie*, 1st ed. 1892], re-edited and updated repeatedly afterwards. See also his *Geschichte der alten Philosophie* [1st ed. 1888], from which later monographs on ancient philosophy were derived (e.g. his *Geschichte der abendländischen Philosophie im Altertum*, published as part of the *Handbuch der Altertumswissenschaft*). To Plato, he devoted a monograph (Windelband (1900). The modern period is covered in his *Die Geschichte der neueren Philosophie in ihrem Zusammenhange mit der allgemeinen Cultur und den besonderen Wissenschaften* [1st ed. 1878, 1880]. He also contributed substantially to standard series in the field of philosophy and cultural analysis (e.g. Windelband (1908)). For an overview see Steindler (2004); Kemper (2006), in the context of the history of pedagogics. Kemper also deals with the internal development of Windelband's thinking (which is not discussed here).
[2] Windelband (1924c).—In this paper, I only translate the more important terms or phrases from the German source texts and, in the relevant cases, I also give the German original.
[3] See Bauch (1915a); Rickert (1915), which gives the substantially extended version of an obituary published in the *Frankfurter Zeitung*, and Ruge (1917), which appeared originally in the *Zeitschrift für Philosophie und philosophische Kritik* 162 (1916–7). For an overview of the early reception of this work, see Kemper (2006), 15–16.

hands, it is claimed, the history of philosophy is more than just a post-factum narration of past philosophy; rather, it becomes inseparable from philosophy itself. A strong statement to this effect can be found in the eulogy that Heinrich Rickert devoted to his teacher where he describes Windelband's *Lehrbuch der Geschichte der Philosophie* as the most forceful "*philosophy* of the history of philosophy" written since Hegel, and at the same time as the "best *introduction to philosophy* [...] that we have".[4] In Windelband's oeuvre, the functions of introducing into philosophy and of studying the history of philosophy are indeed closely intertwined, with an interesting shift in emphasis. Windelband intends his *Einleitung in die Philosophie* to stand in a close relationship to his works on the history of philosophy; it is in the relationship and combination ("*Zusammenstellung*" and "*Beziehung*") between history and systematic philosophy that his philosophical programme is to be fulfilled.[5] Windelband's most systematic treatment of philosophy takes the form of an introduction to which the *Lehrbuch*—hailed by Rickert as the ideal introduction—in turn serves as a bibliographic compendium, and only the two books together in their interrelatedness capture philosophy in its entirety.

The integration of the history of philosophy and of systematic philosophy remains a pressing issue today.[6] Windelband's own integrative claim is at least slightly surprising. He does not present himself as a systematic thinker; his attitude appears to be rather evasive and has rightly been called hermaphroditic in nature.[7] Windelband not only locates philosophy in the combination of introductory texts and historiographic handbooks; he is constantly hybridizing ideas and always retracts the steps he has taken. One particularly clear example (see also section IV) is his tendency to again and again establish distinctions only in order to then pursue both prongs of a distinction: the history of philosophy and systematic philosophy; individual values and general theory; subjective experiences and universal problems; idealism and realism,[8] to name only a few. Summing

---

[4] Rickert (1915), 11; see also Bauch (1915a), VIII: "*jene fruchtbare Verbindung systematischer und historischer Erkenntnis [...], die später Windelbands einzigartige Stellung und Bedeutung in der Geschichte unserer Wissenschaft begründen und sichern sollte.*"
[5] Windelband (1923a), V-VI. The first edition of the *Einleitung* appeared in 1914.
[6] For a few examples of this, see the discussions documented in Sorell a. Rogers (2005); Rorty, Schneewind, Skinner (1984).
[7] A Dutch monograph on Windelband from a 1920s series on "*Groote Denkers* [Great Thinkers]" characterizes his philosophy as "*tweeslachtig*"—as a hybrid, or, more literally, a hermaphroditic enterprise. This doubleness is located right at the heart of Windelband's project, in the very attempt to write a "handbook of principles" that is at the same a "handbook of history" (Van der Vaart Smit (1922), 14).
[8] On this issue, see the discussion in Bauch (1915b).

up, his approach might be called a form of systematic *indecisionism*.[9] The recent research literature on Windelband has rather strongly criticized Windelband on these grounds and has declared his project to have failed.[10] This, however, misses two important points. First, Windelband is very well aware of this element of indecision in his arguments. In the inaugural lecture he delivered when taking his first academic chair at Zürich (on this chair see in more detail section II), he describes the relationship between a philosophical and an empirical treatment of a problem as "wavering [*schwankend*]" and therefore uncertain, and this uncertainty is addressed, in this very terminology, throughout his writings.[11] Secondly, this indecisionist stance is combined—in what might be seen as a kind of self-application of the indecisionist attitude—with a thoroughly *anti-relativist* position.[12] In all his works, Windelband is looking for a fixed framework that saves philosophy and the sciences from relativist arbitrariness. Already in his Zürich inaugural lecture, he explicitly seeks for a "framework of fundamental concepts and problems [*Rahmen von Grundbegriffen und Problemen*]" that serves as a kind of transcendental condition for ordering and classifying knowledge claims.

This combination of indecisionism and anti-relativism is highly remarkable. In terms of philosophical movements, it translates into a joint refutation of both

---

9 How this characterization fits with the established notion of "decisionism" in legal and social philosophy is not addressed here. The thesis may be ventured that the early decisionist ideas, just as Heidegger's *"Entschlossenheit"*, react—at least in part—to the trends that are here dubbed as "indecisionst". Windelband's programme is all the more remarkable given the period's emphasis on the will and its decisions. This issue, too, cannot be pursued here.
10 Most importantly in recent years in a number of texts by Frederick Beiser (see note 13). See also the strong statements in Beelmann (2001), 97: "*Eine zwischen diesen Extremen* [namely a more traditional notion of philosophy and a positivist conception which views history and philosophy as two distinct disciplines, P.Z.] *vermittelnde Position verstrickt sich unweigerlich in Widersprüche, die am Beispiel Windelbands erkennbar werden*"; 98: "*Das philosophische Anspruchsniveau, das auf Notwendigkeit und Deduktion zielt, ist mit dem empirischen Charakter einer historischen Wissenschaft nicht vereinbar.*" Beelmann refers to Windelband's *Lehrbuch* and his rectoral address on "History and Natural Science" to support his claim that Windelband's idiographic notion of history according to which "*die Historie als Sachwalterin des Einmaligen und Einzigartigen eine idiographische Disziplin [ist], die durch diesen Rückfall hinter den mit Vico erreichten Standard ihren Wissenschaftsstatus wieder einbüßt.*" Similar criticism is voiced in Geldsetzer (1968), 136, who also charges Windelband with having compromised history's status as a science by making it an idiographic science that does not deal with generalities. As will be shown in this paper, this reading does not do justice to Windelband's far more nuanced ideas.
11 Windelband (1876), 4. See also Windelband (1923a), 11 ("*Hin- und Herschweben*").
12 Köhnke (1986), 363, calls Windelband a "relativist"; this seems, for the reasons to be discussed in this paper, inadequate.

positivism and relativistic historicism. I intend to read Windelband's philosophy and his ideas concerning the historiography of philosophy, contrary to trends in the literature, as following the strong programme of marrying indecisionism to philosophical truth-claims. In any case, the delicate balance that he seeks to establish refutes criticisms that rather too quickly argue in terms of a strict opposition between truth-claims and empiricist relativism.[13] Viewed this way, Windelband's double programme, as a philosopher and as a historiographer, fits neatly into characteristic trends in his period where a large number of thinkers aimed to detect a level of concepts so general as to be able to incorporate, in a non-reductive fashion, seemingly disparate ways of thinking. One example may suffice here to illustrate this point: Cassirer's early philosophy of mathematics, his study of symbolic forms, and his investigations into the history of philosophy and of science provide an important instance of an integrative approach that brings together all these projects via the search for ever more general structures.[14]

II Empirical History and Supra-Empirical Philosophy: Windelband as an "Inductive Philosopher"

Windelband's best-known text, his rectoral address on "History and Natural Science" from 1894, directly poses a conceptual challenge. This text is mainly concerned with providing a classificatory scheme for the different scientific disciplines. While both history and the natural sciences are explicitly regarded as empirical disciplines, philosophy is a non-empirical science with an a priori method.[15] This raises problems concerning the relationship between the history of philosophy—which is, by virtue of being a form of historiography, an empiri-

---

[13] Recently, Frederick Beiser (2008; 2011, 365–392) has reconstructed Windelband's attitude towards historicism as a combination of simultaneously "resisting" and "accommodating" historicism, again declaring this programme to have failed (Beiser (2008), 563–564). See also the references in note 10.
[14] See the paper by Sebastian Luft in this volume. On the period's search for increasingly more general conceptions which were intended to overcome the differences between the disciplines, see Ziche (2008); Ziche (2006).
[15] Windelband (1924c), 141; English translation: Windelband (1998). For an overview over these aspects of Windelband's work, see again Kemper (2006).

cal discipline—and philosophy itself; after all, how can an empirical discipline be an integrative element of a non-empirical science?[16]

Let's start with the topic of philosophy's reflecting on the other sciences that is central in Windelband's 1894 address. This form of philosophical meta-reflection on the sciences was only becoming institutionalized in those years, with all the openness that comes with a first attempt at institutionalization. These processes of institutionalization are directly related to Windelband's own career: His first chair at the University of Zürich was explicitly dedicated to establishing contact with the special sciences, while at the same time maintaining philosophy's independence.[17] This chair had been instituted only very recently in 1870, and had a decisively innovative character, reacting to the need to newly adjust philosophy and the special sciences. With this purpose in mind, the university established a chair for the "philosophy of the inductive sciences" or, as it was frequently and in significant linguistic shorthand referred to, a chair for "inductive philosophy". Biographies of Windelband typically gloss over his first chair at Zürich in a rather off-hand fashion. Although he held this position for only a year from 1876 to 1877, and thus used Zürich, as many of his colleagues in that period did, as a kind of "waiting-room" for obtaining a professorship in Germany,[18] this position is highly illustrative for the difficulties inherent in understanding philosophy in its relationship to the sciences. It might be worries that such a programme is too closely associated with positivism that has lead biographers be silent about this post. Such a worry, however, would be ill-founded. The very novelty of this chair resulted in its profile being still open for further consolidation. There were no trained "inductive philosophers", and it is therefore not surprising that it was not yet clearly decided—by modern standards—which type of philosophers should fill this chair. The first holders were Friedrich Albert Lange, the neo-Kantian historian of materialism, in Zürich from 1870 to 1872; Wilhelm Wundt, physiologist, philosopher with encyclopaedic ambitions, founding father of experimental psychology, between 1874 and 1875; Windelband; Richard Avenarius, empirio-criticist, between 1877 and 1896. These differences in profile notwithstanding, there are important aspects of continuity among this divergent group of philosophers on the practical level of the appointment procedure. Wundt was appointed upon a recommendation by the great theoretician of the humanities, Wilhelm Dilthey, and Wundt himself drafted a list of

---

16 This, of course, also relates to issues concerning psychologism. Windelband's stance in the psychologism debate cannot be pursued here.
17 The early history of this chair is documented in Ziche (2008), chap. III.1.
18 This term is used in historical discussions of Wundt's development as a psychologist and in the standard history of Zürich university; see the references in Ziche (2008), 331.

possible successors on which Windelband appeared in second place after Fritz Schultze, who was directed far more towards scientific naturalism.[19] Wundt recommends both colleagues as philosophers who "stand squarely within the field of the empirical sciences", thereby explicitly extending the scope of "empirical" to also cover the humanities and the social sciences.[20]

It is perfectly understandable why Windelband could be considered a good candidate for this chair. The course of his studies at Jena, Berlin and Göttingen included the natural sciences, history and philosophy; his two most important teachers were Kuno Fischer in the history of philosophy, and Hermann Lotze under whose supervision Windelband earned his doctoral degree.[21] The topics he taught in Leipzig and Zürich were much the same,[22] which suggests that the academic profile he built up in Leipzig did indeed match what was expected from him in Zürich. He could, apparently, be seen as an inductive, empirical philosopher even with his broad and clearly non-positivist background in philosophy, and with a scientific expertise which lay more in the field of the humanities.

This episode illustrates a number of significant facts about the institutionalization of a philosophical meta-reflection on the sciences, and thus also about the context of Windelband's career. The boundaries that we tend to discern between philosophical movements were virtually non-existent: Wundt, too, could be hired upon Dilthey's recommendation and Wundt himself links his own philosophical profile to that of Windelband. Secondly, this institutionalization took place within and recruited the new professionals from the existing academic fields: academic philosophy was perceived as being able to fill this newly created

---

[19] Schultze (1846–1908) took a position in Dresden instead of accepting the chair in Zürich. He, too, was influenced by neo-Kantian ideas, and published on topics in the philosophy of science, psychology and the problem of materialism.

[20] Further material is available that might help to understand the relationship between Wundt and Windelband. Windelband and Wundt published together in the 1908-volume on the *Allgemeine Geschichte der Philosophie* (Hinneberg 1908), Wundt on the "*Anfänge der Philosophie und die Philosophie der primitiven Völker*" (Wundt 1908), Windelband on the "*Neuere Philosophie*" (Windelband 1908), starting from the Renaissance. For more direct comments, see Windelband (1923a), 18, with critical remarks on Wundt's introductions to philosophy; Windelband (1909b), 99–100. A further, more indirect point of contact is established by the fact that the just-mentioned Fritz Schultze published on the psychology of "*Naturvölker*" while Wundt, in the Hinneberg (1908)-volume, discussed their philosophy.

[21] On the influence of Fischer and Lotze on Windelband, see Rickert (1915). Windelband's dissertation was devoted to the *Lehren vom Zufall* (Windelband 1870). The details of his studies and in particular the way in which and the extent to which he acquainted himself with the natural sciences deserve further attention.

[22] These are conveniently listed in the German wikipedia-entry on Windelband (http://de.wikipedia.org/wiki/Wilhelm_Windelband; January 2014).

profile. Thirdly, it was natural for the meta-reflective stance that was typical for this chair but equally characteristic for other philosophical discourses in this period to focus on issues in methodology. This implies that methodology has to fulfil a double task, in precise agreement with Windelband's larger programme. Methodological reflection has to exert critical control upon the sciences' claims while being open for critically accommodating as wide a variety of sciences as possible.[23] One of the first programmatic statements Windelband makes in his *Einleitung* confirms this openness: the boundary between philosophy and the special sciences is not fixed, but needs to be drawn and re-drawn at each particular moment in history on the basis of recent insights and developments in the sciences.[24] Distinctions are instrumental for clarifying the task and position of philosophy but Windelband explicitly refuses to let himself be caught in clear-cut oppositions. From his first career steps onwards, he was committed to a programme of combining maximal openness in his attitude towards different forms of sciences with an unfoundering adherence to traditional ideals of what philosophy should achieve.

III Individualism and Foundationalism in a Theory of Values: Windelband's Philosophical Programme

Windelband repeatedly places his philosophical programme explicitly in the context of establishing the proper form of a meta-reflection on the special sciences. A concise summary of this programme can be found in the very last paragraph of Windelband's contribution to the volume on the *Allgemeine Geschichte der Philosophie* in Paul Hinneberg's book series *Kultur der Gegenwart*. The progress and success of the individual sciences require philosophy to "pass through the critique of special science".[25] How can this metaphorical way of understand-

---

[23] This is confirmed by a number of statements by Windelband; e.g. Windelband (1909a), 27: "*so muß das Werkzeug in jedem Fall dem Sonderwesen des Gegenstandes angepaßt sein*"; Windelband (1905b), 175, where he views methodology as more open to empiricist ideas than other parts of philosophy. In this context, Windelband's ideas on logic (Windelband (1905a); (1913)) should also be discussed.

[24] Windelband (1923a), 6.

[25] Windelband (1908), 540–541 ("*wird der Weg der Philosophie zur bewußten Gestaltung des Kulturgehaltes ihrer Zeit immer durch die Kritik der besonderen Wissenschaft hindurchgehen müssen*"). A precisely parallel phrase occurs in Windelband (1923a), 334, in the context of a discus-

ing the relationship between philosophy and the sciences to be worked out? Windelband first triangulates his own view between two positions that both are seen as one-sided. He sees Kant's great achievement as having realized the necessity of relating philosophy to the sciences. However, Kant's critical analysis of the sciences remained restricted to taking mathematics and the natural sciences as model disciplines. The other extreme option was taken by Dilthey who developed a critique of historical reason. Both versions lead to mutually related difficulties: Kant cannot account for the historicity of thought,[26] while Dilthey has to embrace a historical relativism.

Windelband himself wants to combine both views, as might already be predicted on the basis of his general integrative strategy. He needs to conceive of a framework that can account for both history (more generally, for all the disciplines dealing with cultural phenomena) and the natural sciences, but philosophy must not be historicized in the way Dilthey suggests and, as Windelband states in his refusal of positivism, it also must not be naturalized. Windelband argues for a *transition* between these types of disciplines that leads from the "change inherent in historical, anthropologically conditioned value judgements to the eternally valid contents [*zu den ewig gültigen Inhalten*]".[27] One might expect Windelband to talk, in the typical neo-Kantian vein, about "values [*Werte*]", but in this passage he does not. Rather, he seems to emphasize that an eternally valid value can no longer be distinguished from a content, and it is indeed difficult to imagine a fact that could be, as it were, harder than an eternal value. These eternal contents have their foundation in a "comprehensive spiritual reality [*übergreifenden geistigen Realität*]".[28] The reform of the critical method that he suggests with these moves leads—and now he uses the key term from a value-oriented form of neo-Kantianism—to a "theory of the generally valid values [*Theorie der allgemeingültigen Werte*]" which form the basis of cultural life as well as of the sciences.

This notion of a "generally valid value" might strike one as exceedingly strange. Indeed, it epitomizes all the tensions that have already surfaced so far. After all, has Windelband not emphasized that generality is the discerning feature of nomothetic natural laws, and that value ascriptions are always idiographically related to an individual's standpoint? This leads to two important

---

sion of the relationship between philosophy and history where the intermediary step linking these fields is seen to lie in the epistemology of the historical sciences.
26 This is lucidly worked out in Beiser (2008) and Beiser (2011).
27 Windelband (1908), 541.
28 Windelband (1908), 541. If, his argument goes, all values are related to consciousness, then absolute values need to be located in a universal consciousness (with God-like features).

questions that shape Windelband's engagement with history and with the history of philosophy: how do we arrive at those most general values? And how does the generality of those values relate to the individuality that is so important in discussions about values?

Before turning to these issues, we should look at whether Windelband does indeed provide a taxonomy of these most general values in his philosophy. The place to look for is his *Einleitung*. This text is, however, not organized along fundamental values, but rather takes a taxonomy of "problems" as its guiding thread, with two main steps, namely "theoretical" and "axiological" problems that are each subdivided into a comprehensive catalogue of problems. This list builds upon the set of "problems" that Windelband sketches in the introduction to his historical *Lehrbuch*. It has already become clear that, for Windelband, values and problems are closely related; a problem-based historiography of philosophy guarantees that values get their adequate role. In the realm of problems, it is "fundamental problems [*Grundprobleme*]" that correspond to the universally valid values. This makes it possible to let the concepts of "values" and "problems" mutually illuminate each other. Problems and, correspondingly, values are in an important sense open-ended, they do not allow for summarization in terms of a finite list, even if there is a comparatively small number of fundamental problems and values that recur over and over again. Put differently, both problems and values are dynamic notions that cannot be captured in the form of definitive results. It is striking to see that problems (and all related notions) appear very consistently in the plural in Windelband's texts.

Windelband answers the question of how we arrive at problems in philosophy in general, and at fundamental problems in particular, by giving a *genetic* account which is, again, double-sided in nature. The material of philosophy is provided by everyday life and philosophy's task is defined by consistently thinking through all the implications raised by everyday problems. However, a kind of filter is required in order to avoid the relativistic overload that would result from taking and accepting everything in everyday life as philosophically relevant. Windelband sees this problem clearly, and offers two strategies—again (in the typically Windelbandian pattern) almost diametrically opposed—for selecting the particularly relevant problems. These strategies can be summarized in a pair of terms: "entanglement [*Verquickung*]" and "shaking or concussion [*Erschütterung*]" (both of which have a slightly negative ring in German, but are essential for Windelband's approach). Philosophical problems are characterized by being "*Verquickungen*", nodal points in which a great variety of ideas and traditions can come together.²⁹ The complexity of these entanglements defies an easy analysis in terms of elements that summatively build up the problem.

These "*Verquickungen*" manifest themselves on an emotional level. They must result from extreme experiences that shatter our expectations or our established ways of thinking. It needs both a special sensitivity to feel these entanglements and a particular intellectual energy to withstand the shattering experiences and to turn them productively into philosophical thinking. It is here that Windelband sees a role for the *great individuals*³⁰ that figure in (traditional) histories of philosophy. The great individuals can tie together the different lines running through the everyday in order to produce or to unveil these entangled knots. Again, problems and values prove strongly related. Not just any value ascription is sufficient for transforming an everyday issue into a (possibly fundamental) problem of philosophy. A strong emotion, a shattering experience is required for transforming an everyday issue into genuine philosophy. Not only is it true that "[a]ll insights transform themselves into ideas of value and motives of the will [*Alle Einsichten setzen sich von selbst in Wertauffassungen und Willensmotive um*]",³¹ but also vice versa: strong checks on our emotive and will-related practices stimulate and necessitate theoretical reflection. Sceptical experiences are a clear example but many other forms of shattering experiences are possible. These strong experiences elevate individual emotional experiences to the realm of general validity. As a methodological side-effect, empathy thereby becomes a legitimate method in an empirically conceived history of philosophy.³²

The stability that philosophy asks for is achieved not on the level of results but in the selection of problems, and here again via strong individual experien-

---

29 These terms are pervasive in Windelband's works; see for instance. Windelband (1957), VII ("*Verflechtung*"), 93: "*In diesem Sinne enthält das platonische System vielleicht die großartigste Problemverschlingung, welche die Geschichte gesehen hat*"; Windelband (1923a), 14 ("*Verschürzung*"); 243 (in all disciplines, idiographic and nomothetic elements "criss-cross" each other); Windelband (1905b), 187: history shows the "*vielverschlungenen*" process through which, over the course of history, the values of reason became recognized. Steindler (2004), 286, sees these passages as discussing "negative factors". I clearly cannot follow him in this point: they are most intimately connected to his philosophical programme.—On "*Erschütterungen*" see, for instance, Windelband (1923a), 8, 246; see also 433: in reality we can detect ruptures or fissures ("*Riß*") which manifest themselves in the theoretical limitations of knowledge, and in the value-problem that values cannot (fully) become manifest in this world.
30 See, for instance, Windelband (1923a), 14, 344, with explicit reference to Hegel.—It should be stated explicitly that these arguments merge into strongly nationalist statements, for instance. in Windelband (1923a), 2.
31 Windelband (1923a), 20.
32 See, for instance, Windelband (1923a), 5; Windelband (1905b), 179.

ces that are, by virtue of their strength and of the greatness of the individuals having those experiences, generalizable. *"Erschütterungen"* translates quite naturally into a *"Schwanken"*,[33] but Windelband clearly intends to turn what may be seen as an epistemological weakness into an argument supporting his own systematic claims in philosophy. Philosophical stability is achieved by concentrating on values; via the experiences of the great individuals, we gain access to the supra-individual dimension of reason within which "eternal validity [*ewige Geltung*]" is possible.[34] The emotional factor is important and Windelband phrases it in terms that directly subvert the idiographic-nomothetic distinction: what would normally appear to be the subject for a detached and intellectualist approach, the "totality", *"das Ganze"*, should also become accessible for a more passionate view.[35] This has an important implication: *The* problem of philosophy does not exist;[36] but all problems prominent in the history of philosophy can be seen as so many complex entanglements.

IV "Problems": Moves to Integrate History and Philosophy

It should be clear by now that Windelband refuses to be caught within neatly ordered and dichotomically structured concepts. In fact, he frequently orders and classifies only in order to directly transgress the boundaries he has erected, and he employs dynamic conceptions that intend to open up the conceptual space within which different methodologies can be accepted without thereby sliding into relativism. In particular, Windelband again and again acts against the most famous distinction he himself introduced, namely the distinction between "nomothetic" and "idiographic" disciplines with which he intended to capture the difference between "history and natural science". On a rather elementary level, these forms of science can cooperate because both proceed empirically. But Windelband goes on looking for connections on a deeper level.

Quite a number of passages in Windelband's works state explicitly that the nomothetic-idiographic distinction does not function as a dihairetic sub-division of forms of science. While his Zürich inaugural lecture explicitly remains neutral

---

33 Windelband (1923a), 7.
34 Windelband (1923a), 344–346. See also Windelband (1905b), 180, 183 with the strong phrase "*Die Vernunft in ihrer überempirischen, allgemeingültigen Bestimmtheit – die Weltvernunft.*"
35 Windelband (1909b), 10.
36 Cf. Windelband (1923a), 10.

as regards the distinction understanding-explaining,[37] in his programmatic text *"Was ist Philosophie?"* with which he opens his collected papers, *Präludien*, he makes it into a definiens of philosophy that it is neither descriptive nor explanatory.[38] The same holds for the discipline of history that Windelband—what is overlooked by some of his more recent interpreters—also views as both stating facts and giving explanations: "History is empirically stating facts and giving empirical explanations [*Geschichte ist empirische Konstatierung und empirische Erklärung*]".[39] In his paper on "History and Natural Science", Windelband translates these ideas into a statement about *explanation* that sounds strangely familiar to philosophers after Hempel and Oppenheim but which, other than the standard readings of the deductive-nomological ideal of explanation, takes as its focal point the *integration* of general statements that express timeless necessity and of particular conditions which describe a particular situation. Only together, these two ingredients can provide a cause and an explanation.[40]

Let us return to the key concept of Windelband's brand of philosophical historiography, the "problem".[41] Given the prominence that this concept gained in characterizing his historical work, it is remarkable that his historical *opus magnum*, his *Lehrbuch*, hardly discusses the notion of a "problem". However, "problems" figure prominently in his writings from early on. His inaugural lecture at Zürich already states the philosophical importance of looking for a "framework of fundamental concepts and problems".[42] Problems, thus, are not only closely related to values, they also relate to concepts and Windelband indeed consistently combines the study of concepts with that of problems in his programmatic statements on the historiography of philosophy. Also, it is important that Windelband when talking about a "framework" in the above citation, employs once again an open terminology: Frameworks are not deductive structures, nor are they an exhaustive list of a priori concepts.

---

37 Windelband (1876), 8.
38 Windelband (1924a), 34.
39 Windelband (1924a), 53. – In other texts, he explicitly combines the explanatory and the descriptive mode; see, for example, Windelband (1905b), 189.
40 Windelband (1924c), 158.
41 On the history of a *"Problemgeschichte"* of philosophy, see Kemper (2006), 156–158, with particular emphasis on Nicolai Hartmann, and p. 65 with an interesting systematic analysis of the notion of a "problem" in philosophy; Geldsetzer (1968), 165–6, with a long list of authors who claimed to have developed, or at least further refined, the *"Problemgeschichte"*, and on 18th-century forms of *"Problemgeschichte"*. Geldsetzer does not devote an extended discussion to the question what problems are.
42 Windelband (1876), 23.

In his *Einleitung*, Windelband gives a definition of what a "problem" is. This definition is rather opaque but at least sums up all the concepts that have already been discussed here: "In any particular moment, there will emerge the structure of the connection between the motives in thought whose relationship is the problem."[43] The motive of an "entanglement" returns here, in the multiple references to "structure", "connection", and "relationship", as does the openness inherent in thinking in terms of problems. History teaches us to discover the "salient points of the problems in the everyday"[44] via the experiential mechanisms discussed in the previous section.

The first thing to be noticed is that problems do indeed provide the solid backbone of philosophy even if they are discovered upon the shakeable grounds of the great persons' shattering experiences. Windelband couches the generality of the problems of philosophy in very strong terms: "they only change the guise of their linguistic form, and their being related to intuitions", for the rest they remain unchanged.[45] This might seem to endanger the openness Windelband seeks, but he has an answer to address this concern. A problem-oriented historiography can only be meaningful if the problems do not directly lead towards clear solutions. However, the answers to these problems also display highly stereotypical patterns even if they are subject to individual evaluative statements. This does not mean that the answers remain stable; but it would be equally illusory to assume that the answers to fundamental problems are arbitrary. The notion of a "framework of problems" perfectly captures this situation: "In the end, it is again and again the same problems and the same oppositions between the attempts at solving them".[46] This unity and continuity is what finally legitimates philosophy as a discipline. It may seem, as Windelband is ready to admit, that philosophers should be "ashamed"[47] because of what could be seen as the systematic poverty of philosophy, but the opposite is the case: The very fact that certain problems return over and over again and that the potential answers are given within a clearly structured framework makes philosophy systematically worthwhile—this stability of problems and types of answers corresponds to phil-

---

43 Windelband (1923a), 9: "*so wird sich daraus in jedem Momente auch die Struktur des Zusammenhanges zwischen den Denkmotiven ergeben, deren Verhältnis das Problem ausmacht*".
44 Windelband (1923a), 8.
45 Windelband (1923a), 10.
46 Windelband (1923a), 11; within Windelband's account of "problems", Darwinian/Machian motives of a mutual adaptation between ideas and facts can be incorporated (Windelband (1923a), 13).
47 Windelband (1923a), 11.

osophy's need for necessary truth—and at the same time guarantees that philosophy remains an emotionally as well as intellectually satisfying endeavour.

Solutions can only be attempted, no definitive solutions to fundamental problems can ever be given. What can be established, however, with surety is the urgency of the problems. Windelband repeatedly refers to a poem by Heinrich Heine in order to circumscribe the status of the real problems of philosophy; they are the "'excruciatingly old problems of existence [*qualvoll uralten Rätsel des Daseins*]'"[48] (as opposed to, as he also repeatedly states, a "mindless collection of curious facts [*geistlose Kuriositätensammlung*]" that only collects individual and neutral facts). The basic characteristics of problems translate into what makes philosophy's relation to its history different from other fields. *The* philosophy as a discipline with rigidly fixed boundaries does not exist: even those problems that are necessary still allow for different answers. Philosophy does not progress by accumulating results, but by letting problems manifest themselves as being inescapable. This happens in a historical process whose course cannot be predicted. It is a matter of historical coincidence that matters of everyday life become raised to the status of philosophical problems, due to "partly individual, and partly general aspects of the life of the mind"—and it is these factors that Windelband sees as essential for a historical approach.[49] Rickert gives this approach a metaphysical dimension and in Windelband, we can see the tension between eternal facts and Heraclitean flux.[50]

A tricky issue, and one to which I cannot give a real answer here, is how Windelband can be sure of the necessity of the problems. One possible line of argument is that he relies on the impressive achievements of the great individuals of the past. Or one could attempt another strategy and look for constants in human experiences. In some passages, in particular in the chapter on history in the *Einleitung* where Windelband discusses both "individual" and "general" historical structures, he seems to come close to such an approach that might be called a history of mentalities. The tension between the historiographical focus

---

48 Windelband (1923a), 10. He quotes from Heinrich Heine's rather pessimistic poem *"Fragen"* from the *Buch der Lieder*: "Am Meer, am wüsten, nächtlichen Meer / Steht ein Jüngling-Mann, / Die Brust voll Wehmut, das Haupt voll Zweifel, / Und mit düstern Lippen fragt er die Wogen: / "O löst mir das Rätsel, / Das qualvoll uralte Rätsel, / Worüber schon manche Häupter gegrübelt, / Häupter in Hieroglyphenmützen, / Häupter in Turban und schwarzem Barett, / Perückenhäupter und tausend andere / Arme schwitzende Menschenhäupter – /Sagt mir, was bedeutet der Mensch? / Woher ist er gekommen? Wo geht er hin? / Wer wohnt dort oben auf goldenen Sternen?" / Es murmeln die Wogen ihr ewges Gemurmel, / Es wehet der Wind, es fliehen die Wolken, / Es blinken die Sterne, gleichgültig und kalt, / Und ein Narr wartet auf Antwort."
49 Windelband (1923a), 11.
50 Rickert (1915), 3–4.

on individuals and the generality required for philosophy and science remains. Windelband aims at providing this generality by transcending individual subjectivity precisely through the particularly strong experiences of the most eminent individuals.

V New Forms of Generality: Turning Indecisionism into a Philosophical Virtue

The focus on the great individuals may sound Nietzschean in tone. The greatest difficulty with reading Windelband as a Nietzschean, however, is—besides the fact that Windelband consistently reads Nietzsche as a poet and not as a philosopher—that a subjectivist worship of the great individuals does not capture the spirit of Windelband's strongly *integrative* programme. In this final section, the lines of argument as presented so far will be summarized under the label of *generality:* how, and where, does Windelband arrive at concepts that are sufficiently general for accommodating the different forms of sciences and different methodologies under one notion? He does so on three levels: the universal validity of the fundamental problems of philosophy that has already been discussed; an "inner connection [*innerer Zusammenhang*]" of philosophy's history, conceived of in an overtly Hegelian fashion;[51] an emphasis on "logical functions [*logische Funktionen*]" as exceedingly general elements of philosophical theorizing. The search for increasingly higher forms of generality directly relates his programme to larger trends in philosophy in his period; Cassirer may again serve as a natural comparison.

The rhetoric of generality is pervasive in his writings.[52] In his analyses of the special sciences, Windelband looks for the most general characteristic of all empirical disciplines that turns out to be methodological as well as metaphysical. Not surprisingly, he finds this characteristic in the integration of elements into a complex, entangled whole: all elements of representations that refer to the same object fit together without contradictions.[53] This relational analysis can be filled in both by laws and by Gestalten, that is, by the paradigmatic objects of both the natural sciences and the humanities. Both forms of science agree

---

51 Windelband states his Hegelian affinities explicitly in for instance Windelband (1924b). See also Beiser (2011), 392.
52 It may suffice to quote one pertinent term, that of "*Gebilde*", which has associations of Gestalt theory and holistic traditions. Compare Windelband (1923a), 8.
53 Windelband (1924c), 149.

in "making the individual knowledge [*Einzelwissen*] fit into a larger whole".[54] We can detect here a strategy that makes use of conceptual distinctions—two different senses of wholeness, namely general laws, and the complex Gestalt-like structures that underlie our evaluative judgements—only in order to stress the compatibility of those notions in the sense that both idiographic and nomothetic disciplines mutually require each other and that both senses of wholeness can be experienced emotionally as well as reconstructed theoretically. The final picture is one we have already encountered: what we require, in the end, is a general notion of lawfulness that provides us with a solid *framework* for our worldview,[55] and within this framework, the "living connection" of all individual forms unfolds itself. The non-deductive openness of "frameworks" and of methodological arguments allows us to integrate the different sciences. This programme is indeed Hegelian in a number of important points, most specifically in the search for an "inner connection [*innerer Zusammenhang*]", a necessary order and a "meaningful totality [*sinnvolles Ganzes*]".[56] Philosophy must indeed be more than just a summary of results. If philosophy's task were nothing but summarizing the general results of the other disciplines into a coherent whole, then the historical dimension would be irrelevant. By explicitly claiming an essentially historical dimension for philosophy, Windelband thereby opposes *both* a positivist reading of philosophy as just a collection of the results of science, and a "popular world-view doctrine [*landläufige Weltanschauungswissenschaft*]".[57] Interestingly, the same argument can be turned against giving metaphysics an overly important role within philosophy.[58] Only when philosophy manages to integrate the empiricist "respect for the details [*Andacht für das Kleine*]" cherished by a historical approach with the focus on general notions, one obtains a form of "cultural history" that is every bit as magnificent as the physical universe.[59] The focus on a broad notion of culture is incorporated in Windelband's winding and self-referential summary of his integration of history and philosophy as he presents it in his programmatic text on the "*Geschichte der Philosophie*": life stands in "intimate relations" (again one of the "*Verquickungs*"-phrases that Windel-

---

[54] Windelband (1924c), 154.
[55] Windelband (1924c), 157.
[56] This is best summarized in Windelband (1905b), 177, again with reference to Hegel. See also Windelband (1909a), 26: a "*synthetisches Bewußtsein*" forms the "*Grundbegriff der kritischen Erkenntnistheorie*".
[57] Windelband (1905b), 181.
[58] Windelband (1905b), 181.
[59] Windelband (1909b), 86–7.

band repeats frequently) with the "*Kulturinteressen*" of an epoch.⁶⁰ This epoch, even more broadly, the "entire development of the cultural activities in history" needs to be studied if we want to arrive at a "historical self-knowledge of human reason" which, in turn, is a methodological pre-condition for philosophy.⁶¹ Thus, according to Windelband, what is immediately given for a philosophical theory of principles (Windelband is not very precise in his statements here; what he probably means, is a system of philosophy, based upon principles) is its own history.

Windelband is highly consistent in applying the ideas developed here. Perhaps the clearest test case lies in his treatment of the idea of *progress* in the history of philosophy. If he is indeed presenting the history of philosophy as an analysis of the eternal problems and generally valid values in philosophy, one would rather expect him to disregard the notion of progress. This is indeed what one finds. Philosophy does not proceed via a "continuous progress [*stetiger Fortschritt*]" that would let it approximate a final result more and more closely.⁶² Philosophy's processuality is a processuality of putting down the "entire harvest [*Gesamtertrag*]" of European culture in scientific terms.⁶³ Changes in philosophy, especially those occasioned by philosophy's reacting to the progress of the natural sciences (with respect to the natural sciences, Windelband uses the notion of progress without further reservation) do not imply that philosophy itself is fundamentally progressive.

History's task, then, is indeed intimately related to that of philosophy itself. But Windelband takes an extra step towards a further philosophical analysis of the form of generality required by his integrative philosophical programme of combining individual experience with scientific generality. The very terminology in which Windelband and his early exegetes try to capture the highest level of generality is again influenced by Hegelian ideas. Bruno Bauch characterizes Windelband's ultimate unifying idea as an investigation into "logical functions [*logische Funktionen*]".⁶⁴ What characterizes these functions, according to Bauch, is that they can be differentiated, but that they still belong together in virtue of being logical functions. Differentiating between logical forms, but at

---

60 Windelband (1905b), 186.
61 Windelband (1905b), 186. See also 185: "Man as rational being is not given naturalistically [*naturnotwendig*], but is given us as a historical task [*historisch aufgegeben*]". This phrase occurs again word for word in Windelband (1924b), 283.
62 Windelband (1957), 8.
63 Windelband (1957), 8. Cf. also loc. cit. 10 on the "pragmatic" character of philosophy's progress.
64 Bauch (1915b), 102, 112.

the same time recognizing them as such, is a way to overcome the wavering motion, the "*Schwanken*" between the fundamental dichotomies of philosophy.[65] A similar terminology is employed by Windelband in his essay on the "*Wille zur Wahrheit*". Windelband's discussion of the will focuses on the "autonomy of mental functions [*Selbständigkeit der geistigen Funktionen*]" that prevents the will from becoming an organ of capricious arbitrariness.[66] Again, this combination of autonomy and structure is confirmed in the "development of methodology" which shows that in any case the "instrument needs to be adapted to the particular nature of the object". Under the over-arching label of "mental functions" or "logical structures" it thus becomes possible to integrate the openness of methodologies, the autonomy of the will, and the stability in intellectual and practical matters that philosophy aims for. What he thinks he has achieved can be described, to use his own term, as a "double unfolding [*Doppelentfaltung*]" of philosophy and the history of philosophy,[67] in the sense of being directed towards empirical history and idealistic system-building at the same time. What the "logical functions" are supposed to achieve coincides with what the methodological stance does: methodology needs to do justice to all disciplines (and thus also to both poles in such a "double unfolding") and at the same time methodology can understand the individual characteristics of both through unveiling their most profound differences".[68]

Windelband's programme, when reconstructed in this fashion, can be easily linked with, for instance, Cassirer's functional arguments. We may still feel his approach to be lacking in precision or conceptual ambition. However, this does not come from his violating conceptual distinctions that he himself introduced, or from a naive lapse into contradictions. Rather, the difficulty seems to be that his integrative programme hints at new levels of generality that might indeed account for new forms of integrating philosophy and the sciences, but does not work out those categories in detail. A second problem can be put in Hegelian terms: Windelband's project remains in many respects a conciliatory programme that—in an insufficiently Hegelian fashion—is always intent on doing justice to both sides of a conceptual distinction without much of a dialectical transformation. This is anything but naive: it is the result of a very serious

---

[65] In Bauch's text, it is realism and idealism which have to be related (with reference to a critical discussion between Windelband and August Messer), but the same holds for all the tensions mentioned so far.
[66] Windelband (1909a), 27. – Note that even where he discusses the will, Windelband is searching for general features, not for an understanding of individual decisions.
[67] Windelband (1905a), 175.
[68] Windelband (1905a), 175.

search, over a frequently tantalizingcourse, for giving history an integral role within philosophy.

Bibliography

Bauch (1915a): Bruno Bauch, "Wilhelm Windelband †", in: *Kant-Studien* 20, VII-XIV.
Bauch (1915b): Bruno Bauch, "Idealismus und Realismus in der Sphäre des philosophischen Kritizismus. Ein Verständigungsversuch", in: *Kant-Studien* 20, 97–116.
Beelmann (2001): Axel Beelmann: *Theoretische Philosophiegeschichte. Grundsätzliche Probleme einer philosophischen Geschichte der Philosophie*, Basel: Schwabe.
Beiser (2008): Frederick C. Beiser, "Historicism and neo-Kantianism", in: *Stud. Hist. Phil. Sci.* 39, 554–564.
Beiser (2011): Frederick C. Beiser: *The German Historicist Tradition*, Oxford: OUP.
Geldsetzer (1968): Lutz Geldsetzer: *Die Philosophie der Philosophiegeschichte im 19. Jahrhundert. Zur Wissenschaftstheorie der Philosophiegeschichtsschreibung und -betrachtung*, Meisenheim am Glan: Anton Hain.
Hinneberg (1908): Paul Hinneberg (Ed.), *Die Kultur der Gegenwart. Ihre Entwicklung und ihre Ziele*. Series I, Part V: *Allgemeine Geschichte der Philosophie*, Berlin/Leipzig: B.G. Teubner.
Kemper (2006): Matthias Kemper: *Geltung und Problem. Theorie und Geschichte im Kontext des Bildungsgedankens bei Wilhelm Windelband*, Würzburg: Königshausen & Neumann.
Köhnke (1986): Klaus Christian Köhnke, *Entstehung und Aufstieg des Neukantianismus. Die deutsche Universitätsphilosophie zwischen Idealismus und Positivismus*, Frankfurt a. M.: Suhrkamp.
Rickert (1915): Heinrich Rickert: *Wilhelm Windelband*, Tübingen: J.C.B.Mohr (Paul Siebeck).
Rorty, Schneewind, Skinner (1984): Richard Rorty, Jerome B. Schneewind and Quentin Skinner, *Philosophy in History. Essays in the Historiography of Philosophy*, Cambridge: CUP.
Ruge (1917): Arnold Ruge: *Wilhelm Windelband*, Leipzig: Barth.
Sorell a. Rogers (2005): Tom Sorell and G.A.J. Rogers (Eds.) *Analytic Philosophy and History of Philosophy*, Oxford: Clarendon.
Steindler (2004) Larry Steindler, "Wilhelm Windelband (1848–1915)", in: Giovanni Santinello a. Gregorio Piaia (Eds.), *Storia delle storie generali della filosofie*, vol. 5, *Il secondo ottocento*, Roma and Padova: Antenore, 270–294.
Van der Vaart Smit (1922): Hendrik Willem van der Vaart Smit, *Windelband*, Baarn: Hollandia.
Windelband (1870): Wilhelm Windelband, *Die Lehren vom Zufall*, Berlin: A.W. Schade.
Windelband (1876): Wilhelm Windelband, "Über den gegenwärtigen Stand der psychologischen Forschung", Leipzig: Breitkopf & Härtel.
Windelband (1878, 1880): Wilhelm Windelband, *Die Geschichte der neueren Philosophie in ihrem Zusammenhange mit der allgemeinen Cultur und den besonderen Wissenschaften*, 2 vols., Leipzig: Breitkopf & Härtel.
Windelband (1888): Wilhelm Windelband, *Geschichte der alten Philosophie*, Nördlingen: Beck.
Windelband (1900): Wilhelm Windelband, *Platon*, Stuttgart: Frommann.

Windelband (1905a): Wilhelm Windelband, "Logik", in: Wilhelm Windelband (Ed.), *Die Philosophie im Beginn des zwanzigsten Jahrhunderts. Festschrift für Kuno Fischer*, vol. 1, Heidelberg: Carl Winter, 163–186.

Windelband (1905b): Wilhelm Windelband, "Geschichte der Philosophie", in: Wilhelm Windelband (Ed.), *Die Philosophie im Beginn des zwanzigsten Jahrhunderts. Festschrift für Kuno Fischer*, vol. 2, Heidelberg: Carl Winter, 175–200.

Windelband (1908): Wilhelm Windelband, "Die neuere Philosophie", in: Paul Hinneberg (Ed.), *Die Kultur der Gegenwart. Ihre Entwicklung und ihre Ziele*, Berlin/Leipzig: B. G. Teubner, 382–543.

Windelband (1909a): Wilhelm Windelband, *Der Wille zur Wahrheit. Rede bei der akademischen Feier der Universität Heidelberg am 22. Novemeber 1909*, Heidelberg: Carl Winter.

Windelband (1909b): Wilhelm Windelband, *Die Philosophie im Deutschen Geistesleben des XIX. Jahrhunderts. Fünf Vorlesungen*, Tübingen: J.C.B. Mohr (Paul Siebeck).

Windelband (1913): Wilhelm Windelband, "Die Prinzipien der Logik", in: Wilhelm Windelband a. Arnold Ruge (Eds.), *Enzyclopädie der philosophischen Wissenschaften*, vol. 1, *Logik*, Tübingen: J.C.B. Mohr (Paul Siebeck), 1–60.

Windelband (1923a): Wilhelm Windelband, *Einleitung in die Philosophie*, 3rd ed., Tübingen: J. C.B. Mohr (Paul Siebeck).

Windelband (1923b): Wilhelm Windelband, *Geschichte der abendländischen Philosophie im Altertum*, published as part of the *Handbuch der Altertumswissenschaft*, 4th ed., München: Beck.

Windelband (1924a): Wilhelm Windelband, "Was ist Philosophie?", in: Wilhelm Windelband, *Präludien. Aufsätze und Reden zur Philosophie und ihrer Geschichte*, vol. 1, Tübingen: J. C.B. Mohr (Paul Siebeck), 1–54.

Windelband (1924b): Wilhelm Windelband, "Die Erneuerung des Hegelianismus", Wilhelm Windelband, *Präludien. Aufsätze und Reden zur Philosophie und ihrer Geschichte*, vol. 1, Tübingen: J.C.B. Mohr (Paul Siebeck), 273–289.

Windelband (1924c): Wilhelm Windelband, "Geschichte und Naturwissenschaft." In: Wilhelm Windelband, *Präludien. Aufsätze und Reden zur Philosophie und ihrer Geschichte*, vol. 2, Tübingen: J.C.B. Mohr (Paul Siebeck), 136–160.

Windelband (1957) Wilhelm Windelband, *Lehrbuch der Geschichte der Philosophie*, 15th ed., edited and updated by Heinz Heimsoeth, Tübingen: J.C.B. Mohr (Paul Siebeck).

Windelband (1998): Wilhelm Windelband, "History and Natural Science", in: *Theory and Psychology* 8, 5–22.

Wundt (1908): Wilhelm Wundt, "Die Anfänge der Philosophie und die Philosophie der primitiven Völker", in: Paul Hinneberg (Ed.), *Die Kultur der Gegenwart. Ihre Entwicklung und ihre Ziele*, Berlin / Leipzig: B. G. Teubner, 1–31.

Ziche (2006): Paul Ziche, "'Wissen' und 'hohe Gedanken'. Allgemeinheit und die Metareflexion des Wissenschaftssystems im 19. Jahrhundert", in: Michael Hagner a. Manfred D. Laubichler (Eds.), *Der Hochsitz des Wissens. Das Allgemeine als wissenschaftlicher Wert*, Zürich / Berlin: Diaphanes, 129–150.

Ziche (2008): Paul Ziche, *Wissenschaftslandschaften um 1900. Philosophie, die Wissenschaften und der "nicht-reduktive Szientismus"*, Zürich: Chronos.

Tim-Florian Goslar
On the Culturalization of Philosophical Historiography: Hermeneutics and Philosophical Historiography in Feuerbach, Dilthey and Blumenberg

It isn't quite "hermeneutics" when an author has to be understood against himself—as well as against the one who reads him in a hermeneutical fashion.[1]

The history of philosophy is always also the history of a discipline that has been overwhelmingly concerned with its own history. Philosophy provides methodological access to its history and writes a history that is, in its self-understanding, a history of philosophy's progress. In the closing years of the 19th century, however, a hermeneutic and self-reflective approach to the field of philosophical historiography arises which noticeably refers to subjects that lie outside the limits of philosophical history. In the course of this, the thought of a continually progressive history of philosophy is set aside. The hermeneutical and self-reflective thinking of history orients itself henceforth to human-social-historical reality and thus to a reality that is permanently changing and developing. The aims set by progress oriented thinking cannot accommodate this openness. And while Wilhelm Dilthey's hermeneutics was originally outlined as a methodological foundation for the humanities that was to be developed by philosophy, nowadays hermeneutics increasingly subsumes philosophy. In view of this the question arises to what extent, since the end of the 19th century, did hermeneutics' increasing claim to universality modify a historiography that hitherto had been the exclusive concern of philosophy.[2]

While no compendium on hermeneutics fails to mention Dilthey and while Hans Blumenberg's way of thinking is even described as a "radically immanent

---

[1] Blumenberg (2001), 17.
[2] In the earlier years of his work, Friedrich Schleiermacher, who will not be specifically considered in the following, still understands hermeneutics as a method of textual exegesis and as a set of rules detached from historical implications. In later years, however, he further develops a hermeneutics as the doctrine of an art [Kunstlehre] which centres around a historically conditioned process of understanding. Being influenced to some degree by Scheiermacher, Dilthey develops a hermeneutics that raises a claim to universality and which henceforth is essentially tied to history. On the origin of Dilthey's universal hermeneutic as well as its relation to Schleiermacher, see Grondin (2009), 17–29.

thinking [of] hermeneutics"[3], there is a whole plethora of divergent opinions regarding Ludwig Feuerbach's hermeneutics. Its colourful variety seems to resist unification almost entirely.[4] But without wanting to reach unity with regard to this issue, Feuerbach's hermeneutical advances are of interest in the following because there is, in the context of his philosophical historical writings, an immediate, methodological dependence on philosophical historiography.[5] The juxtaposition of the Feuerbachean approach on the one hand and Dilthey's hermeneutics and consequently Blumenberg's on the other generates an additional heuristic benefit. In a systematic regard it makes visible that with hermeneutics' increasing claim to universality, the relation between hermeneutics and philosophical historiography is to be determined anew.

From very early on, Ludwig Feuerbach characterizes his methodological procedure as a genetic process. He does so specifically in his 1837 Leibniz monograph which is part of his three-volume historiography on philosophy, *Geschichte der neuern Philosophie*. When encountering Leibniz in the course of this history he wonders how such an extensive and varied thought can be transferred into a philosophical historiographical representation without unduly and illegitimately restricting its content. At this point Feuerbach develops a hermeneutic whose fundamental category is *development*.

Philosophy, according to Feuerbach, is in its core the *"capacity for development"*—and precisely this *capacity for development* is in the centre of the *"formal*

---

3 Müller-Funk (1990), 65.
4 Thus, the interpretations range from assuming hermeneutics to be an "essential moment" and "the main theme of Feuerbach's work" (Serrão (1998), 16f.) to the conception that Feuerbach "neither initially nor later found access to the hermeneutic problem" but in "his one-sided enthusiasm for speculative theology and philosophy" was still looking towards "the question of a historical-critical Biblical exegesis" (Schott (1973), 166). According to Serrão in Feuerbach's later writings the "hermeneutic interest" was "not relinquished" but merely "shifted to other enigmatic areas of human nature: those of religion and anthropology" (Serrão (1998), 32). However, the question whether and to what extent Feuerbach's naturalistic, sensualistic and materialistic basic conceptions following his philosophical historiography, could be reconciled with a hermeneutic approach without, at the end of this road, completely suspending hermeneutics, is not pursued any more.
5 According to Serrão, Feuerbach's "reflections on the problem of interpretation" first originate "from his philosophical historiography" (Serrão (1998), 17). It also needs to be considered, however, that the passages in his 1837 Leibniz monograph that are decisive for a hermeneutics in part correspond with his examination of Hegel, such as can be found in his *Kritik des 'Anti-Hegel'* as well as in his review of *Hegels Geschichte der Philosophie*, both of which appeared in 1835 and thus after the publication of the first and second volume of his *Geschichte der neuern Philosophie*. On Feuerbach's philosophical historiography against the background of his examination of Hegel, see Wartofsky (1982), 49–88.

activity of representation" which philosophical historiography is obliged to undertake.[6] Reconstructing the development should grant access to what implicitly underlies philosophy. Development is "the deciphering of the true *sense* of a philosophy" and with that nothing more than the "*representation* of its *idea*".[7] This methodological reflection, which at this point precedes the representation of philosophical history, arises from the demand [*Anspruch*] placed on the object itself: it requires a methodological procedure that is capable of looking beneath the surface.

Analytic as well as synthetic activity is required to extrapolate the implicitly underlying idea and hence the true sense of a philosophy. Analytic activity "develops out of the said that which is *not said* but still implicitly [...] lies in it".[8] Analytic activity is thus the mediating activity between the explicit, that is to say, the superficially realized and that which implicitly underlies it. Hence it is "only the object of *meditation*".[9] As a meditating activity between the expressed and the unexpressed it uncovers the implicit and hands it over the care of the synthetic activity. The latter brings together what initially, after the analysis, stands side by side in an unconnected fashion. It reconstructs the core of a philosophy by exploring the idea "through connecting the different, isolated ostensibly unrelated, or at least not expressly related, yet essentially still related thoughts."[10]

Only after this synthetic activity is the depiction capable of bringing out the idea.[11] Despite the detour via analysis and synthesis to the idea of a philosophy, the depiction remains obliged to the surface of the said so as not to drift into the boundless. The last safeguard is and remains the text. Genetic activity "must always be based on *definite data*" in order to make sure "that this development, this genesis is really in accord with the true, unmistakeable sense and spirit of a philosopher".[12] Critique, in turn, is only possible on the basis and respectively in the implementation and reconstruction of development—first genesis, then critique. The alternative, a critique without genesis, lacks legitimacy. This is because a preceding critique could also only remain external and, without a previous understanding of the immanent development, must inevitably be unsuccess-

---

6 Feuerbach (1981), 3.
7 Feuerbach (1981), 4.
8 Feuerbach (1981), 4.
9 Feuerbach (1981), 4.
10 Feuerbach (1981), 4.
11 Feuerbach's demand for depiction and explication of that which is immanent to a philosophy creates aside from his materialistic attitude a room for the idea. For what is still underlying the matter is still "undeveloped" (Feuerbach (1981), 4, remark 1), it is not a component of "empirical perception" (Feuerbach (1981), 4) and remains yet to be developed.
12 Feuerbach (1981), 5.

ful: "Refutation is very easy; but understanding is very difficult".[13] Feuerbach's hermeneutics should, in the course of the representation of the history of philosophy, elucidate what could be misunderstood without the help of a hermeneutic procedure. With such a misunderstanding, the philosophy could not be represented or could at best be depicted falsely. However, through a process in which development and historical representation are closely related, development is always bound to *"pure historical* depiction" and moreover one "in which the philosopher—as far as *possible—speaks,* and becomes explicable *through* and *out of himself"*.[14] Thus, hermeneutic access is dependent on philosophical historiography, since it was initially the character of the investigated object that evoked the necessity of a hermeneutic procedure.

> Depending on the nature of the object and the quality of the respective material, present in the works of the philosopher, the pure historical depiction can be developmental or take their place. Development can only ever cover the essentials: it is only appropriate where it is *needed*.[15]

A general necessity for the hermeneutic exploration of texts is thus rejected. Such a necessity is only present where the transposition of a philosophy into representation threatens to fail. Thus Locke can "not be essentially misunderstood or be treated superficially, but Leibniz [can]".[16] Only the risk of discrepancy and irreconcilable differences between the implicit and the explicit and, subsequent to that, the difficulty of translating the results gained through analytic and synthetic extrapolation in the form of a depiction evokes a hermeneutics. What first suggests itself as a restriction of the hermeneutical process broadens to an exclusion of the interpreter in favour of "hermeneutical objectivity".[17]

> Development should be *reproduction, metamorphosis*. The developer should not represent the strange *as strange* but rather, as though it was his, he should reflect it as meditated and

---

13 Feuerbach (1960), 346.
14 Feuerbach (1981), 6.
15 Ibid. A "primacy of the hermeneutic over the historical" (Serrão (1998), 31) is thus difficult to maintain – what can be determined as hermeneutic in Feuerbach, remains ever referred to philosophical historiography.
16 Feuerbach (1981), 3.
17 "True to a Hegelian tradition the explicit identification with hermeneutic objectivity was maintained to the point of self-denial." (Geldsetzer (1968), 204) Feuerbach's approach with regard to the relationship of hermeneutics and philosophical historiography would thus have to be seen in close relation to Schleiermacher's hermeneutics. Precisely in his *hermeneutical objectivity* he is very close to the "Schleiermacher-school" (see ibid.).

assimilated through his own activity. His model is not the bee who gathers pollen and bears it homeward but the bee who *exudes* the gathered pollen as wax.[18]

Feuerbach sees in this the justification of an essential moment of critique that, at this point, complements the genetic procedure: "the true critique lies in the development itself", since development in its turn is only possible "through the separation of the essential from the contingent, the unconditioned from the conditioned, the objective from the subjective", a separation which is carried out by critique itself.[19] Feuerbach's genetic-critical developmental model launches a hermeneutics that brings out the implicit sense of a philosophy and which seeks to establish objectivity by means of sundering the objective from the subjective. Hermeneutics stands in the background as an independent method for the sake of hermeneutical objectivity, conveying if necessary the basic idea of a philosophy and thus remains always directed to philosophical historiography. Its task is reproduction, although pure historical depiction may in some cases be sufficient.

However this relationship between hermeneutics and philosophical historiography is stood on its head as soon as hermeneutics steps out of the spell of being a mere auxiliary discipline and rises to claim universal applicability for the whole realm of intellectual creation. Not only is the method of hermeneutics subjected to decisive modifications but also the interest of hermeneutics undergoes a lasting alteration in the course of this. And these changes themselves have an effect on the self-understanding of philosophical historiography.

Wilhelm Dilthey's endeavour to provide a foundation of the humanities aims at instantiating an independent method that is capable of appropriately grasping the object of the humanities. The positivism and empiricism of his day had considered it their task to impose natural scientific methods on the historical and spiritual disciplines. Consequently the very object of the humanities threatens to slip under inappropriate natural-scientific models. The humanities cannot wholly avoid a share of the responsibility for this status quo in that they have hitherto neglected to supply "a foundation upon the only, in essence, secure

---

18 Feuerbach (1981), 5.
19 How close Feuerbach is to Hegel in his philosophical historiography can be seen in the following citation from his *Kritik des 'Anti-Hegel'*: "The true critique is therefore that which seeks out the idea of a philosophy, using it as a measure for its assessment and explores afterwards if and how far the philosopher corresponds or contradicts this idea in his conception, expression, depiction and development. [...] It only really explicates what the philosopher in question already had on the tip of his tongue or in his mind, but for which he had found no or only extremely awkward conceptions and expressions" (Feuerbach (1969a), 65f.), see also remark 5.

knowledge, in brief, a philosophical groundwork" for their own actions.[20] For Dilthey it is necessary to develop this basis "from out of the tasks of life" from which all the sciences have emerged and to which they remain constantly related.[21] The humanities in particular always refer to "the same fact", namely, "human-social-historical reality".[22] And with this the question of the constitution of objective, social structures comes into view and further Dilthey's hermeneutics finds itself oriented towards history. Both aspects correlate directly with one another.

Hermeneutics is needed to bring our reality to understanding and its three methodological steps consist of the "relation of experience [*Erlebnis*], expression and understanding".[23] In the process of understanding we recognize "an internal out of the signs that are externally and sensibly given",[24] in other words, experience [*Erlebnis*]. As to the question regarding what constitutes our reality, nothing can be established here "that does not involve a r e l a t i o n to life of the I".[25] At the basis of this is life, from out of which the *I's respective relations to life*, understood as "individual life unities"[26], constitute our reality in their interactions: "Life consists in the interaction of life-unities".[27]

Thus, Dilthey's hermeneutics unfolds in an interplay between individuals and the structures emerging from their interactions, from the "product[s] of the collective spirit [...], in which human consciousness becomes objective and in this way withstands dismemberment". It withstands dismemberment into incomprehensible and unrelated parts of a subjective nature but primarily it withstands dismemberment in time: "One cannot experience what the human is through brooding reflection on oneself nor through psychological experiments but rather through history".[28] Individual immanent experiences [*Erlebnisse*] should become disclosed starting from the objective products of the collective spirit which, in their re-enactment, become expressed anew: "the whole of philological and historical science is grounded on the presupposition that this subsequent understanding of the singular can be raised to objectivity".[29]

---

20 Dilthey (1959), XVI.
21 Dilthey (1958), 79.
22 Dilthey (1958), 81.
23 Dilthey (1958), 131.
24 Dilthey (1957b), 318. The "epitome of what comes to us in experience and understanding is the life of the human race in its comprehensive unity" (Dilthey (1958), 131).
25 Dilthey (1958), 131.
26 Dilthey (1958), 131.
27 Dilthey (1958), 228.
28 Dilthey (1957a), 180.
29 Dilthey (1957b), 317.

Dilthey's interest in objective spirit includes reality as a historical-social and intersubjective life-process, however, "immediate inner reality in its own right [...], especially as an internally experienced coherence [*erlebter Zusammenhang*]",[30] is the object of investigation. Immanence, itself, which is to be traced, comprehended and made explicit, is conditioned by history. Therefore, the declared purpose is the "complete recognition of immanence [...] in historical consciousness".[31] Inversely, it is necessary that we win an "insight into the essence of the historical"[32] on the basis of the "objectification of life".[33]

Dilthey's hermeneutics is universal in its demand to comprehend reality in all its facets as emerging from immanence and also inversely in the demand to understand immanence as emerging from the objectification of life because the humanities understand reality as a product of our experiencing, expressing and understanding. In the course of this process, reality itself opposes an exclusively conceptual determination and opposes in particular the construction of concepts of the natural sciences.[34] However it does require a suitable conceptual inventory which can appropriately describe the objectified structures of the humanities and the processes of their formation. That is why the concepts of the humanities must express "the tendency that dwells in life, its variability and its unrest". These concepts are "fixed representations of a progressive solidification of thought, which itself is a process or a direction of movement".[35] The task of the humanities, owing to the "dynamic of life",[36] is "immanent life-interpretation". "Life is free of conceptual knowledge, spirit is sovereign in the face of all cobwebs of dogmatic thinking".[37] A translation of immanence by means of hermeneutics can never completely succeed and always means only an approximation of the dynamic ground-structure of life from out of which our reality emerges. While unambiguous clarity can never be reached, the permanent attempt to help immanence to language is the task and goal of philosophy. As Blumenberg writes:

> Philosophy [is] nothing other than the emerging self-awareness of humanity [...]. That might sound highly speculative but it implies something very elementary, namely, that human beings comprehend themselves in what is "vital" in their life, that they become aware of

---

30 Dilthey (1957b), 317 f.
31 Dilthey (1958), 290.
32 Dilthey (1958), 147.
33 Dilthey (1958), 147.
34 On the critique of concepts in Dilthey's life-philosophy, see Misch (1967), in particular 88 – 94.
35 Dilthey (1958), 157.
36 Misch (1967), 100.
37 Dilthey (1958), 291.

themselves in their drives, conditionalities and possibilities, in a word: that they bring their cause to language within their own awareness. This is as elementary as it is difficult, and perhaps in the end unattainable.[38]

The concept attempts to ascertain the vital interest that was originally contained in the form of expression. For this reason the conceptual determination is to be placed once again into its originary movement, development itself, and hence within life, to generate meanings within the understanding that make humanity visible in its vitality. It is necessary "to translate the immeasurably expanding external historical-social reality back into spiritual vitality from out of which it emerged".[39] It is possible to associate Blumenberg with Dilthey's hermeneutics in his desire to disclose human spaces of immanence [Immanenzräume] in their historical conditionality. In methodological terms the professed goal is therefore to find a suitable descriptive inventory that is capable of comprehending that which is vital within humans.

With the publication of *Paradigmen zu einer Metaphorologie* Hans Blumenberg enters an internal academic debate concerning the range of and potential of conceptual-historical approaches. Also, Blumenberg's hermeneutical access is preceded by a critique of concepts.[40] Metaphors as the central, non-conceptual components of language are able to reveal far more about humanity and its history than a conceptual-historical analysis.[41] A conceptual-history, presented as ideal-typical, already undermines its own project: "in a rigorous sense" a pure conceptual language strives towards a "hypothetical 'final result'", the "completeness of a terminology", "that catches the presence and precision in definite

---

38 Blumenberg (1961), 128.
39 Dilthey (1958), 119 f.
40 Blumenberg first published *Paradigmen zu einer Metaphorologie* in 1960 in the *Archiv für Begriffsgeschichte* and this choice already brought the debate that was unfolding between metaphor theory and conceptual history within the *Paradigmen zu einer Metaphorologie* into academic discourse.
41 Blumenberg himself, in his continuation of his metaphorology—the *Theorie der Unbegrifflichkeit*, which remained a rough scheme –, refers to the fact that the early explications of metaphorology are as yet closely oriented towards the confrontation between metaphor theory and conceptual history. In this regard, the *Theorie der Unbegrifflichkeit* is also the attempt to extend metaphorology beyond the confrontation between metaphor theory and conceptual history because metaphor is now only considered merely as "a narrow and special case of unconceptuality" (Blumenberg (1997a), 87). Nevertheless metaphors keep their potential as "indicative fossils of an archaic layer of processes of theoretical curiosity" (Blumenberg (1997a), 87) and the access that metaphors grant to humanity's spaces of immanence [Immanenzräume] is also still maintained here.

concepts".⁴² A purely conceptual-terminological language denies the possibility of its own history: "In achieving its final conceptual state, philosophy must lose every justifiable interest in researching the *history* of its concepts".⁴³ Concepts, strictly speaking, do not even possess their own history—what allows conceptual-history to be the history of its own concepts is the ground on which the concepts are founded and this ground is provided by metaphors. The elucidation of the permutations of metaphorical ground, in turn, allows the elucidation of conceptual-historical transitions.⁴⁴

The concept remains on the surface, the metaphor, however, is able to view the underlying stratum: the spaces of immanence [*Immanenzräume*]. Metaphor has the potential, as Blumenberg claims in reference to Ernst Cassirer's *animal symbolicum*, "to come to re-interpret the external 'impression' as 'expression' of the inner and thus to replace the strange and inaccessible with something sensible and graspable".⁴⁵ The bridge, that the metaphor proposes from the internal to the external and simultaneously from the external to the internal, allows precisely this access to immanence that was already intended by Dilthey's hermeneutic ground-structure of experience [*Erleben*], expression and understanding. An inherent component of metaphorology is to arrive at a hermeneutics that considers itself obliged to history.

The analytic framework of metaphorology weaves a continuum between concept and metaphor. Metaphors that do not let themselves be transferred to conceptuality are irreducible and as such absolute. That absolute metaphors "prove to be resistant in the face of the terminological demand" does not mean, however, that "a metaphor cannot be replaced, represented or corrected through another more accurate metaphor".⁴⁶

---

42 Blumenberg (1998), 7. "Viewed from the ideal of a conclusive terminology, even conceptual history can generally only have a critical-destructive value, a role, that is played out and exhausted in the achievement of the goal" (Blumenberg (1998), 8).
43 Blumenberg (1998), 7f.
44 Nevertheless Blumenberg is aware of the necessity for the cooperation of conceptual history and metaphorology and indeed his approach envisions such a cooperation. Metaphorology is "nothing more [...] than playing off metaphor and concept against each other. He considers conceptuality, to expose the prior involvement and the space of expectation of the unconceptual, and he considers unconceptuality in order to lead up to the genesis of the conceptual." (Konersmann (1999), 129).
45 Blumenberg (1981), 114.
46 Blumenberg (1998), 12f.

Thus even absolute metaphors have a *history*. They have a history in a more radical sense than concepts, because the historical permutation of a metaphor foregrounds the meta-kinetic horizon of meaning and perspectives, within which concepts are being modified.[47]

Metaphorology wants to elucidate "the substructure of thinking, [...] but it also wants to make comprehensible the boldness [*Mut*] with which the spirit advances itself in its images and how its history is projected in the boldness of surmising [*Mut zur Vermutung*]".[48] The structural moment inherent to metaphors and genuinely oriented towards history thus elevates metaphors to the status of key witnesses of historical development and lays open historically conditioned paradigms of orientation. Metaphorology extends its claim beyond the conceptually realized surface structure, to which it remains constantly referred, to the *substructure of thinking*. Metaphorology is the analysis of human spaces of immanence [*Immanenzräume*] against the background of historical horizons of meaning. Thus, philosophy, whatever its direction, seeks "to bring to language what is human and what shows itself in humanity".[49] Philosophy, in the face of an immanence that can never be conceptually defined, is assigned the task of providing a knowledge that offers sufficient security for the elucidation of human thinking in its historical performance. Elucidation is, then, always the elucidation of its own historical standpoint: an emerging self-awareness to take its own impulses, conditionalities and possibilities into view.

Quite apart from the options popular at the time, Dilthey's hermeneutics wants to advance a new self-understanding of the humanities: it should neither act as the place holder of the natural sciences nor should it fall into a conventional "ideological dilettantism [*Weltanschauungsdilettantismus*]".[50] Historically evolved reality as a product of our processes of experience [*Erlebensprozesse*], expression and understanding thus suspends every externally given, absolute standpoint in favour of the development of a historical consciousness as an *emerging self-awareness*—"a relativity of each kind of belief".[51] This suspension as well as the sustained openness in the movement of the historical process on the basic level manifests itself in the previously mentioned resistance to conceptual determination. With this, any possibility of ideology [*Weltanschauung*] is dismissed. Supposedly coherent overall interpretations of reality are regarded only as historical artefacts. "There is an antagonism between the historical consciousness of the present and every kind of

---

47 Blumenberg (1998), 13.
48 Blumenberg (1998), 13.
49 Blumenberg (1961), 128.
50 Landgrebe (1984), 200.
51 Dilthey (1958), 290.

metaphysics as scientific ideology [*wissenschaftlicher Weltanschauung*]". The historical development of a competing and almost "limitless number of such metaphysical systems" has shown that "each one at each time it existed has excluded and struggled against the others such that to this day a decision could not be reached".[52] While the creation of world-pictures has always occupied a "quasi-metaphysical role in our spiritual household",[53] historical consciousness no longer delegates the orientation towards reality to metaphysical structures. The "metaphysical tradition" "has, as it is, basically nothing to say about the human, which is being asserted as exceptional".[54]

The "validity and possibility of the world-picture", according to Blumenberg, has been suspended. The "effect of the most intimate achievement of what is today called a 'humanities' attitude" [*geisteswissenschaftliche Einstellung*], which means an attitude of "historical reflection", consists in the fact that "historical knowledge about the power of the world-picture was already the dismantling of this power" and ever since has become "the reason for the futility of its renewal."[55] The world-picture establishes, according to Blumenberg, "the meaningful relatedness of reality and humanity" and accordingly is "relevant for humanity's self-understanding and a representation of totality directing its actions".[56] On the other hand, the world-model depends "on the current state of knowledge in the sciences" and systematizes the "entirety of its propositions" as the "representation of the totality of empirical reality".[57] Blumenberg believes that world-picture and world-model part ways for the first time with Descartes. Hence, the "total representation of nature on the one hand and the mapping and interpretation of the knowledge of nature on the other" can no longer

---

52 Dilthey (1960), 3, see also Blumenberg: "[T]he function of the world-picture is in its essence monistic, a world-picture does not tolerate other world-pictures in its vicinity" (Blumenberg (1961), 136). "In confrontation with their kind the pictures fade and their validity is consumed" (Blumenberg (1961), 136).
53 Blumenberg (1961), 135.
54 Blumenberg (1981), 108.
55 Blumenberg (1961), 135. It is the *humanities attitude* [*geisteswissenschaftliche Einstellung*] which allows Dilthey's and Blumenberg's points of view to be brought into line with one another, although Blumenberg emphasizes early that his thoughts are close to those in Heidegger's essay *Die Zeit des Weltbildes* (see Blumenberg (1950), 9 f.). Apart from his early works, Blumenberg distances himself increasingly from Heidegger. Implicit in the given text is a plea for a hermeneutical approach which is open to an infinite historical development so that it neither provokes a teleological abolition of historical development nor is determined by underlying absolute structures. It seems as if the latter, in the form of the *Seinsgeschichte*, gives Blumenberg grounds for criticizing Heidegger (see for example Blumenberg (1997b)).
56 Blumenberg (1961), 135.
57 Blumenberg (1961), 135.

agree.[58] World-model has since replaced world-picture, such that reality's meaningful relations to the human has been excluded. Hence the reference to Dilthey's hermeneutics as an exploration of spaces of immanence [*Immanenzräume*] is possible: that meaningful relations to reality, relations which are so important for humanity, should be established again is an enterprise that the (natural-) scientific world-model by definition cannot achieve. The "experienced pluralism of world-pictures" has reduced "the tension that produced historical reflection".[59] Thus, claims to absolute validity move to the background since these claims can no longer be delivered from an exterior. Genesis and validity henceforth remain referred to one another.

Feuerbach also seems to agree with this diagnosis since the history of philosophy "viewed superficially" offers no more "than a change of different systems".[60] However, for him the underlying truth is "unchangeable and one".[61]

> The diversity of systems is founded on the idea of truth itself. The history of philosophy is nothing other than the temporal exposition of the different determinations that together constitute the content of truth. The true, objective category in which they must be regarded is the idea of *development*.[62]

Feuerbach does not yet forsake the delegation of the philosophical-historical development to an external, absolute structure. His developmental model should, by way of a hermeneutic procedure, bring out the core and the idea of a philosophy.[63] The particular core is, however, always only the expression from a unique perspective of a core that is common to all philosophy. That is why the philosophical history is a *"system"* in which the "absolute idea" underlying all philosophies can only be glimpsed if the history of philosophy is "stripped of the form of temporality and external historical conditions".[64] Representation "in the field of the history of philosophy" has for its object "not external but internal, *immanent* activities of the spirit—*thought*".[65] It is necessary to picture and reproduce these by means of an organic representation. However within *reproduction* the task of an organic depiction is exhausted. Feuerbach's hermeneutic thought sells on what has been reproduced to the historiography of philosophy, which

---

58 Blumenberg (1961), 135.
59 Blumenberg (1961), 136.
60 Feuerbach (1969b), 49.
61 Feuerbach (1969b), 49.
62 Feuerbach (1969b), 49.
63 See also Feuerbach's examination of Hegel in Feuerbach (1969a), 65f.
64 Feuerbach (1969b), 50.
65 Feuerbach (1981), 5.

in turn is subject to the requirements of an *absolute idea*.⁶⁶ Any claim to exceed the limits of this servitude would mean to place oneself in a "mechanical relation" to the "activities of the thinking spirit" and represent "them as a recounting of external activities in the frame of a narrative ".⁶⁷

Both Feuerbach's and Dilthey's conception seem, first of all, to converge in Dilthey's understanding of hermeneutics as "the *aesthetic doctrine* [*Kunstlehre*] of the *interpretation of written memorials*".⁶⁸ Both positions criticize mere conceptualities, as that which is necessary to see lies hidden under the surface—be it the idea underlying a philosophy in Feuerbach or be it the immanence and vitality of the human in Dilthey. Feuerbach's approach is decisively exceeded, however, when hermeneutics proves itself to be historically conditioned and bound to history. It thus steps out of an internal monologue with individual works and thinkers who stand within the framework of one underlying philosophical history, and into a historically conditioned dialogue between individuals and productions of collective spirit. Hermeneutics, then, no longer gravitates around the interpretation of written memorials but rather around "the exegesis or *interpretation of the remnants of human existence contained in these writings*".⁶⁹

Feuerbach delegates the results he gained through the application of hermeneutics to philosophical historiography. The movement of hermeneutic interpretation is captured in the representation of the one, underlying, absolute idea. However, with Dilthey immanence is only understood within renunciation and

---

66 "[F]or Feuerbach the history of philosophy is not mere chronicle, but rather the very process of the unfolding of the truth itself" (Wartofsky (1982), 54). Feuerbach thus far remains still within the paradigm of the history of philosophy as a history of progress. Schott therefore comes to the conclusion that a "historical relativism" (Schott (1973), 166) underlays Feuerbach's later writings. The question is to what extent Feuerbach's own undertaking denies the openness of the historical path that is of significance for hermeneutics in the sense of Dilthey and Blumenberg. With the third volume of his philosophical historiography, *Pierre Bayle. Ein Beitrag zur Geschichte der Philosophie und Menschheit* (1839), Feuerbach gradually approachs a sensualistic and materialistic anthropology. Feuerbach had in the first two volumes of his philosophical historiography still attempt to take an "historical-objective standpoint" but he now leaves this, according to Rawidowicz, in his examination of Bayle—the "polemicist" takes "the place of the historian and researcher". This volume is said to be an early "confessional book" of Feuerbach: "The name 'Bayle' is to some extent a 'pseudonym' for Feuerbach himself, a 'cloak' for the naturalism that was gradually maturing in him" (Rawidowicz (1964), 63). However the first signs of this development can be found in the second volume of his philosophical historiography "The *Leibniz* [...] forms the basis for Feuerbach's distinctive materialism and so-called anthropologism" (Wartofsky (1982), 90); see also remark 4.
67 Feuerbach (1981), 6.
68 Dilthey (1957b), 320.
69 Dilthey (1957b), 319.

is brought back to the internal in understanding before being renounced anew.[70] In contrast to Feuerbach, Dilthey founds a hermeneutic access to spaces of immanence [*Immanenzräume*]. He claims to access immanence in a permanent oscillation between the superficially realized and immanence. Immanence is transcended, and in order to prevent giving it over completely to conceptualization, is re-translated and relocated into its own immanence. The interpreter is always at the same time an essential part of the interpretation—Feuerbach's claim to hermeneutic objectivity, on the contrary, culminates in the "self-denial"[71] of the interpreter, the purely historical depiction leaves the thought "always in its homeland, its origin".[72]

Dilthey, in his programme outlined in the *Einleitung in die Geisteswissenschaften*, had promised to combine "a historical with a systematic procedure" in order to discuss "the question concerning the philosophical basis of the humanities". Yet in its development, this this procedure is subject to a momentum of its own.[73] As the "connecting link"[74] between philosophy and the historical sciences both disciplines together should provide a methodological foundation of the humanities. This, however, also means that hermeneutics, once developed and entrusted to the humanities, determines the methodological approach—including that of philosophy. If philosophical historiography too should henceforth proceed hermeneutically, it must inevitably overstep its limits, not least because a subcutaneous stratum of worldviews [*Weltanschauung*] underlies philosophy, a layer "which is not grounded in conceptual thought but in the vitality of the persons who produced it".[75] When "a system [is] considered in its historical development", the corresponding worldview [*Weltanschauung*] is unmasked and shelved.[76]

The suspension of heterogeneous, self-conflicting world-views [*Weltanschauungen*] deprives philosophy of the exclusive right to the analysis of the basic hermeneutic structures of experience [*Erlebnis*], expression and understanding. Even philosophy can no longer provide the measure for coherent interpretations of reality and thus it takes its place within the canon of the human-

---

70 "[E]ven the most rigorous attention can only attain a controllable degree of objectivity and become quasi-aesthetic procedure if the expression of life is fixed and we can thus always return to it. Such quasi-aesthetic understanding of enduringly fixed expressions of life we call exegesis or interpretation" (Dilthey (1957b), 319).
71 Geldsetzer (1968), 204.
72 Feuerbach (1981), 5.
73 Dilthey (1959), XV.
74 Dilthey (1957b), 331.
75 Dilthey (1960), 30.
76 Dilthey (1960), 30.

ities. All the while hermeneutics emerges as "a kind of *prima philosophia*".[77] The "question of the philosophical foundations of the humanities" prepares the way for the hermeneutic foundation of the humanities, to which philosophy belongs.[78] The "introduction and growing influence of hermeneutics on philosophy" has also resulted in a broadening of perspective beyond the limits of philosophical historiography: philosophical historiography becomes cultural historiography. In this regard Blumenberg continues "the increasing tendency to amalgamate general and philosophical historiography to the history of the humanities or cultural history" which began to emerge in the 19th century and which "was finally represented most consistently in Dilthey's work".[79] Perhaps then it is no wonder that Feuerbach is disturbed by this narrative representation [*Darstellung*], given the fact that Blumenberg's writings were early on described as large-scale narratives of cultural history.[80] This, according to Feuerbach, is no longer philosophical historiography.

Bibliography

Blumenberg (1950): Hans Blumenberg, *Die ontologische Distanz. Eine Untersuchung über die Krisis der Phänomenologie Husserls* (Habilitationsschrift), Kiel (unpublished).
Blumenberg (1961): Hans Blumenberg, "Die Bedeutung der Philosophie für unsere Zukunft", in: Amt für Kultur, Volksbildung und Schulverwaltung der Stadt Wien (Ed.), *Wiener Schriften*, vol. 16, *Europa-Gespräch 1961. Die voraussehbare Zukunft*, Wien: Jugend und Volk, 127–140.
Blumenberg (1981), Hans Blumenberg, "Anthropologische Annäherung an die Aktualität der Rhetorik" (1971), in: Hans Blumenberg, *Wirklichkeiten in denen wir leben. Aufsätze und eine Rede*, Stuttgart: Reclam, 104–136.
Blumenberg (1997a): Hans Blumenberg, "Ausblick auf eine Theorie der Unbegrifflichkeit" (1979), in: Hans Blumenberg, *Schiffbruch mit Zuschauer. Paradigma einer Daseinsmetapher*, Frankfurt a. M.: Suhrkamp Verlag, 85–106.
Blumenberg (1997b): Hans Blumenberg, "Was wäre, würde Heidegger verstanden?", in: Hans Blumenberg, *Ein mögliches Selbstverständnis. Aus dem Nachlaß*, Stuttgart: Reclam, 34–36.
Blumenberg (1998): Hans Blumenberg, *Paradigmen zu einer Metaphorologie* (1960), Frankfurt a. M.: Suhrkamp Verlag.

---

77 Fellmann (1991), 21.
78 Dilthey (1959), XV.
79 Geldsetzer (1968), 225.
80 So Blumenberg is considered by Eckhard Nordhofen as a "philosopher of infinite narration, […] who has amalgated thinking in history with the history of thinking in a way that no longer allows us to separate these territories". Compare (Nordhofen (1996), 47.

Blumenberg (2001): Hans Blumenberg, *Lebenszeit und Weltzeit* (1986), 4th edition, Frankfurt a. M.: Suhrkamp Verlag.
Dilthey (1957a): Wilhelm Dilthey, "Ideen über eine beschreibende und zergliedernde Psychologie" (1894), in: Wilhelm Dilthey, *Gesammelte Schriften*, vol. 5, *Die geistige Welt. Einleitung in diePhilosophie des Lebens. Erste Hälfte. Abhandlungen zur Grundlegung der Geisteswissenschaften*, ed. by Georg Misch, 2nd edition, Stuttgart und Göttingen: B. G. Teubner Verlagsgesellschaft und Vandenhoeck & Ruprecht, 139–240.
Dilthey (1957b): Wilhelm Dilthey, "Die Entstehung der Hermeneutik" (1900), in: Wilhelm Dilthey, *Gesammelte Schriften*, vol. 5, *Die geistige Welt. Einleitung in die Philosophie des Lebens. Erste Hälfte. Abhandlungen zur Grundlegung der Geisteswissenschaften*, ed. by Georg Misch, 2nd edition, Stuttgart und Göttingen: B. G. Teubner Verlagsgesellschaft und Vandenhoeck & Ruprecht, 317–331.
Dilthey (1958): Wilhelm Dilthey, "Der Aufbau der geschichtlichen Welt in den Geisteswissenschaften" (1927), in: Wilhelm Dilthey, *Gesammelte Schriften*, vol. 7, ed. by Bernhard Groethuysen, 2nd edition, Stuttgart und Göttingen: B. G. Teubner Verlagsgesellschaft und Vandenhoeck & Ruprecht.
Dilthey (1959): Wilhelm Dilthey, *Einleitung in die Geisteswissenschaften. Versuch einer Grundlegung für das Studium der Gesellschaft und der Geschichte. Erster Band* (1883), in: Wilhelm Dilthey, *Gesammelte Schriften*, vol. 1, ed. by Bernhard Groethuysen, 4th edition, Stuttgart: B. G. Teubner Verlagsgesellschaft und Göttingen: Vandenhoeck & Ruprecht.
Dilthey (1960): Wilhelm Dilthey, "Das geschichtliche Bewußtsein und die Weltanschauungen" (1931), in: Wilhelm Dilthey, *Gesammelte Schriften*, vol. 8, *Weltanschauungslehre. Abhandlungen zur Philosophie der Philosophie*, ed. by Bernhard Groethuysen, 2nd edition, Stuttgart und Göttingen: B. G.Teubner und Vandenhoeck & Ruprecht, 1–71.
Fellmann (1991): Ferdinand Fellmann, *Symbolischer Pragmatismus. Hermeneutik nach Dilthey*, Reinbek bei Hamburg: Rowohlt Taschenbuch Verlag.
Feuerbach (1960): Ludwig Feuerbach, "Nachgelassene Aphorismen", in: Ludwig Feuerbach, *Sämtliche Werke*, ed. by Wilhelm Bolin und Friedrich Jodl, vol. 10, *Schriften zur Ethik und nachgelassene Aphorismen*, ed. by Friedrich Jodl, 2nd edition, Stuttgart / Bad Canstatt: Frommann Verlag Günther Holzboog, 297–346.
Feuerbach (1969a): Ludwig Feuerbach, "Kritik des ‚Anti-Hegels'. Zur Einleitung in das Studium der Philosophie" (1835), in: Ludwig Feuerbach, *Gesammelte Werke*, vol. 8, *Kleinere Schriften I* (1835–1839), ed. by Werner Schuffenhauer, bearbeitet von Wolfgang Harich, Berlin: Akademie Verlag, 62–127.
Feuerbach (1969b): Ludwig Feuerbach [Rezension], "Hegels Geschichte der Philosophie. Herausgegeben von Michelet" (1835), in: Ludwig Feuerbach, *Gesammelte Werke*, vol. 8, *Kleinere Schriften I* (1835–1839), ed. by Werner Schuffenhauer, bearbeitet von Wolfgang Harich, Berlin: Akademie Verlag, 44–61.
Feuerbach (1981): Ludwig Feuerbach, "Geschichte der neuern Philosophie. Darstellung, Entwicklung und Kritik der Leibnizschen Philosophie" (1837), in: Ludwig Feuerbach, *Gesammelte Werke*, vol. 3, ed. by Werner Schuffenhauer, bearbeitet von Werner Schuffenhauer and Wolfgang Harich, 2nd edition, Berlin: Akademie Verlag.
Geldsetzer (1968): Lutz Geldsetzer, *Die Philosophie der Philosophiegeschichte im 19. Jahrhundert – Zur Wissenschaftstheorie der Philosophiegeschichtsschreibung und -betrachtung*, Meisenheim am Glan: Verlag Anton Hain.

Grondin (2009): Jean Grondin, *Hermeneutik*, Aus dem Französischen übersetzt von Ulrike Blech. Göttingen: Vandenhoeck & Ruprecht.
Kimmerle (1974): Heinz Kimmerle, "Einleitung", in: Friedrich Schleiermacher, *Hermeneutik*. Nach den Handschriften neu herausgegeben und eingeleitet von Heinz Kimmerle. Zweite, verbesserte und erweiterte Auflage, Heidelberg: Carl Winter Universitätsverlag, 9–24.
Konersmann (1999): Ralf Konersmann, "Vernunftarbeit. Metaphorologie als Quelle der Historischen Semantik", in: Franz Josef Wetz a. Hermann Timm (Eds.), *Die Kunst des Überlebens. Nachdenken über Hans Blumenberg*, Frankfurt a. M.: Suhrkamp Verlag, 121–141.
Landgrebe (1984): Ludwig Landgrebe, "Wilhelm Diltheys Theorie der Geisteswissenschaften (Analyse ihrer Grundbegriffe)" (1928), in: Frithjof Rodi a. Hans-Ulrich Lessing, *Materialien zur Philosophie Wilhelm Dilhteys*, Frankfurt a. M.: Suhrkamp Verlag, 199–210.
Misch (1967): Georg Misch, *Lebensphilosophie und Phänomenologie. Eine Auseinandersetzung der Diltheyschen Richtung mit Heidegger und Husserl. Mit einem Nachwort zur 3. Auflage* (1930), 3rd edition, Darmstadt: Wissenschaftliche Buchgesellschaft Darmstadt.
Müller-Funk (1990): Wolfgang Müller-Funk, *Die Enttäuschungen der Vernunft. Von der Romantik zur Postmoderne. Essays*, Wien: Deuticke Verlag.
Nordhofen (1996): Eckhard Nordhofen, "Zum Tode des Philosophen Hans Blumenberg. Hans Blumenberg, geboren am 13. Juli 1920 in Lübeck, gestorben am 28. März 1996 in Altenberge/Westfalen", in: *Die Zeit* 16/1996, 47.
Rawidowicz (1964): Simon Rawidowicz, *Ludwig Feuerbachs Philosophie. Ursprung und Schicksal* (1931), 2nd edition, Berlin: De Gruyter.
Schott (1973): Uwe Schott, *Die Jugendentwicklung Ludwig Feuerbachs bis zum Fakultätswechsel 1825. Ein Beitrag zur Genese der Feuerbachschen Religionskritik. Mit einem bibliographischen Anhang zur Feuerbach-Literatur*, (Studien zur Theologie und Geistesgeschichte des Neunzehnten Jahrhunderts, vol. 10). Göttingen: Vandenhoeck & Ruprecht.
Serrão (1998): Adriana Veríssimo Serrão, "Hermeneutik in der Geschichtsschreibung. Feuerbach über das Problem der Interpretation." Translated by Manuela Ribeiro Sanches, in: Walter Jaeschke a. Francesco Tomasoni (Eds.), *Ludwig Feuerbach und die Geschichte der Philosophie*, Berlin: Akademie Verlag, 16–33.
Wartofsky (1982): Marx W. Wartofsky, *Feuerbach* (1977), Cambridge et al.: Cambridge University Press.

Index

Anaxagoras 124, 129, 141
Anaximander 119, 129, 146
Angehrn, Emil 2, 4, 45, 53
Apelt, Ernst Friedrich 91
Aristoteles 10f., 47, 55, 57f., 70, 77, 118f.,
 122–125, 129, 131, 136, 151f., 166, 188
Ast, Friedrich 33, 99
Avenarius, Richard 211

Bacon, Francis 109
Bauch, Bruno 207f., 223f.
Baur, Ferdinand Christian 161–165
Becker, Immanuel 10
Beelmann, Axel 2, 55, 209
Beiser, Frederick 5, 81f., 84, 120, 123, 188,
 204, 209f., 214, 221
Beneke, Friedrich Eduard 5, 82–91, 93–95
Bernal, Martin 143, 145
Bernays, Jacob 128
Biedermann, Carl 18
Biese, Franz 11
Blumenberg, Hans 6, 227f., 233–239, 241
Boeckh, August 28f., 144
Bona Meyer, Jürgen 91, 93f.
Bondeli, Martin 4f., 63, 67
Brandis, Christian August 10f., 142, 173
Braniß, Christian Julius 33f.
Bräuniger, Ines 7
Büchner, Ludwig 109
Burnouf, Eugène 144
Busse, Wilhelm 109

Cassirer, Ernst 6, 13, 181, 184f., 191–196,
 198–204, 210, 221, 224, 235
Chalybäus, Heinrich Moritz 27
Champollion, Jean-François 144
Choerilus of Iasus 152
Clemens of Alexandria 163
Cohen, Hermann 94, 193–196, 201, 203
Colebrooke, Henry Thomas 141
Copleston, Frederick 82

Daly, Aengus 7
Degérando, Joseph Marie 109

Democritus 128f.
Derrida, Jacques 56
Descartes, René 11, 20, 171, 237
Diderot, Denis 168, 171
Diels, Hermann 127f.
Dilthey, Wilhelm 5f., 14–16, 19, 26, 28, 31,
 37–40, 59, 64, 100, 110–113, 204,
 211f., 214, 227f., 231–241
Diogenes Laërtius 119, 128, 136
Droysen, Gustav 13

Engels, Friedrich 5, 108–110, 112f.
Erdmann, Johann Eduard 12f., 81f., 102f.
Eucken, Rudolf Christoph 4, 10, 19–22

Feuerbach, Ludwig 6, 108–110, 227–231,
 238–241
Fichte, Immanuel Hermann 11, 29, 81–91,
 93, 95, 101
Fischer, Kuno 12f., 81f., 93, 176, 212
Flasch, Kurt 2, 50, 52f., 60
Forster, Michael 5, 12, 130, 141
Frege, Gottlob 5, 92, 113
Fries, Jakob Friedrich 5, 82–95, 99–103,
 105, 108f., 112f.

Gadamer, Hans-Georg 6, 13, 126, 133, 184,
 189, 192
Gauss, Karl Friedrich 91
Geldsetzer, Lutz 26, 64, 71, 102f., 105, 111,
 120f., 126, 141, 209, 218, 230, 240f.
Gladisch, August 5, 130, 141, 143f.
Goclenius, Rudolphus 26
Gorgias 157
Goslar, Tim-Florian 6, 227
Griesheim, Karl Gustav Julius von 107
Grohmann, Johann Christian August 5, 71,
 102–105, 107–109, 111, 113
Grünkorn, Gertrud 7

Hartmann, Eduard von 82, 218
Hartung, Gerald 1, 4, 9–11, 13–15
Hegel, Georg Wilhelm Friedrich 1, 3–6, 9,
 11–17, 20, 22, 26f., 33, 41, 46–49, 52,

54f., 60, 63f., 71–79, 81–87, 89f., 93, 95, 101, 105–109, 111–113, 117f., 120–127, 129f., 132, 134–136, 142f., 163f., 182f., 186, 208, 216, 222, 228, 231, 238
Heidegger, Martin 39, 209, 237
Heine, Heinrich 220
Heit, Helmut 5, 117f., 120, 126, 130
Helmholtz, Hermann 91
Henrich, Dieter 50
Heraclitus 37, 40f., 127–130, 133, 141, 176
Herbart, Johann Friedrich 5, 82–95, 101
Herder, Johann Gottfried 33, 90
Hermes Trimegistos 153
Herodotus 47, 146–148, 150f., 153–156
Hinneberg, Paul 212f.
Hölderlin, Friedrich 82
Holzhey, Helmuth 7, 94
Homer 148f., 157, 166
Hösle, Vittorio 183
Humboldt, Wilhelm von 27, 141, 143f.
Hume, David 70, 89
Husserl, Edmund 59, 92, 197

Iamblichus 153
Isocrates 153f.

Jacobi, Friedrich Heinrich 33, 35, 101
Jaeschke, Walter 60, 82, 120
Julien, Stanislas 144

Kant, Immanuel 4, 9, 11–13, 18, 20, 25f., 30, 32, 63–68, 70f., 75–79, 81f., 84–91, 93f., 100–102, 104f., 108, 111, 113, 133, 189, 195–197, 199f., 214
Koenig, Heike 7
Köhnke, Klaus Christian 9, 12, 94, 209
Köstlin, Karl Reinhold von 16
Kranz, Walther 127f.
Kraus, Christian Jacob 66
Kroner, Richard 82
Kronfeld, Arthur 91

La Rochefoucauld, François de 170
Lakatos, Imre 26
Lange, Friedrich Albert 18, 91, 93, 128, 211
Lavoisier, Antoine Laurent de 133

Leibniz, Gottfried Wilhelm 65, 70, 228, 230, 239
Lespinasse, Julie de 168, 170
Liebmann, Otto 93f., 97
Locke, John 11, 70, 230
Lotze, Hermann 82, 212
Löwith, Karl 117
Luft, Sebastian 6, 181, 210

Mansfeld, Jaap 2, 126
Marx, Karl 18, 49, 110
Mauthner, Fritz 15
Meiners, Christopher 66, 128
Messer, August 224
Meyerhoff, Otto 91
Michelet, Karl Ludwig 11, 120
Micraelius 26

Nelson, Leonard 91
Niehues-Pröbsting, Heinrich 132
Nietzsche, Friedrich 4–6, 15, 20, 22, 36–41, 56, 117f., 123f., 127–136, 144, 161, 166–169, 172–177, 221
Novalis (Georg Philipp Friedrich von Hardenberg) 81f.

Origenes 163
Otto, Rudolf 84, 91
Overbeck, Franz 6, 160–167, 169, 177f.
Overbeck, Ida 167–170, 172, 178

Paracelsus (Philippus Theophrastus Aureolus Bombastus von Hohenheim) 133
Parmenides 129f., 133, 157
Paul the Apostle 164
Pherecydes 146f., 153, 155
Philolaus 157
Plato 11, 17, 20f., 23, 25, 47, 57, 70, 124, 129, 131f., 136, 141, 163, 166, 174, 178, 207, 225
Pluder, Valentin 1, 5, 99
Prantl, Karl 128
Protagoras 129, 157
Proust, Marcel 168f.
Pythagoras 111, 130, 141f., 145–150, 152–157

Ranke, Leopold 13, 29
Rapp, Christof 132
Reinhold, Karl Leonhard 4, 63, 67–72, 74–79, 81–85, 88f., 91, 95, 101
Rickert, Heinrich 193, 207f., 212, 220
Ricoeur, Paul 15f.
Ritter, August Heinrich 10, 16, 27, 128, 142, 173
Rohde, Erwin 129
Rompf, Daniel 7
Rorty, Richard 2, 56, 182, 196, 198, 208
Röth, Eduard 5, 141–157
Ruge, Arnold 207

Sacy, Sylvestre de 144
Said, Edward 143
Sainte-Beuve, Charles-Augustin 6, 167–173, 176f.
Salomé, Lou von 174f.
Schelling, Friedrich Wilhelm Joseph 11, 27, 34–36, 81–91, 93, 95, 101
Schlegel, Friedrich 4, 10, 30–32, 39f., 81f., 141, 143
Schleiden, Matthias 91
Schleiermacher, Friedrich Daniel 4, 10, 16, 26–29, 41, 227, 230
Schlömilch, Oskar 91
Schmeitzner, Ernst 166–169
Schmid, Heinrich 91
Scholtz, Gunter 4, 25, 29, 32, 34, 38
Schopenhauer, Arthur 36f., 82, 84, 162, 172f., 175, 188
Schröter, Manfred 35
Schultze, Fritz 212
Schulze, Gottlob Ernst 101
Schwegler, Friedrich Karl Albert 11f., 15–18, 20
Sellars, Wilfred 46
Socrates 129, 131, 157, 166
Sommer, Andreas Urs 6, 159, 168, 174, 176
Spinoza, Baruch de 25, 35, 175f.

Stahl, Friedrich Julius 35
Steenblock, Volker 22
Stekeler-Weithofer, Pirmin 48, 53, 59f.

Telauges 157
Tennemann, Wilhelm Gottlieb 10, 71, 109
Thales of Miletus 118, 122, 133
Theophrastus 122
Thucydides 47
Treitschke, Heinrich von 160
Trendelenburg, Friedrich Adolf 11, 13f., 82, 109

Ueberweg, Friedrich 13, 124f., 127f., 130, 169
Ulrici, Hermann 12, 27, 29

Vauvenargues, Luc de Clapiers, Marquis de-
Voltaire (François Marie Arouet) 168, 170
Vogt, Carl 109

Wagner, Richard 174
Walch, Georg 26
Wartenburg, Paul Yorck von 38f., 41
Windelband, Wilhelm 1, 3f., 6, 10, 14, 19, 94, 126, 181, 183–194, 204, 207–224
Windischmann, Carl Joseph Hieronymus 31, 33, 141
Wolff, Christian 65, 68, 77, 80
Wundt, Wilhelm 40, 211f.

Xenophanes 147, 154, 157

Zeller, Eduard 5, 11–14, 16–18, 20f., 36, 64, 91, 93, 117f., 124–130, 133–136, 142–144, 148–157, 173, 175
Zeno 157
Ziche, Paul 6, 207, 210f.
Ziegler, Theobald 18

www.ingramcontent.com/pod-product-compliance
Lightning Source LLC
Chambersburg PA
CBHW050858160426
43194CB00011B/2206